Pies & Pastries

APPETIZERS, MAIN DISHES & DESSERTS

ANOTHER BEST-SELLING VOLUME FROM HPBooks

Publisher: Helen Fisher; Executive Editor: Rick Bailey;
Editorial Director: Veronica Durie; Editor: Carlene Tejada
Art Director: Don Burton; Book Design: Ken Heiden
Food Stylist: Janet Pittman; Photography: George de Gennaro Studios—
George de Gennaro, Tom Miyasaki, Dennis Skinner, David Wong

Published by HPBooks, P.O. Box 5367, Tucson, AZ 85703
602/888-2150
ISBN: 0-89586-163-1
Library of Congress Catalog Card No. 81-85986
©1982 Fisher Publishing, Inc. Printed in U.S.A.

Cover photo: Cheddar-Apple Pie with Raisins, page 91, and French Puff Tart, page 105.

A Worldwide Tradition

Hear the word "pie" and the image that comes to mind may be a double one—an everyday humble dish and the final delight of a formal dinner.

Pastry has traditionally been a container for the workingman's lunch. Miners in England's Cornwall left home every morning with a pastry-wrapped meat mixture in their pockets. The farmer in America came home at noon to chicken pot pie—a kind of chicken stew topped with a pastry lid.

At one time, London was full of shops selling deep-dish meat pies and turnovers. Meat pies were a sign of prosperity. Today's Thanksgiving mince pie is actually a carryover from these earlier English pies made from minced or chopped meat.

It is as sweets that pies and pastries have reached their glory. For centuries, sugar and spices were a luxury only the most wealthy could afford. Rich noble families could not only buy expensive sugar and spices, but could pay chefs to do nothing but create rich, sweet, melt-in-your-mouth pastry delights.

Chefs of continental Europe contributed elegant puff pastry and *choux* pastry, or cream-puff pastry. They carried elegance to its finest degree and developed the art of pastry decoration. For this they created pastry cutouts and crimping techniques. They extended the use of the pastry tube to decorating with meringue and whipped cream.

Thin flaky pastry sheets, called *filo*, or *phyllo*, crossed the Mediterranean with travelers journeying from the East. These pastry sheets were usually layered with dried fruits and nuts and steeped in syrup. Their influence on the pastries of the Western World can be seen in the strudels of Eastern Europe.

Pies, probably more than any other type of food, show that necessity is the mother of invention. A thrifty housewife in New England, trying to stretch her meager staples, discovered that a shallow pan needs less filling than a deep dish. And that was the beginning of the basic round, shallow pie.

Pastry making is considered an art, but unlike other art forms, it is one that everyone can do. If you are new to preparing pies and pastries, this book will give you detailed instructions for making each type of pastry dough. As you become more familiar with the various pastries and techniques, you will develop skills that ensure success every time. If you are already experienced in preparing pies and pastries, you'll find ideas that will help make your finished product look more professional, and techniques to bring ease and convenience to pastry making. ◆

A holiday dessert buffet is pictured on the previous pages. From left to right: Frozen Nesselrode Tarts, pages 162 and 168, and Pumpkin Chiffon Tarts, pages 155 and 168; Christmas Wreath, page 183; Pistachio Coils, page 186, and Cranberry-Apple Relish Pie, page 91.

Janet Pittman

Janet grew up in California's San Joaquin Valley—one of the richest fruit and vegetable regions in the United States. Three generations lived close together. Both Mother and Grandma shared their cooking skills with the youngest cook. Experimentation was encouraged so Janet's career began at an early age. One of her earliest memories is of shaping pie dough!

In 1966, Janet received her Bachelor of Science in Home Economics from the University of California. After several years of working for major food companies in quality control, recipe develop-

ment and food styling, she became a freelance home economist specializing in food styling and recipe development. Janet's talents have been in demand by leading restaurant chains, packaging companies, food companies and the wine industry. She has been a food stylist for eleven HPBooks cookbooks—including this one.

Janet's family and home are in Wyoming. She divides her working days between her kitchen, which looks out onto snow-capped mountains, and photography studios in metropolitan areas across the country.

Equipment

Very few special utensils are needed for making pies and pastries. The indispensable utensils are relatively inexpensive and easy to find.

♦ A wooden spoon is necessary for stirring fillings and sauces.
♦ A wire whip or a rotary beater makes quick work of mixing liquid ingredients until smooth.
♦ A portable or standard electric mixer is essential for making meringue toppings.
♦ A pastry cutter is not essential but it will help make straight and curved cuts in flaky pastries. Many pastry cutters have both a straight knife edge and a rickrack edge.
♦ The ideal pastry brush has soft bristles and is 1 inch wide. It is sometimes called a *basting brush.* Its soft bristles will not mar delicate pastry with unsightly grooves.

Pie Pans

Measure a pie pan inside the rim across the middle of the pan. This measurement may differ from pan to pan according to where and when a pan was manufactured. Even standard 9-inch glass pie plates may differ as much as 1/4 inch.

Glass or dull-metal pans absorb heat and make a crisp crust. This is especially important for custard pies.

Lightweight, pressed-aluminum pans and freezer-to-oven baking dishes are useful for freezer pies and for preparing frozen pies for baking later. Pressed-aluminum pans are usually smaller than standard pans. If you use one of these pans and have leftover filling, freeze it for a quick single-serving meal or dessert.

Saucepans

Sturdy saucepans that are made to conduct heat evenly across the bottom are essential for cooking pudding and cream fillings. If your pans have hot spots, or areas on the bottom where food tends to burn, reduce the heat and cook the mixture a little longer. Be sure to follow stirring instructions given in the recipe.

Pastry Cloth & Sleeve

A pastry cloth and a sleeve for your rolling pin are optional. They make rolling out standard pastry easier and less messy. Pastry cloths are usually made of heavyweight woven cotton. Pastry sleeves are made of a tube-knit cotton. Your pastry cloth may come with a frame to keep it taut while you are working on it. To use, sprinkle the cloth generously with flour and roll the sleeve-covered rolling pin over it. This distributes the flour evenly into both materials. Shake the cloth and sleeve lightly after using. They do not need to be washed after each use. Store them with your rolling pin and other pastry equipment.

Ovens

Ovens used to develop recipes in this book were conventional gas and electric ovens. If you have a convection oven, follow the manufacturer's suggestions for baking times.

Baking characteristics vary among ovens, depending on size and type of oven, placement of heating elements and racks, and type of heat. Get to know your oven. Use an oven thermometer to check the thermostat so you can make any necessary adjustments in the temperature setting.

If food frequently browns unevenly in your oven, give pastry half a turn about halfway through the baking time.

Basic Doughs & Crumb Crusts

Pastry falls into two categories: flaky and non-flaky. When flour, fat and water are combined in a certain way and cooked, flakes of pastry are formed. Some flaky pastry may contain egg. Non-flaky pastries are usually more chewy than flaky because they contain more liquid.

There are three major types of flaky pastry:

Standard Pastry is also called *flaky pastry, rich pastry, pie dough, short crust, pâte brisée* and *pâte sucrée*. This is the pastry Grandma made and the one that lends itself to so many flavor variations.

Puff Pastry, a layered wonder, is found around the world in pastry shops and fine restaurants.

Strudel and Filo, from Eastern Europe and the Middle East, are large thin sheets of pastry rolled, folded or piled into many layers.

There are two major types of non-flaky pastry.

Choux Pastry is used for cream puffs and éclairs. It has many large holes rather than flakes.

Crumb Crusts are included as a pastry only because they are shells for fillings. They are the most popular shells for chiffon and freezer pies.

Standard Pastry

Standard pastry is the easiest and most versatile of the pastry family.

Tenderness of standard pastry depends on the correct proportions of flour, fat and water and as little mixing and handling as possible. When wheat flour is mixed with water, gluten is formed. Gluten acts as an adhesive and is needed to hold pastry together. But too much gluten results in tough pie crust. To prevent excess gluten, the flour is mixed with fat before water is added. The fat coats some of the flour, protecting it from the water and decreasing the chance of excess gluten. It is important to use a small amount of water and to mix only until the ingredients are combined. Rolling out dough a second or third time encourages the development of more gluten and frequently accounts for tough pie crusts.

Flakiness of standard pastry is influenced by fat particles distributed throughout the flour. These fat particles can range from the size of cornmeal grains to the size of small peas. During baking, the fat particles melt. They are replaced by expanding hot air, and layers of crust are created. Sometimes the fat particles are too small and air pockets do not form. This happens in oil pastry and in pastry made with hot water that melts the fat before it has a chance to create layers. The crust will be very tender but will crumble rather than flake. Chilling the water, shortening or dough is necessary only if your kitchen is warm enough to melt fat particles in the dough.

Flavor and texture of a standard pastry may be changed by adding herbs, cheese or nuts, or by using shortening, lard or butter. See the recipes on pages 14 to 20.

Most standard pastry recipes in this book can be used interchangeably. Some recipes give a choice of pastry dough. If the pie you are making calls for only Basic Pastry but you think Cheddar Pastry would enhance the pie's flavor, go right ahead and try it.

Standard Pastry Techniques

Single-Crust Pies

Pies that are not topped with a crust are called *single-crust pies.* The crust, or shell, may be filled before or after baking, according to the recipe.

Rolling Out

If you are preparing a dough circle for a round pan, shape the dough into a flat ball. If you are

Turning dough during the rolling-out process.

Placing the folded circle of dough in the pie pan.

preparing a rectangle or a square, shape the dough into a thick rectangle or square.

Lightly flour a pastry cloth, breadboard or countertop. Place the dough in the center of the floured surface. Lightly sprinkle it with flour. Roll the rolling pin over the floured surface. Place dough on the floured surface and sprinkle it lightly with flour.

To make uniformly thick pastry, roll out the dough with light, even strokes from the center of the dough to the edge. Lift the rolling pin as it approaches the edge. Do not roll it off the edge or the edge will become too thin. Roll the rolling pin away from you 2 or 3 times and then toward you 2 or 3 times. Give the dough a 1/4 turn and roll away and toward you 2 or 3 more times. Continue rolling and turning until the dough reaches the desired size. As you roll out, keep the dough as close to the basic shape as possible by frequent quarter turns. As the shape becomes larger, it may be easier to turn the rolling pin than to turn the dough. If necessary, sprinkle the dough or work surface with flour to prevent sticking. Do not use more flour than needed. Too much flour may cause a dry, tough crust.

Unbaked Pie Shells

Roll out the dough to a 12-inch circle for a 9-inch pie, or about 3 inches larger than the inside diameter of the pie pan measured across the top. Fold the circle in half. Place the pie pan next to the folded edge. Gently lift the folded dough and place it in one side of the pie pan with the fold across the center. Unfold the dough. Or, wrap the dough around the rolling pin and unroll it over the pie pan. Ease the dough into the pie pan, being careful not to stretch it. Repair any tears by moistening the torn edges with water and pressing one edge on top of the other. Use a small sharp knife to trim the edge of the dough to a 3/4-inch overhang.

Finish your pie shell with a raised edge, page 10, and decorative fluting, pages 10 and 11.

Baked Pie Shells

Prepare an unbaked pie shell, above, with a raised edge and fluting. Preheat the oven to 475F (245C). Use a fork to prick sides and bottom of the unbaked shell at 1/2-inch intervals. This helps prevent large bubbles from forming in the crust. Bake blind and glaze as directed on page 9.

If you use a metal pie pan or a refrigerator-to-oven pie pan, baking blind is not necessary. Refrigerate the unbaked shell 15 to 20 minutes before baking. Then bake 8 to 10 minutes until the shell is golden brown.

Baking blind. Rickrack Fluting is on page 11.

Baking Blind

To lessen shrinkage of the crust as it bakes, use the *baking-blind* technique. Fit a 12-inch square of foil into the unbaked pie shell, molding it to fit the shell. Pour 1 to 1-1/2 cups of dried beans evenly onto the foil. Or, use a double sheet of heavy-duty foil and no beans. Bake 8 minutes. Remove foil and beans or foil. If your oven browns foods unevenly, rotate the pie pan after removing the foil. Bake 4 to 5 minutes longer until the shell is golden brown. Glaze the shell with a sugar glaze, below, or place it on a rack to cool.

Keep beans for baking blind in an attractive glass container and use them whenever you are baking blind. Label the container. Do not try to cook these beans.

Glazing

To help prevent a baked crust from becoming soggy when filled, brush it with a sugar glaze as soon as you remove it from the oven. To make the glaze, mix 2 teaspoons sugar and 1 teaspoon hot tap water in a small bowl until most of the sugar is dissolved. Brush the mixture onto the hot crust. Cool the glazed crust on a rack.

If you make baked pie shells frequently, prepare the glaze with 1/2 cup sugar and 1/4 cup boiling water, stirring until the sugar is dissolved. Pour the cooled glaze into a labeled jar and refrigerate it.

Double-Crust Pies

Pies that have a top and bottom crust with a filling in between are *double-crust pies*. They are always baked after they are filled.

Rolling Out the Bottom Crust

Divide the dough into 2 equal portions. Roll out 1 portion to an 11-inch circle for a 9-inch pie or 2 inches larger than the pie pan measured across the top. See Rolling Out, pages 7 and 8.

Fold the circle in half. Place the pie pan next to the folded edge. Gently lift the folded dough and place it in one side of the pie pan with the fold across the center. Unfold the dough and ease it into the pie pan without stretching. Repair any tears by moistening the torn edges with water and pressing one edge on top of the other. The weight of the filling will settle the dough deeper into the pan. To prevent too little crust at the edge, do not trim the dough until after the pie is filled.

Filling

Fill the crust with the filling. If you have about 4 cups of filling, spread or arrange it evenly. If you have 6 to 7 cups, mound it slightly in the center. Lift the pie pan in one hand. Hold a small knife at an angle and trim the edge of the dough even with the rim of the pan. Or carefully break off excess dough with your fingers.

Top Crust

Roll out the other half of the dough to a 12-inch circle for a 9-inch pie. Cut eight 2-inch slits radiating from the center to 2 to 3 inches from the edge. Or, make decorative slits:
♦ If you are making fruit pies, make the slits in the shape of the first letter of the fruit filling. Or, make slits as if sketching the fruit.
♦ A 4-inch curve with radiating 3/4-inch slits will resemble the branch of a fruit tree; see the photo on page 12.
♦ Make as many as twenty 1/2- to 1-inch slits in any desired pattern.
♦ Make 4 to 6 evenly spaced cutouts with hors d'oeuvre cutters.

Fold the dough circle in half. Place the filled

pie pan next to the fold. Gently place the circle over the filling with the fold across the center. Unfold. Trim the edge with a small knife to a 3/4-inch overhang.

Your pie is now ready to be finished with a raised edge, fluting, glaze and topping.

Finishing Your Pie

Pie—whether it's double-crust or single-crust—needs a raised edge and fluting to give it a professional look.

How to Make a Raised Edge

A raised edge can be made on a single-crust pie or on a double-crust pie after the top has been placed over the filling.

Starting on the side away from you, place your thumbs pointing toward each other on the inside of the pie shell. Your index fingers should be on the outside of the pie pan pointing toward each other. For a single-crust pie, fold the 3/4-inch overhang under itself so the edge of the shell is even with the rim of the pie pan. For a double-crust pie, fold the 3/4-inch overhang under the edge of the bottom crust. Press the folded edge gently between your thumbs and index fingers to make a raised edge. Turn the pie pan as you work, so your fingers are always on the side away

from you. Make the raised edge as even as possible. Reinforce any thin spots by placing a small dough scrap under that spot before folding it under.

If the overhang extends more than 3/4 inch, trim off the excess with a small knife. For an overhang less than 3/4 inch, press the dough between your thumb and index finger to thin and extend it. Place a small dough scrap under the thinned spot and fold it under as part of the raised edge.

Your pie is now ready for decorative fluting.

Decorative Fluting

A pie that looks inviting makes the difference between everyone clamoring for a wedge or agreeing half-heartedly to try a sliver. One way to make an attractive pie is to flute, or shape, the edge.

Spiral Fluting—Push your thumb into the raised edge on the diagonal. Bring bent index finger from outside of the raised edge and press directly toward your thumb. Remove both fingers and place your thumb where your index finger was and repeat around edge. Repeat the process to make very crisp and distinct edges along the top of each ridge.

Crimping or Straight-Tines Fluting—Use the back of a floured fork to make the pattern.

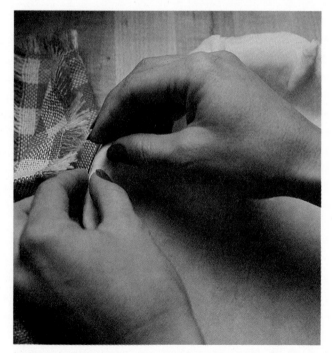

Making a raised edge on a single-crust pie shell.

Making Spiral Fluting on a double-crust pie. Cherry Pie is on page 103.

Hold the fork so the tines point toward the center of the pie and press the tines into the raised edge. Space evenly between each fork print. See the photo below.

Herringbone Fluting—Use the back of a floured fork. Press the fork tines diagonally onto the raised edge. Turn the tines 90 degrees and press next to the previous mark. Repeat around the edge. See the photo below.

Cutouts—Roll out dough slightly thinner than specified to allow extra dough for cutouts. Trim edge of dough to a 1/2-inch overhang and roll under. Press with your thumb to make a smooth flat edge. Using an hors d'oeuvre cutter or a small knife, cut out 1/2- to 1-inch circles, leaves or other shapes from the dough scraps. Lightly brush the flat edge around pie with water. Arrange cutouts around the edge of the pie. Overlap slightly, if desired. See the photo below.

Flower-Petal Fluting—Make a Scalloped Fluting, below. Then press bowl of scallop with lightly floured fork tines. See pages 94, 100 and 101.

High Flutings

When a deep pie shell is desired, make a high fluting. Quiches and custard pies usually require a deep pie shell.

Scalloped Fluting—Place your left thumb flat against the inside edge of the pie shell. Your left hand will be over the shell. Place the thumb and index finger of your right hand on either side of your left thumb. Press your left thumb out and over the edge of the pan. Place your left thumb on the other side of your right index finger. Move your right thumb where your index finger was and repeat around edge. To make inside edge more distinct, pinch the points. Or, use a spoon instead of your left thumb to make the scallop.

Rickrack Fluting—Use the same process as for Scalloped Fluting but use your left thumb on its side instead of flat. Pinch both inside points and outside points to make a distinct edge. See the photo on page 9.

Star Fluting—Follow the directions for making Scalloped Fluting, but shape only 8 to 12 evenly spaced points. Star Fluting enhances pumpkin or custard pies. See page 122.

Top-Glazes & Toppings

For a glossy brown top on a double-crust pie, lightly brush the unbaked pie with water, milk or cream. For extra crispness, sprinkle a sweet pie with 1 tablespoon sugar or cinnamon sugar. Sprinkle a savory pie with 2 teaspoons sesame seeds, poppy seeds or caraway seeds.

Do not brush glaze on the fluting until the last 10 minutes of baking. Do not let pools of glaze accumulate or these spots will brown too quickly.

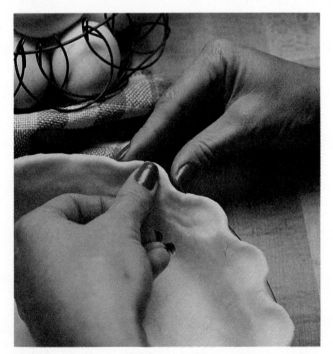

Making Scalloped Fluting on a single-crust pie shell.

Glazing a Quick Lattice, page 13, with milk. The Straight-Tines Fluting and Cutouts are on page 10 and above. Blueberry Pie is on page 99.

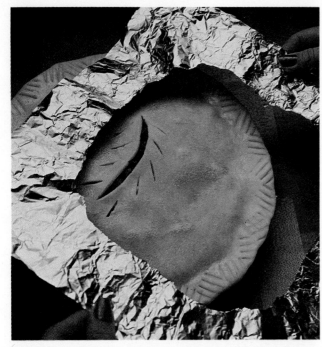

Covering edges of a double-crust with foil. The fluting is Herringbone, page 11. Traditional Mince Pie is on page 116.

Baking the Pie

The edge of a pie tends to brown faster than the center. To prevent overbrowning, construct a foil shield. For a 9-inch pie, fold a 12-inch square of foil in half and then in half again, making a 6-inch square. Cut or tear the folded corner 3-1/2 inches from the point. Unfold the foil. Discard the foil circle and place the circle frame over the fluted edge of your pie.

Bake the pie according to the specific recipe directions. Some recipes direct you to cook a pie until the fruit or vegetable it contains is tender. Test for tenderness by inserting the tines of a fork through a slit in the top crust.

Lattice Tops

Lattice-top pies require the same amount of dough as double-crust pies. Follow directions for Rolling Out the Bottom Crust, page 9.

Lattices for dessert pies are not as closely woven as those for pot pies. The spacing between strips for pot pies depends on the size of the casserole.

How to Weave a Lattice

Place 5 parallel strips about 3/4 inch apart on the filled pie. Use longer strips in the center and shorter strips on the sides. Fold back every other strip a little more than halfway. Place 1 of the remaining 5 strips across the center of the pie at right angles to the first 5 strips. Carefully unfold the folded strips and fold back the flat strips. Place 1 strip parallel to the center strip, leaving a 3/4-inch space between the 2 strips. Unfold and fold every other strip as you did for the center strip. Repeat with a strip parallel to the last strip near the edge of the pie. Fold back every other strip on the other side of the pie and repeat weaving with the 2 remaining strips. See the photo on page 67.

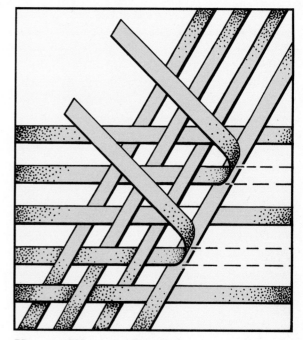

How to Weave a Lattice

Woven Lattice Method 1

Fill pie and trim bottom crust to edge of pie pan. Roll out remaining dough to a 12" x 10" rectangle. With a pastry cutter or knife, cut ten 10" x 3/4" strips and three 10" x 1" strips. Set aside the three 1-inch wide strips. They will be used around the edge of the pie after the lattice is finished. Weave a lattice with the 3/4-inch strips. Press lattice strips to edge of shell and trim off at edge of pie pan. Brush edge with water. Fit the 1-inch strips around edge, overlapping slightly and cutting off any excess length. Press gently to edge. If desired, press edge between your thumbs and index fingers to make a raised edge, page 10. Finish with decorative fluting, pages 10 and 11. Glaze and top as desired, page 11. Bake as directed in recipe.

Woven Lattice Method 2

Fill bottom crust. Do not trim edge. Roll out remaining pastry to an 11-inch circle. With a pastry cutter or knife, cut ten 3/4-inch strips from the circle. Lightly brush edge of bottom shell with water. Weave lattice and press lattice strips to edge of shell. Trim strips even with edge of bottom crust. Fold under and make a raised edge, page 10. Finish with decorative fluting, pages 10 and 11. Glaze and top as desired, page 11. Bake as directed in recipe.

Diamond Lattice

This is a non-woven lattice. Follow directions for Method 2 but do not weave lattice strips. Place 6 strips about 3/4 inch apart in one direction across the filling. Place the remaining 6 strips so a diamond pattern is produced where the filling shows through. Twist strips if desired. Proceed as for Woven Lattice Method 2.

Quick Lattice

Fill bottom crust and trim dough to edge of the pie pan. Roll out remaining dough to a 12-inch circle. Using a small (about 1-inch) hors d'oeuvre cutter, make a cutout in the center of the circle. Make more cutouts at 1/2-inch intervals in a regular pattern, creating a lattice of cutouts about 7-1/2 to 8 inches in diameter. Center over filling. Make a raised edge, page 10. Make a decorative edge using cutouts or decora-

Making a Diamond Lattice. Fresh-Rhubarb Lattice Pie is on page 97.

tive fluting, pages 10 and 11. Glaze and top as desired, page 11. See the photo on page 11. Bake as directed in recipe.

Freezing Pies & Pastries

Pies and pastries should be frozen as quickly as possible. If your freezer has a quick-freeze shelf, take advantage of it. Place food uncovered on the quick-freeze shelf with as much surrounding space as possible for air flow. You don't have to cover food while it is being quick-frozen, but it must be covered for storage in the freezer. Remove quick-frozen foods from the freezer as soon as they are frozen solid. Wrap them securely in freezer paper or foil, or place them in a freezer container with a tight-fitting lid. Label each package with the name of the food, the date, and baking or heating instructions.

If You Have a Food Processor

Standard pastry dough can be mixed in a food processor. Use these directions for:

Almond Pastry
Basic Pastry
Cheddar Pastry
Chocolate Pastry
Rich Butter Pastry
Sweet Butter Pastry
Wheat Pastry

Chill shortening or butter about 5 minutes in the freezer. Fit the steel knife blade into the work bowl. Process flour, salt and any other dry ingredient with 1 quick on-off turn. Cut chilled shortening or butter into 12 or 24 pieces and add to dry mixture. Process until pieces are the size of large peas, 5 to 10 seconds. Add the smaller amount of water. Process until mixture begins to gather on the blades, about 5 seconds. The action of the blade softens the shortening or butter, decreasing the need for more moisture. Do not process so long that dough forms a ball or your pie crust will not be flaky. Shape dough into 1 or 2 flat balls.

Use these directions for:

Cream-Cheese Pastry
Process-Cheese Pastry

Fit the steel knife blade into the work bowl. Place cheese and butter or shortening in work bowl. Process until blended, 5 to 10 seconds. Remove from work bowl. Chill in the freezer 5 minutes.

Basic Pastry

Flaky, tender pastry for both main dishes and desserts.

Use These Ingredients	To Make	
	Single Crust	**Double Crust**
all-purpose flour	1 cup	2 cups
salt	1/2 teaspoon	1 teaspoon
vegetable shortening or lard	1/3 cup	2/3 cup
water	3 to 4 tablespoons	7 to 8 tablespoons

Single Crust: Stir flour and salt together in a medium bowl. With a pastry blender or fork, cut in shortening or lard until pieces are the size of small peas. Add the smaller amount of water and toss with a fork until all flour is moistened and mixture starts to form a ball. If necessary, add remaining water to crumbs in bottom of bowl. Gather dough in your hands and gently shape into a flat ball.
Double Crust: Prepare as for Single Crust, shaping dough into 2 equal balls.

Variation

Herb Pastry: For each 1 cup of flour, stir 1/4 teaspoon poultry seasoning into flour-salt mixture.

How to Make Basic Pastry

1/The bowl with the pastry blender shows pieces of shortening the size of small peas.

2/Mixture in bowl has started to form a ball. Gently shape it into a flat ball.

Six-Crust Basic Pastry

Each portion makes one single crust.

6 cups all-purpose flour
2 teaspoons salt

2 cups vegetable shortening
1-1/4 to 1-1/2 cups water

Stir flour and salt in a large bowl. With a pastry blender or fork, cut in shortening until mixture resembles small peas. Add the smaller amount of water and toss with fork until all flour is moistened and mixture starts to form a ball. If necessary, add remaining water to crumbs in bottom of bowl. Gather dough in your hands and gently shape into a ball. Divide into 6 equal portions. Gently shape each portion into a flat ball. Wrap portions not being used immediately in plastic wrap. Wrap each portion separately and tightly. Dough may be refrigerated 2 days or frozen 6 months. Thaw as directed for Multi-Crust Basic Pastry, page 16. Makes dough for 3 double-crust pies or 6 single-crust pies.

Multi-Crust Basic Pastry

Make a two- or three-month supply all at once.

20 cups all-purpose flour
   (5 lbs. plus 2 cups)
3 tablespoons salt

3 lbs. vegetable shortening
3-1/2 to 3-3/4 cups water

In a 2-gallon or larger bowl, stir flour and salt. Spoon half the shortening over top of flour. With a pastry blender, cut in shortening until mixture resembles small peas. Toss with a wooden spoon to mix well and bring all flour up from bottom. Spoon remaining shortening over top and continue cutting in. Mix well. Pour 2 cups water over flour mixture. Toss to mix well and bring mixture up from bottom of bowl. Repeat with 1-1/2 cups water. Toss to mix, then mix with your hands, incorporating all flour. If necessary, add more water to crumbs in bottom of bowl. Measure 1 cup dough and gently shape into a flat ball. Repeat with remaining dough. Wrap each ball separately in plastic wrap. Or, place on a baking sheet, freeze uncovered until solid and place in an airtight container. Store in freezer. To thaw, place frozen dough ball in refrigerator overnight, at room temperature about 1 hour, or in microwave 1 minute at 10% (LOW). Makes dough for 20 to 22 single-crust pies or for 10 or 11 double-crust pies.

Wheat Pastry

Use this pastry the next time you make a vegetable or meat pie.

Use These Ingredients	To Make	
	Single Crust	**Double Crust**
all-purpose flour	1/2 cup	1 cup
whole-wheat flour	1/2 cup	1 cup
salt	1/2 teaspoon	1 teaspoon
vegetable shortening	1/3 cup	2/3 cup
water	3 to 4 tablespoons	7 to 8 tablespoons

Single Crust: Stir all-purpose flour, whole-wheat flour and salt together in a medium bowl. With a pastry blender or fork, cut in shortening until pieces are the size of small peas. Add the smaller amount of water and toss with a fork until all flour is moistened and mixture starts to form a ball. If necessary, add remaining water to crumbs in bottom of bowl. Gather dough in your hands and gently shape into a flat ball.
Double Crust: Prepare as for Single Crust, shaping dough into 2 equal balls.

Variation

Double-Wheat Pastry: Stir 2 tablespoons wheat germ into flour mixture for each 1/2 cup whole-wheat flour.

Cheddar Pastry

Sharp Cheddar cheese gives the best flavor.

Use These Ingredients	To Make	
	Single Crust	**Double Crust**
all-purpose flour	1 cup minus 2 tablespoons	1-3/4 cups
salt	1/2 teaspoon	1 teaspoon
Cheddar cheese	1/2 cup finely shredded	1 cup finely shredded
vegetable shortening	1/4 cup	1/2 cup
water	3 to 4 tablespoons	7 to 8 tablespoons

Single Crust: Stir flour, salt and cheese together in a medium bowl. With a pastry blender or fork, cut in shortening until pieces are the size of small peas. Add the smaller amount of water and toss with a fork until all flour is moistened and mixture starts to form a ball. If necessary, add remaining water to crumbs in bottom of bowl. Gather dough in your hands and gently shape into a flat ball.

Double Crust: Prepare as for Single Crust, shaping dough into 2 equal balls.

Cream-Cheese Pastry

Traditional for Russian Piroshki, page 43, it can also be used for fruit and main-dish pies.

Use These Ingredients	To Make	
	Single Crust	**Double Crust**
cream cheese	1 (3-oz.) pkg.	2 (3-oz.) pkgs.
butter	1/4 cup	1/2 cup
all-purpose flour	1 cup	2 cups
salt	1/2 teaspoon	1 teaspoon
water	3 to 4 tablespoons	7 to 8 tablespoons

Single Crust: Place cream cheese and butter in a medium bowl. Mash with a fork until smooth. Push to one side of bowl. Add flour and salt. Use fork to lift cheese mixture on top of flour. With a pastry blender or fork, cut cheese mixture into flour until pieces are the size of small peas. Add the smaller amount of water and toss with fork until all flour is moistened and mixture starts to form a ball. If necessary, add remaining water to crumbs in bottom of bowl. With your hands, gently shape into a flat ball.

Double Crust: Prepare as for Single Crust, shaping dough into 2 equal balls.

Process-Cheese Pastry

Vary the flavor of cheese spread used to complement the flavor of the filling.

1 (5-oz.) jar process-cheese spread
2/3 cup vegetable shortening
2 cups all-purpose flour

1/2 teaspoon salt
6 to 7 tablespoons water

Place cheese spread and shortening in a medium bowl. Mash with a fork until mixture is smooth. Push to one side of bowl. Add flour and salt. Use a fork to lift cheese mixture on top of flour. With a pastry blender or fork, cut cheese mixture into flour until pieces are the size of small peas. Add the smaller amount of water and toss with a fork until all flour is moistened and mixture starts to form a ball. If necessary, add remaining water to crumbs in bottom of bowl. Gather dough in your hands and gently shape into 2 flat equal balls. Makes dough for 1 double-crust pie.

Oil Pastry

Especially for those who are reducing their intake of shortening and butter.

Use These Ingredients	To Make	
	Single Crust	**Double Crust**
all-purpose flour	1 cup plus 2 tablespoons	2-1/4 cups
salt	1/2 teaspoon	1 teaspoon
vegetable oil	6 tablespoons	3/4 cup
cold water	2 tablespoons	1/4 cup

Single Crust: Stir flour and salt together in a medium bowl. Add oil and water at the same time. Stir quickly until mixture forms a ball. If necessary, add 1 or 2 teaspoons water to crumbs in bottom of bowl. Shape into a flat ball. Because oil pastry absorbs flour very quickly, place the un-floured dough ball between two 12-inch squares of waxed paper. Place on a lightly dampened surface to keep the bottom paper from slipping. Roll out dough between waxed paper to desired size. Peel off top paper. Flip over dough and remaining waxed paper. Center dough over pie pan. Gently peel off paper. Ease dough into pan.

Double Crust: Prepare as for Single Crust, shaping dough into 2 equal balls. If second ball of dough is to be a top crust, cut slits or other decorations before flipping and placing over filling. For a lattice top, use Quick Lattice, page 13.

Rich Butter Pastry

When you make a pie for a special occasion, indulge yourself with this buttery treat.

Use These Ingredients	To Make	
	Single Crust	**Double Crust**
all-purpose flour	1 cup	2 cups
salt	1/4 teaspoon	1/2 teaspoon
butter, slightly softened	1/2 cup	1 cup
water	3 to 4 tablespoons	7 to 8 tablespoons

Single Crust: Stir flour and salt together in a medium bowl. With a pastry blender or fork, cut in butter until pieces are the size of small peas. Add the smaller amount of water and toss with a fork until all flour is moistened and mixture starts to form a ball. If necessary, add remaining water to crumbs in bottom of bowl. Gather dough in your hands and gently shape into a flat ball.
Double Crust: Prepare as for Single Crust, shaping dough into 2 equal balls.

Sweet Butter Pastry

European-style pastry for tarts. The French call it pâte sucrée.

1-1/2 cups all-purpose flour	**1/2 cup butter**
2 tablespoons sugar	**1 egg yolk**
1/2 teaspoon salt	**1/4 cup milk or half and half**

Stir flour, sugar and salt together in a medium bowl. Work the butter into the flour mixture by rubbing between your thumb and fingers until butter pieces are the size of small peas. Combine egg yolk and milk or half and half. Add to flour mixture and toss with a fork until mixture starts to form a ball. If necessary, add more milk or half and half, 1 teaspoon at a time, to crumbs in bottom of bowl. Gather dough in your hands and gently shape into a flat ball. Makes dough for one 11-inch tart.

Chocolate Pastry

For a chocolate-flavor baked pie shell, pages 8 and 9, reduce the baking time by 2 or 3 minutes.

1 cup all-purpose flour	**2 tablespoons unsweetened cocoa powder**
1/4 teaspoon salt	**1/3 cup vegetable shortening**
1/4 cup packed brown sugar	**3 to 4 tablespoons water**

Stir flour, salt, brown sugar and cocoa powder in a medium bowl. With a pastry blender or fork, cut in shortening until mixture resembles small peas. Add 3 tablespoons water and toss with a fork until all flour mixture is moistened and starts to form a ball. If necessary, add remaining water to crumbs in bottom of bowl. Gather dough in your hands and gently shape into a flat ball. Makes dough for 1 single-crust pie.

Almond Pastry

Nut pastries are especially delicious filled with fruit.

Use These Ingredients	To Make	
	Single Crust	**Double Crust**
all-purpose flour	1 cup	2 cups
salt	1/2 teaspoon	1 teaspoon
Ground Almonds, see below	1/4 cup	1/2 cup
vegetable shortening	1/3 cup	2/3 cup
water	3 to 4 tablespoons	7 to 8 tablespoons

Single Crust: Stir flour, salt and Ground Almonds together in a medium bowl. With a pastry blender or fork, cut in shortening until pieces are the size of small peas. Add the smaller amount of water and toss with a fork until all flour is moistened and mixture starts to form a ball. If necessary, add remaining water to crumbs in bottom of bowl. Gather dough in your hands and gently shape into a flat ball.
Double Crust: Prepare as for Single Crust, shaping dough into 2 equal balls.

Ground Almonds:
Place 1 (2-3/4-ounce) package slivered almonds in blender. Process about 15 seconds, stopping twice to stir. Makes about 1/2 cup.

Variation
Pecan Pastry: Substitute pecan pieces for slivered almonds.

Egg Glaze

This mixture is used as a glaze for pastries and as a sealer to hold them together.

1 egg
1/4 teaspoon salt

Beat egg and salt with a fork or whisk until smooth. Salt will cause the egg to become thin, making a smooth liquid. Glaze may be frozen if it has been at room temperature 5 minutes or less. Freeze and thaw only once. Makes about 3 tablespoons glaze.

Puff Pastry

The French call this *pâte feuilletée,* the pastry of little leaves. This classic layering technique results in such rich delights as Napoleons, page 174, and Cream Horns, page 173.

Classic Puff Pastry contains between 500 and 800 layers of pastry and 250 to 400 layers of butter, depending on the number of folds you give the dough. When baked, the butter in the dough melts and is replaced by expanding hot air. The result is a light, high, crisp and flaky pastry.

Quick Puff Pastry is an easier version of the traditional Classic Puff Pastry. It does not have as many distinct layers so it may not puff quite as high. The recipes are generally interchangeable, but it's best to use Classic Puff Pastry with recipes that depend on the many pastry layers expanding upward to form a shell.

Puff pastry shells may be frozen unfilled to be baked later. If the shell is frozen unbaked, it will be crisp after baking and there will be less danger of breakage. Thaw unbaked puff pastry shells for about 30 minutes before baking.

If you must freeze a baked shell, put it in a freezer container and place it in the freezer in a spot where there is little chance of damage. Thaw a baked shell at room temperature for about 30 minutes and then crisp it in a 425F (220C) oven for 3 to 5 minutes before serving.

I prefer to make the dough ahead of time, wrap it well and store it unshaped and unbaked in the freezer.

Some supermarkets carry 17-1/4-ounce packages of frozen puff pastry. Each package contains 2 sheets. One sheet equals 1 cup of puff pastry. The sheets can be thawed and used in all puff pastry recipes in this book except Bouchées, Vol-au-Vent and Kulebiaka, which need a thicker pastry.

Puff Pastry Techniques

Puff pastry is more difficult to work with than standard pastry because it needs frequent resting and chilling. The proportions of butter, flour and water result in a low gluten content. Cake flour, which has a low wheat-protein content and tends to form less gluten, may be used in place of a fourth of the flour. The less gluten the dough contains, the easier it is to work with and the more tender the pastry will be. Chilling the dough gives gluten a chance to rest and relax, promoting tenderness in the dough. If you fold and roll out continuously, completing all the turns at one time without chilling, the dough will become too firm to roll out as directed. Chilling also helps keep the butter in distinct layers. Always chill when indicated in the recipe.

While working with puff pastry, keep the work surface smooth and lightly floured. Scrape the work surface occasionally with a dough scraper or broad knife. Roll out the dough evenly without stretching one side more than the other. This is essential for even expansion and shrinking during baking.

When cutting most shapes, stay 1/2 to 1 inch away from folded edges. They do not have a uniform thickness and may not expand evenly.

Cut puff pastry with an up-and-down motion. A dragging motion may stretch the dough. A large butcher knife or a sharp pizza cutter is efficient for long straight lines. A small chef's knife or a paring knife works well for cutting circles or for trimming edges. The back of the blade of a small knife is used to make indentations and grooves. If the recipe calls for 1/16-inch cuts, use a small knife because it is lighter and easier to manage.

Most puff pastries are glazed with Egg Glaze, opposite. Brush it on lightly. Use a soft brush so you do not make grooves in the dough. Do not let any glaze drip over a cut edge or it may prevent the layers from expanding evenly.

How to Store Puff Pastry Dough

Wrap the dough in plastic wrap or place it in a freezer container or a food storage bag. Refrigerate it for 3 days or freeze it for 3 months. If refrigerated longer than 30 minutes, let the dough stand at room temperature 3 to 5 minutes before rolling out. Thaw frozen dough for 3 to 5 hours in the refrigerator or for 30 minutes at room temperature.

Classic Puff Pastry

If you need only 1 cup of puff pastry, see the variation below.

1 cup butter
2 cups all-purpose flour or
   1-1/2 cups all-purpose flour and
   1/2 cup cake flour

1/4 teaspoon salt
3/4 cup cold water

Let butter stand at room temperature 15 minutes. Cut off 2 tablespoons of butter and set aside. Place the remaining butter between 2 pieces of lightly floured waxed paper. Pound with a rolling pin to make butter pliable, with the consistency of firm dough. As butter flattens, replace top paper and pound again. If paper breaks, use a new piece. Use a small spatula to shape butter into a 5-inch square with slightly rounded edges. Wrap in plastic wrap. Refrigerate while making dough. Combine flour and salt in a medium bowl. Work reserved 2 tablespoons butter into flour by rubbing together with your fingers. Add cold water and stir to a pliable dough. Knead on a lightly floured surface 30 times. Cover by inverting bowl over dough. Let rest 10 minutes. Lightly flour a smooth surface. Roll out dough to an 8-inch circle. Then roll out only the 4 sides and not the center until dough measures 9 inches through the middle, both in length and width, and resembles a flower with 4 petals. Center of dough will be thick. Place chilled butter square on center. Fold dough over butter, bringing corners to center and overlapping slightly. Wrap in plastic wrap and refrigerate 15 minutes. Lightly flour work surface and add flour as necessary during *turning* process: Place dough flat side down on work surface. Press rolling pin firmly on dough 7 times, once in center and 3 times above and below center to flatten dough and seal edges. Roll out dough away from and toward you, not sideways. Keep thickness of dough as even as possible, gradually making it thinner all over. Do not let rolling pin roll off edge of dough. Keep corners as square as possible. Roll out to a rectangle 14 to 15 inches long and 6 to 7 inches wide. Fold in thirds like a letter. Give it a quarter turn so the long opening is to your right. Press with rolling pin to seal edges. This process of pressing, rolling out, folding and sealing is called a *turn.* Complete a second turn and refrigerate 15 minutes. Repeat the turn 4 more times, refrigerating 15 minutes after each 2 turns. The completed dough will have been through a total of 6 turns. Refrigerate 15 minutes or longer after last turn before using for a recipe. If dough becomes difficult to roll out, wrap it in plastic wrap and refrigerate 10 minutes. Makes 2 cups.

Variation

To make two 1-cup portions: After 6 turns have been made, cut dough rectangle in half crosswise. Wrap each piece separately. Refrigerate or freeze and use as directed.

Puff Pastry Scraps

Save scraps from puff pastry. Freeze them in a freezer container or food storage bag. When you have 1-1/4 cups of scraps, let them thaw in the refrigerator for 3 to 5 hours or at room temperature for 30 minutes. Place the scraps side-by-side and slightly overlapping on a lightly floured surface. Roll out to a 10" x 4" rectangle. Fold in thirds. Wrap in plastic wrap and refrigerate. Use the dough in any recipe that calls for 1 cup of puff pastry and does not depend on high even expansion. These recipes are: Tarte Tatin, page 92; Blue Cheese Twists, page 40; Cream Horns, page 173; Jalousie, page 176; and any turnover recipe including Appetizer Calzone, page 45.

How to Make Classic Puff Pastry

1/Use a small spatula to shape butter into a 5-inch square with rounded edges.

2/Placed chilled butter in center of dough and fold dough petals over butter.

3/To flatten dough, firmly press with rolling pin in several different places.

4/After rolling out dough to a rectangle, fold it in thirds like a letter.

Quick Puff Pastry

As good as Classic Puff Pastry, page 22, for most recipes and easier to make.

2 cups all-purpose flour or
   1-1/2 cups all-purpose flour and
   1/2 cup cake flour

1/4 teaspoon salt
3/4 cup cold butter
2/3 cup cold water

Combine flour and salt in a medium bowl. Cut butter into about 60 pieces. Drop into flour and toss lightly to break butter pieces apart and coat with flour. Add cold water all at once and mix quickly. Mixture will be lumpy. Turn onto a lightly floured surface and knead 10 times to form a rough ball. Shape into a rectangle and flatten slightly. The following process of rolling out, folding and turning the dough is called a *turn:* Adding flour to work surface as necessary, roll out dough away from you and toward you, not sideways, making a 15" x 6" rectangle and keeping dough as uniformly thick as possible. Fold in thirds like a letter. Give dough a quarter turn so the long opening is to your right. Repeat the *turn* twice for a total of 3 turns. If butter begins to break through dough, sprinkle that spot generously with flour. If dough becomes difficult to roll, wrap in plastic wrap and refrigerate 10 minutes. If dough has streaks after the third turn, give 1 more turn. Makes 2 cups.

Variation

To make two 1-cup portions: After 3 turns have been made, cut dough rectangle in half cross-wise. Wrap each piece separately. Refrigerate or freeze and use as directed.

How to Make Quick Puff Pastry

1/Knead dough 10 times to form a rough ball.

2/After folding in thirds, roll out to a rectangle and fold again.

Strudel

Central and Eastern Europe, which includes Austria, Hungary, Yugoslavia and Czechoslovakia, have always been famous for pastry. One reason is the delicate strudel served in the outdoor cafés of such romantic cities as Vienna and Budapest. If you order strudel in a Viennese café, it will be topped with a mountain of rich whipped cream. What could be more luxurious and delicious!

Strudel is a tissue-thin sheet of pastry that is rolled several times around a filling. This results in several light flaky layers of crisp pastry. In this case, melted butter and breadcrumbs between the layers are responsible for the flakiness. The thinness of strudel is achieved by stretching. For the dough to have enough elasticity to be stretched, gluten must be present. This occurs when flour that is high in wheat protein, such as bread flour, is mixed with water. Kneading the dough encourages the gluten to develop, providing the elasticity necessary for stretching the dough.

The first time you make strudel you will wonder that many housewives in Central Europe make strudel almost daily. But as you become proficient in lifting and stretching the dough, you will find it's easier than you thought. If two or three people are involved, the stretching goes faster and is more fun than work.

As with any dish originating in country kitchens, there are as many versions of strudel as there are cooks and available ingredients. Apple strudel or *Apfelstrudel* is the most traditional, but a many seasonal fruits and other ingredients are widely used.

We usually think of strudel as a dessert. It can also be an appetizer, a luncheon or supper dish, or a side dish served at a hearty meal. See the vegetable strudels on pages 88 and 89.

Strudel Pastry Techniques

The rolling out and stretching of strudel dough must be done on a large surface. A table 4 feet long and 3 feet wide will be large enough and still let you reach all sides of the dough. A patterned sheet makes a good cloth for covering the work surface. As you stretch the dough, you will see the pattern showing through. If you cannot clearly see the pattern through the dough, you know that area needs more stretching. After completing the strudel, shake out the sheet, fold it up and store it with your other pastry equipment.

Oiling or buttering the top of the dough before and during stretching prevents it from drying out and sticking. This is especially important the first few times until you have learned how to handle the dough easily and quickly.

Lift and stretch the dough over the backs of your hands. The palm side of your fingertips may be used if you have short fingernails and can keep the tips of your fingers together so they do not puncture the dough.

Let the dough rest after kneading and again after rolling out. This relaxes the gluten so the dough will be easier to stretch without tearing. If you overstretch an area and it tears, pinch the dough together immediately to close the hole. Continue stretching, being cautious around the patched spot. If there are any large holes, thin out some of the edge trimmings and pinch them around edges of the holes. Small holes don't need to be patched.

For any strudel recipe, you can use 1 pound of purchased filo sheets in place of Strudel Pastry, page 26. First, prepare the filling and cover the work surface with a cloth or sheet. Place 1 layer of filo sheets in a rectangular area about 4 feet long and 2 feet wide, overlapping about 2 inches at any seam. Use the amount of melted butter and breadcrumbs specified in the recipe. Lightly brush with melted butter and sprinkle with about half the breadcrumbs. Repeat the filo layer, slightly staggering the sheets so the seams are in different places. Brush with melted butter and sprinkle with the remaining breadcrumbs. Continue layering the filo sheets, brushing each layer with melted butter, until you have used all the sheets. Proceed as directed in the recipe, placing the filling the length of the 4-foot side.

Strudel Pastry

Paper-thin dough to roll around sweet or savory fillings.

1 egg
2/3 cup water
2 tablespoons butter, melted

1-3/4 cups bread flour
1/2 teaspoon salt
About 1 tablespoon butter, melted

Combine egg, water and 2 tablespoons melted butter in a small bowl. Combine flour and salt in a large bowl. Add egg mixture to flour. Stir by hand 3 minutes. On a lightly floured surface, knead dough until smooth and elastic, about 8 minutes. Place on a floured surface and cover with inverted bowl. Let rest 15 minutes. Prepare desired filling. Cover a surface that is about 4 feet long and 3 feet wide with a cloth that is 4 feet square or larger. Lightly flour the cloth, rubbing with your hands to distribute flour evenly. Place dough on cloth and roll out as thin as possible, about 1/8 inch thick and 15 inches square. Cover with plastic wrap. Let rest 10 minutes. Remove plastic wrap. Lightly brush dough with melted butter. Working quickly so dough will not dry out, stretch it to a 4-foot square: Starting near center, place back of your hands under dough. Slowly lift and move your hands apart to stretch dough. This may also be done by holding a section of dough firmly to the cloth with one hand and gently stretching in the opposite direction with back of the other hand. Stretch dough so it gradually becomes thinner all over rather than very thin in one spot and not in others. Stretch until almost paper-thin. Trim off thick edges with scissors. Let stand to dry 10 minutes. Then use immediately. Makes dough for one 4-foot strudel.

How to Make Strudel Pastry

1/Knead dough until smooth and elastic, about 8 minutes.

2/Roll out dough to a 15-inch square.

Filo Pastry

Filo, or *phyllo*, has been used for centuries in the countries bordering the Mediterranean Sea. From Greece and Turkey, through Lebanon and around to Egypt, shelves in pastry shops are lined with all shapes, sizes and flavors of filo pastries. Many of the sweet pastries are filled with nuts and dried fruits. These pastries are often soaked in honey syrup.

I do not recommend making your own filo if you can buy it. The label on one brand of filo lists the ingredients as "flour, water, salt and SKILL!" Fresh or frozen filo sheets or leaves may be purchased in 1-pound packages in some supermarkets and in specialty stores. You may even discover a Greek or Turkish bakery where filo is made on the premises and sold fresh.

Frozen strudel leaves may be substituted for frozen filo. If filo sheets or strudel leaves are not available in your area, prepare Strudel Pastry, page 26. Stretch it to a 5-foot square. Trim and cut the square into twenty 15" x 12" sheets. This will be the equivalent of 1 pound of purchased filo sheets. Use these homemade filo sheets immediately.

Filo Pastry Techniques

Filo pastry is very delicate and requires gentle handling. Be careful not to handle packages of frozen filo roughly because the frozen sheets are brittle and easily broken. Thaw as directed on the package, usually overnight in the refrigerator. If the pastry is not completely thawed, the sheets will tear. Read the recipe carefully before starting and have all other ingredients ready before opening the package of filo.

If the recipe you are using requires only 1/2 pound of filo, unroll the thawed filo sheets. Remove the sheets you need. Immediately rewrap the unused filo and cover the sheets you will be using with plastic wrap.

As filo dries it becomes brittle and will not roll up easily. If your kitchen is very dry, place a damp towel over the plastic wrap covering the filo. Do not let the towel come in contact with the filo or the sheets may soften and have to be discarded. Torn and broken pieces of filo may be used in Spanakopita, page 59, and Baklava, page 184, which are layered in large pans.

Thawed filo sheets may be refrozen but this increases their chances of drying and breaking.

3/Lift and stretch dough with the back of your hands.

4/Trim off thick edges with scissors.

Choux Pastry

Choux pastry is also called *cream-puff pastry*. Choux, pronounced *shoo*, is the French word for cabbage. If you look closely at the shape and texture of the outside of a cream puff, it does resemble cauliflower, a member of the cabbage family.

Water, butter and flour—the same ingredients used for other pastries—are combined in choux pastry. But the proportions of these ingredients, the addition of eggs, and the method of combining make it distinctively different from other pastries. Choux pastry contains more liquid than standard pastry and puff pastry. When choux is baked, this liquid becomes steam and expands. The dough, made soft and elastic by eggs, holds the steam. The result is baked pastry with large holes inside. The holes may be filled with a savory filling of meat or cheese and enjoyed as an appetizer, or filled with a sweet filling and served as a dessert.

Although cream puffs and éclairs receive the most attention, choux can be shaped and filled in a number of ways. Appetizer Balls, page 33, with meat or fish filling will delight the cocktail crowd. Fill a large Christmas Wreath, page 183, with whipped cream or pudding and decorate it with a holiday theme. Stir cheese into the pastry before it is shaped into an appetizer ring to make Gougère, page 47.

Choux freezes best after it is baked. Wrap it in plastic wrap and place it in a freezer container or food storage bag and freeze. Thaw the pastry at room temperature for about 30 minutes. Preheat the oven to 425F (220C). Place the thawed pastry on a baking sheet and crisp it in the oven for 2 to 4 minutes, depending on the size and shape of the pastry. Do not fill it before freezing unless the filling is ice cream. Choux pastry filled with a cream mixture then frozen may be soggy when it's thawed and served.

How to Make Choux Pastry

1/Add flour and salt all at once to butter and water mixture.

2/Stir until dough leaves side of pan. Then add 1 egg.

Choux Pastry

Unsweetened egg pastry is also called cream-puff pastry.

Use These Ingredients	To Make	
	3-Egg Pastry	**4-Egg Pastry**
water	3/4 cup	1 cup
butter	6 tablespoons, cut in 6 pieces	1/2 cup, cut in 8 pieces
all-purpose flour	3/4 cup	1 cup
salt	1/4 teaspoon	1/2 teaspoon
large eggs	3	4

Place water and butter in a medium saucepan. Bring to a full boil over medium heat. Boil until butter is melted. Add flour and salt all at once. Stir vigorously until dough forms a ball and leaves side of pan, about 1 minute. Remove from heat. Add eggs one at a time, mixing thoroughly after each addition. After last egg is thoroughly incorporated, mix vigorously 30 seconds longer. Shape dough as directed in recipe. Cool away from drafts.

3/Mix well after adding each egg.

4/After beating in last egg, beat 30 seconds longer. Mixture will be shiny and smooth.

Crumb Crusts

It was probably a frugal pastry chef in Europe who created the first crumb crust with leftover bread or cake. Today, our crisp crumb crusts are usually made with cookie or cracker crumbs and melted butter. Although not a pastry, crumb crusts have become a basic shell for chiffon and freezer pies. Their flavor can vary as easily as you can crush hard cookies or crackers or add chopped nuts, coconut or spices. Most crumb crusts are interchangeable. The exception is Chocolate-Cookie Crust. Its strong flavor may overwhelm a lightly flavored filling.

For a smooth compact crust, the crumbs must be fine and uniform in size. Most crumb crusts are baked so they will hold together. Chilling the crust after baking hardens the butter and makes a firm crust.

To make your own crumbs, break graham crackers or cookies into uniform pieces. Place the pieces in a food processor fitted with the steel knife blade or in a blender. Process to fine crumbs. Or, place the broken crackers or cookies in a plastic bag and roll a rolling pin over them until they are crushed fine. Four 2-1/2-inch graham crackers will yield about 1/4 cup of crumbs.

Crumb crusts are best for freezer pies because they are not as brittle as standard pastry. A frozen standard crust becomes even more brittle. A frozen crumb crust becomes firmer. Crumb crusts are easier to wrap and freeze because they don't have breakable fluted edges.

Purchased crumb crusts are smaller than the recipe for 9-inch crusts in this book. If you use one, you will have about 1 cup of extra filling. Put it in a freezer container and chill or freeze it as indicated in the recipe. Or, put it in tart-size purchased crumb shells—about 1/3 cup to each shell—and you'll have a ready-made frozen dessert.

How to Make Crumb Crusts

1/Make a firm crust by pressing crumbs with the back of a spoon.

2/Or, press crumbs with the bottom and side of a custard cup.

Crumb Crusts

Crust	Crumbs	Melted Butter	Sugar	Other Ingredients	Oven Temperature	Baking Time
Graham-Cracker	1-1/4 cups graham-cracker crumbs	1/3 cup	1/4 cup		375F (190C)	8 minutes
Gingersnap	1-1/4 cups gingersnap crumbs	1/3 cup	1/4 cup		375F (190C)	8 minutes
Vanilla-Wafer	1-1/2 cups vanilla-wafer crumbs	1/3 cup	1/4 cup		375F (190C)	8 minutes
Nutty-Graham	1 cup graham-cracker crumbs	1/3 cup	1/4 cup	1/3 cup finely chopped walnuts or pecans	375F (190C)	8 minutes
Coconut-Graham	1 cup graham-cracker crumbs	1/3 cup	1/4 cup	1/2 cup flaked or shredded coconut	375F (190C)	8 minutes
Coconut	2 cups flaked or shredded coconut	1/4 cup			325F (165C)	20 minutes
Chocolate-Cookie	1-1/2 cups chocolate-cookie crumbs	1/3 cup	2 table-spoons		375F (190C)	8 minutes

Preheat oven. Combine all ingredients in a medium bowl. Use a spoon to mix well. Spread mixture evenly over bottom of a 9-inch pie pan. Use a smaller pie pan, the back of a large spoon, a custard cup or your hands to press mixture against bottom and up sides of pan 1/2 inch higher than rim of pan. Bake and cool. Makes one 9-inch crust.

 *tip*

Margarine can be substituted for butter in most recipes in this book, but there may be a difference in the texture of the finished dish. Recipes in this book were developed with lightly salted butter in cube or stick form—not with whipped butter.

Distinctive Appetizers

Little tidbits to whet your appetite.

Gourmands around the world regularly demonstrate a weakness for savory fillings in crisp miniature crusts. In the Middle East, people gather for pre-dinner conversation around platters of filo pastries with their aromas of nuts, lamb, chicken and cheese. These hors d'oeuvres are represented here by Filo Triangles and Sigaras. In France, tiny cream puffs filled with seafood and spiced cheese disappear as soon as they make their entrance. I've called them *Appetizer Balls.*

Many cultures share a love of tiny savory turnovers. In Spain and Mexico, they're filled with spicy beef or chicken mixtures and called *empanadas.* In Russia, *piroshki* contain beef or cabbage filling and are flavored with dill. Italian *calzone* show their origins with a mozzarella and salami or pepperoni filling.

Begin your next formal dinner with continental flair. Surprise your guests with a savory French pastry such as Ham Pithiviers or Gougère as a first course. Both may be served before or with a green salad. If you're having only a few guests in for a light lunch or supper, serve double portions of either Ham Pithiviers or Gougère as the main course with a hearty vegetable salad.

For buffet-style appetizers, arrange little pastries on platters. Garnish the platters liberally with cherry tomatoes, radish roses, carrot curls or lemon wedges. Accent the arrangement with sprigs of parsley or watercress. Plan differences in textures, shapes and flavors. The crispness and biting flavor of radishes go well with Filo Triangles and Piroshki. Cucumber and carrot sticks with Avocado Dip, Deviled Western Cutouts and Empanadas de Queso are another appetizing selection.

The larger the party, the more advance planning and preparation you'll need to do. Appetizers to be served at room temperature can be prepared a few hours ahead and arranged on platters. Cover them with plastic wrap until the first guests arrive. Prepare hot appetizers ahead but do not bake them. Place them on the baking sheets, cover and refrigerate. They can go in the oven any time after the guests arrive so they'll be served piping hot. Prepare garnishes and fresh accompaniments several hours ahead. Refrigerate them until the trays are ready to be garnished.

When an appetizer recipe calls for refrigeration before baking, the appetizer can be frozen at that point in airtight containers. About 30 minutes before baking, arrange the frozen appetizers on a baking sheet to give them time to thaw.◆

South-of-the-Border Cocktail Party

Empanadas de Queso, page 41
Beef Empanadas, page 42
Avocado Dip, page 35
Appetizer Balls, page 33
with
Olive-Chili Spread, page 34
Papaya, Pineapple & Strawberry
Fruit Platter
Tortilla Chips with Bean Dip
Sangría
Margaritas

Sesame-Cheese Diamonds

Make two batches. Flavor one with Parmesan cheese according to the variation below.

3/4 cup butter, softened
1-1/2 cups shredded sharp Cheddar cheese
  (6 oz.)
1-1/4 cups all-purpose flour

1/4 teaspoon onion salt
Dash red (cayenne) pepper
2 tablespoons toasted sesame seeds,
  page 73

Preheat oven to 375F (190C). Place butter and cheese in a large bowl. Beat with electric mixer until fluffy and almost smooth. Stir in flour, onion salt, red pepper and sesame seeds. Shape into a ball and refrigerate about 30 minutes until no longer sticky. Review Rolling Out, page 8. Divide dough into 2 equal portions. On a lightly floured surface, roll out 1 portion 1/8 inch thick. To make 1-1/2-inch diamonds, cut parallel lines 1-1/2 inches apart. Then cut parallel lines 1-1/2 inches apart at a slight angle across the first set of lines. Repeat with remaining dough. Shape scraps into a ball, roll out and cut more diamonds. Place on an ungreased baking sheet. Bake 10 to 12 minutes until lightly browned. Serve warm or at room temperature. Baked diamonds may be frozen in an airtight container. Thaw and serve at room temperature. Or heat 3 minutes in a 325F (165C) oven. Makes about 60 appetizers.

Variation

Parmesan Diamonds: Omit sesame seeds. Substitute 1/2 cup grated Parmesan cheese for 1/2 cup Cheddar cheese. Sprinkle diamonds with additional Parmesan cheese before baking.

Appetizer Balls

Rich and delectable miniature puffs filled with savory mixtures.

Choux Pastry made with 4 eggs, page 29
1/4 cup grated Parmesan cheese (3/4 oz.)

Crab Pâté, page 36,
Olive-Chile Spread, page 34

Preheat oven to 400F (205C). Prepare dough for pastry. Stir in Parmesan cheese after beating in last egg. Drop dough by slightly rounded teaspoonfuls about 2 inches apart on ungreased baking sheets. Bake 30 minutes or until puffed and dry. Remove or loosen from baking sheets. Cool. Prepare Crab Pâté and Olive-Chile Spread. Cut off tops of balls. Fill with pâté and spread. Replace tops. Serve within 2 hours or pastry may become soggy. Makes 48 appetizers.

Variation

Substitute Shrimp Pâté, page 37, for Crab Pâté.

Deviled Western Cutouts

Use this savory pastry as the dough for canapé bases.

1-1/2 cups all-purpose flour
1/2 teaspoon salt
1/4 teaspoon dry mustard
1/4 teaspoon garlic salt
1/8 teaspoon white pepper

1/4 cup grated Parmesan cheese (3/4 oz.)
1/2 cup butter or shortening
1 (4-1/2-oz.) can deviled ham
3 tablespoons water

Combine flour, salt, mustard, garlic salt, white pepper and Parmesan cheese in a medium bowl. With a pastry cutter or fork, cut in butter or shortening until pieces are the size of small peas. Stir in deviled ham and water until mixture begins to form a ball. Gather dough into your hands and gently shape into 2 equal balls. Preheat oven to 375F (190C). Review Rolling Out, page 8. On a lightly floured surface, roll out 1 ball to a 12" x 8" rectangle. Cut into twenty-four 2-inch squares. Shape as directed below and place on ungreased baking sheets. If desired, refrigerate until about 15 minutes before ready to serve. Bake 10 to 12 minutes until lightly browned. Repeat with remaining dough. Serve warm or cooled. Makes 48 appetizers.

Shield: Make a 2-inch cut from one corner toward the opposite corner. Mark the center point on one side adjoining the cut corner. Make a 1-inch cut from that point toward the corner opposite the 2-inch cut. Repeat on the other adjoining side. Place on baking sheet. Separate slightly at cuts.

Fish: Make 1-inch cuts from opposite corners toward the center. From the center point of each side, make a 5/8-inch cut parallel to the first cuts. Place on baking sheet. Push both corners with long cuts in the same direction to resemble fins.

Maltese Cross: Make 1-inch cuts from each corner toward the center. Place on baking sheet. Pinch each point slightly to make a curve in each 2-inch side.

Pine Tree: On one side of the square, make 3 cuts perpendicular to the edge, equally spaced and in the following order: 1/4-, 1/2- and 3/4-inch long. On the side nearest the 1/4-inch cut, make the same 3 cuts. Place on baking sheet. Separate slightly at cuts.

Olive-Chile Spread

For a more spicy filling, replace 1 to 2 tablespoons of milk with hot salsa.

1 (8-oz.) pkg. cream cheese, softened
1 chicken bouillon cube, crushed
2 to 3 tablespoons milk
1/4 cup finely chopped green onions
   with tops

1/4 cup finely chopped ripe olives
2 tablespoons finely chopped green chilies

With a fork, mash cream cheese in a small bowl. Gradually add bouillon cube and 2 tablespoons milk. Mix until smooth and spreadable. If necessary, add more milk. Stir in remaining ingredients. Refrigerate 1 hour or longer. Makes filling for 24 Appetizer Balls.

How to Make Deviled Western Cutouts

1/Cut and shape dough squares to resemble shields and fish.

2/Cutouts are done when lightly browned. Pine trees and Maltese crosses are shown here.

Avocado Dip

Especially good with Empanadas de Queso, page 41.

1 large avocado	**Generous dash red (cayenne) pepper**
2 tablespoons finely chopped onion	**Generous dash black pepper**
1 teaspoon lemon juice	**1 large tomato**
1/8 teaspoon garlic salt	**1 tablespoon chopped cilantro, if desired**
1/8 teaspoon salt	

Cut avocado in half. Remove seed. Scoop out pulp with a spoon and place in a small bowl. Mash with a fork until almost smooth. Stir in onion, lemon juice, garlic salt, salt, red pepper and black pepper. Cover and refrigerate 2 to 3 hours to blend flavors. Place tomato, stem end down, on work surface. Cut off top third. Scoop out pulp, leaving shell about 1/4 inch thick. Reserve pulp. Scoop pulp from top of tomato. Remove as many seeds as possible from all pulp and discard. Chop pulp. Stir into avocado mixture. Stir in cilantro, if desired. Spoon into tomato shell. Serve in the center of an appetizer tray. Makes about 1 cup.

Variation

Omit large tomato. Cut 1 small tomato into 1/4-inch pieces. Stir into avocado mixture. Serve in a bowl.

Peppy Appetizer Flan

Spiced pepper cheese gives this filling special zip.

Double-Crust Rich Butter Pastry, page 19
1/2 cup whipping cream
2 eggs, separated
1 (4-oz.) pkg. Rondelé cheese spiced with
  pepper, 1 (5-oz.) pkg. Boursin spice
  cheese or 4 oz. Roquefort cheese

1 tablespoon all-purpose flour
1 cup shredded Monterey Jack cheese
  (4 oz.)
1 teaspoon water
1/2 teaspoon poppy seeds

Prepare dough for pastry. Review Baked Pie Shells, pages 8 and 9, and Diamond Lattice, page 13. Preheat oven to 400F (205C). Divide dough into 3 equal portions. Put 2 portions together and shape into 1 large flat ball. On a lightly floured surface, roll out large ball to a 13-inch circle. Fit into an 11-inch flan pan with a removable bottom. Trim edges even with top of pan. Refrigerate 15 minutes or bake blind. To bake blind, line pie shell with foil and fill with beans. Bake chilled shell or bean-filled shell 10 minutes; remove foil and beans. In a medium bowl, combine cream and egg yolks. Set aside 1 tablespoon cream mixture in a small bowl. Crumble Rondelé, Boursin or Roquefort cheese into cream mixture in medium bowl. Add flour. Mix well. Beat egg whites until soft peaks form. Fold into cheese mixture. Sprinkle Monterey Jack cheese over bottom of partially baked shell. Pour cheese mixture evenly over Monterey Jack cheese. On a lightly floured surface, roll out remaining dough to a 12'' x 6'' rectangle. With a pastry cutter or a knife, cut rectangle into 12 strips 1 inch wide. Add water to reserved 1 tablespoon of cream mixture. Use as a glaze to brush over strips. Arrange strips glazed side up on flan in a diamond pattern. Trim edges of strips even with rim of pan. Sprinkle flan with poppy seeds. Bake 20 minutes or until golden. Makes 12 appetizer servings.

Crab Pâté

This pâté may be a filling for Appetizer Balls, page 33, or a spread for cocktail bread.

6 oz. fresh or frozen crab
2 tablespoons dry white wine
2 tablespoons vegetable oil
2 large sprigs fresh parsley

1/4 teaspoon salt
2 tablespoons toasted sesame seeds,
  page 73

Rinse crab and remove any shell or fiber. Place all ingredients except sesame seeds in blender or food processor. Process on low speed until just blended but not a paste. Spoon into a medium bowl. Stir in sesame seeds. Refrigerate 1 hour or longer. Makes filling for 24 Appetizer Balls.

Hors d'Oeuvre Puffs

There's a surprise inside each one. Mix and match your favorite fillings and toppings.

**1 cup Classic Puff Pastry, page 22, or
    Quick Puff Pastry, page 24**
Fillings, see below

Egg Glaze, page 20
Toppings, see below

Fillings:
Halved anchovy fillets
Deviled ham
**Finely chopped ham and Swiss cheese or
    Cheddar cheese**
Smoked oysters or clams

**Cooked crumbled bacon and chopped
    green onions**
Halved stuffed olives
1/2-inch slices smoked link sausages

Toppings:
Sesame seeds
Caraway seeds

Poppy seeds
Grated Parmesan cheese

Review Puff Pastry Techniques, page 21. Prepare dough for pastry. On a lightly floured surface, roll out dough 1/8 inch thick. With 2-1/2- to 3-inch cookie cutters or hors d'oeuvre cutters, make an even number of cutouts. Gather scraps into a ball and let rest 3 to 5 minutes. Roll out and cut more shapes, keeping an even number of cutouts for each shape. Half the cutouts will be bases for puffs. Include cutouts made from scraps as bases. Place bases on ungreased baking sheets. Prepare Egg Glaze. Brush over each base. Place 1/2 teaspoon filling in center of each base. Top with a matching shape. Press edges together with your fingers. Brush tops with glaze, being careful not to let glaze drip over edges. Sprinkle with desired toppings. Use the same topping to indicate puffs that have the same filling. Leave some puffs plain, if desired. Refrigerate 10 minutes or longer. Preheat oven to 425F (220C). Bake 10 to 12 minutes until golden brown. Baked puffs may be frozen. Reheat in preheated oven at 425F (220C) about 5 minutes. Makes about 18 appetizers.

Shrimp Pâté

Delightful as an appetizer or a sandwich spread.

3/4 cup cooked fresh or canned shrimp
1 (8-oz.) pkg. cream cheese, softened
2 to 3 tablespoons milk

2 tablespoons finely chopped green onion
1/8 teaspoon garlic salt

Rinse and drain shrimp. Place cream cheese and shrimp in a medium bowl. Mash with a fork. Gradually add 2 tablespoons milk, mixing until almost smooth. Stir in green onion and garlic salt. Refrigerate 1 hour or longer. If necessary, stir in 1 tablespoon milk to make mixture spreadable. Makes filling for 24 Appetizer Balls.

Sigaras

Cigar-shaped Turkish appetizers can be filled with one of three Middle Eastern fillings.

1/2 lb. fresh or thawed frozen filo sheets　　　　**About 1/2 cup butter, melted**
Spinach-Cheese Filling, page 39,
　　Chicken-Walnut Filling or
　　Meat Filling, page 40

Review Filo Pastry Techniques, page 27. Prepare desired filling. Lightly brush baking sheets with butter. Preheat oven to 400F (205C). Work with 2 sheets of filo at a time, keeping remaining filo covered with plastic wrap. Lightly brush 1 filo sheet with butter. Top with a second filo sheet and lightly brush with butter. Cut crosswise into four 4-inch strips about 12 inches long. Place 2 teaspoons filling about 1 inch from the end of each strip and 1/2 inch from each side. Fold end over filling. Fold sides over filling and make 1/2-inch folds the length of the strip, rolling up jelly-roll fashion. Place seam side down on prepared baking sheet. Brush lightly with butter. Melt more butter if necessary. Repeat with remaining filo sheets. If desired, refrigerate Sigaras until about 20 minutes before serving. Bake 15 to 20 minutes until golden brown. Serve hot. Makes 24 appetizers.

Filo Triangles

Crisp, flaky tidbits.

1/2 lb. fresh or thawed frozen filo sheets　　　　**About 1/2 cup butter, melted**
Spinach-Cheese Filling, page 39,
　　Chicken-Walnut Filling or
　　Meat Filling, page 40

Review Filo Pastry Techniques, page 27. Prepare desired filling. Lightly brush baking sheets with butter. Preheat oven to 400F (205C). Work with 1 sheet of filo at a time, keeping remaining filo covered with plastic wrap. Lightly brush filo sheet with butter. Cut into 2-inch strips about 12 inches long. Place 1 teaspoon filling about 1 inch from top of each strip. Fold corner over filling, making a triangle. Continue folding strip as in a flag fold, maintaining triangle shape. Place seam side down on prepared baking sheets. Repeat with remaining strips and remaining filo sheets. Brush tops of triangles with butter. Melt more butter, if necessary. If desired, refrigerate triangles until about 20 minutes before serving. Bake 15 to 20 minutes until golden brown. Serve hot. Makes 48 appetizers.

How to Make Sigaras

1/Place 2 teaspoons filling on each strip. Chicken-Walnut Filling is on page 40.

2/Fold end and sides over filling. Make 1/2-inch folds the length of the strip.

Spinach-Cheese Filling for Filo

If you don't have frozen chopped spinach, use frozen leaf spinach and chop it yourself.

2 tablespoons olive oil
1/2 cup finely chopped onion
1 (10-oz.) pkg. frozen chopped spinach,
    thawed
3/4 cup cottage cheese (6 oz.) or
    crumbled feta cheese (2-1/4 oz.)

1/2 teaspoon salt
1/8 teaspoon pepper
1/4 teaspoon dried dill weed
1 egg

Heat olive oil in a small saucepan over medium heat. Add onion. Sauté until tender, stirring frequently. Remove from heat. Add remaining ingredients. Stir to mix well. Makes about 2 cups.

Chicken-Walnut Filling for Filo

Everyday ingredients combine to make a slightly exotic filling.

3 tablespoons butter
1/2 cup thinly sliced green onions
1/2 cup finely chopped walnuts
1-1/2 cups finely chopped cooked
   chicken or turkey

1/4 teaspoon paprika
1/8 teaspoon pepper

Melt butter in a medium skillet over medium heat. Add green onions and walnuts. Stir frequently until onions are tender. Add remaining ingredients. Stir to mix well. Makes about 2 cups.

Meat Filling for Filo

Spicy Middle Eastern beef or lamb for filling Filo Triangles or Sigaras, page 38.

2 tablespoons olive oil
1 lb. lean ground beef or lamb
1/2 cup chopped onion
2 tablespoons chopped green pepper
1/2 teaspoon salt

1/4 teaspoon ground allspice
1/4 teaspoon garlic salt
1/8 teaspoon black pepper
Dash red (cayenne) pepper

Heat olive oil in a medium skillet over medium heat. Add meat, onion and green pepper. Cook until meat is no longer pink, breaking meat up with a spoon. Stir in remaining ingredients. Cool slightly before using. Makes about 2 cups.

Blue-Cheese Twists

Chopped pecans add special crunch to these pastry sticks.

1 cup Classic Puff Pastry, page 22, or
   Quick Puff Pastry, page 24
2 oz. blue cheese, crumbled

2 tablespoons butter, softened
3 tablespoons finely chopped pecans
Egg Glaze, page 20

Review Puff Pastry Techniques, page 21. Prepare dough for pastry. Mix blue cheese and butter with a fork until smooth. On a lightly floured surface, roll out dough to a 12-inch square. Spread cheese mixture on upper two-thirds of the square. Sprinkle nuts over cheese mixture. Fold bottom third over middle third. Fold top third down. Lightly roll out to a 12" x 5" rectangle. Cut into twenty-four 5" x 1/2" strips. Twist each strip 3 or 4 times. Place strips about 1 inch apart on ungreased baking sheets. Flatten slightly to help hold the twist. Prepare Egg Glaze. Lightly brush twists with glaze. Refrigerate 15 minutes or longer. Preheat oven to 400F (205C). Bake twists 12 to 15 minutes until lightly browned. Serve warm. Makes 24 appetizers.

Pissaladière

If Greek or Italian olives are not available, use pimiento-stuffed green olives.

3 large onions
1/4 cup olive oil
1 garlic clove, crushed
1/4 teaspoon salt
1/4 teaspoon pepper

1/2 teaspoon crushed oregano leaves
Double-Crust Basic Pastry, page 14
2 (2-oz.) cans flat anchovy fillets
9 Greek or Italian cured olives
1/2 cup grated Parmesan cheese (1-1/2 oz.)

Peel onions and cut in half lengthwise. Thinly slice crosswise to make about 4 cups. Place olive oil and sliced onions in a large skillet. Stir frequently over medium-low heat until onions are tender but not browned, 20 to 25 minutes. Add garlic the last 5 minutes. Stir in salt, pepper and oregano. Remove from heat. Prepare dough for pastry. Review Rolling Out, page 8. On a lightly floured surface, roll out dough to a 16'' x 11'' rectangle. Place in a 15'' x 10'' jelly-roll pan. Roll edge under, keeping dough inside pan. Press edge against inside of pan with a fork to make a slightly raised rim. Spread cooked onion mixture over dough. Preheat oven to 425F (220C). Drain anchovies. Crisscross anchovies on top of onion mixture, making a diamond pattern. Halve and pit olives. Place 1 olive half in center of each diamond. Sprinkle with Parmesan cheese. If desired, refrigerate until about 30 minutes before serving. Bake 20 to 25 minutes until bottom of crust is browned well. Cut into 2-1/2-inch squares. Serve hot. Makes 24 appetizers.

Empanadas de Queso

Queso is Spanish for cheese. These delicious turnovers are filled with cheese and chilies.

2 tablespoons butter
1/4 cup finely chopped onion
2 tablespoons all-purpose flour
1/4 teaspoon salt
3/4 cup milk
2 tablespoons chopped green chilies

1-1/2 cups shredded Cheddar cheese or
  Monterey Jack cheese (6 oz.)
Double-Crust Basic Pastry, page 14
Egg Glaze, page 20
Avocado Dip, page 35, if desired

Preheat oven to 400F (205C). Melt butter in a small saucepan over medium heat. Add onion. Sauté until onion is tender, stirring occasionally. Do not brown. Stir in flour and salt until blended. Add milk and chilies. Stir constantly over medium heat until mixture comes to a full boil. Stir and boil 1 minute. Stir in cheese. Set aside. Prepare dough for pastry. Review Rolling Out, page 8. Cut dough into 2 equal portions. On a lightly floured surface, roll out 1 portion 1/8 inch thick. Using a plastic lid or inverted bowl as a guide, cut dough into 3-inch circles. Lightly knead scraps and let rest 3 to 5 minutes. Continue rolling out and cutting circles until 1 portion of dough is used. Stack circles, if desired. Repeat with remaining dough. Prepare Egg Glaze. Place about half the circles on a flat surface. Lightly brush glaze around edges of circles to make 1/4-inch borders. Place 1 rounded teaspoon of filling on each circle. Fold in half over filling, bringing edges together. Do not let filling go into glazed area, or dough will not be securely sealed and filling will leak out during baking. Press edges with a fork. Use a knife to make 1 or 2 small slits in the top of each empanada. Lightly brush tops with glaze. Place on ungreased baking sheets. Repeat with remaining circles and filling. If desired, refrigerate until 15 minutes before serving. Bake 10 to 12 minutes until golden brown. Serve with Avocado Dip, if desired. Makes 30 to 35 appetizers.

Beef Empanadas

In Spain and Mexico, appetizers are often in the form of turnovers.

Sour-Cream Salsa, see below
Avocado Dip, page 35
1 lb. ground beef or pork
2 tablespoons olive oil
1/2 cup finely chopped onion
1 tablespoon all-purpose flour
1 teaspoon salt

1 teaspoon paprika
1/4 teaspoon ground cumin
1/8 teaspoon garlic powder
1/2 cup water
2 tablespoons chopped raisins
Double-Crust Cheddar Pastry, page 17
Egg Glaze, page 20

Sour-Cream Salsa:
1/2 cup dairy sour cream
2 tablespoons green chile salsa

Prepare Sour-Cream Salsa and Avocado Dip. Preheat oven to 400F (205C). Cook meat in a medium skillet over medium heat until no longer pink, breaking up with a spoon. Drain off all drippings. Add olive oil and onion to meat. Sauté until onion is tender, stirring occasionally. Add flour, salt, paprika, cumin and garlic powder. Stir until blended. Add water and raisins. Stir constantly over medium heat until mixture is thickened. Set aside. Prepare dough for pastry. Review Rolling Out, page 8. Cut dough into 2 equal portions. On a lightly floured surface, roll out 1 portion 1/8 inch thick. Using a plastic lid or inverted bowl as a guide, cut into 3-inch circles. Lightly knead scraps and let rest 3 to 5 minutes. Continue rolling out and cutting circles until 1 portion of dough is used. Stack circles, if desired. Repeat with remaining dough. Place about half the circles on a flat surface. Prepare Egg Glaze. Lightly brush glaze around edges of circles. Place 1 rounded teaspoon of filling on each circle. Fold circles in half over filling, bringing edges together. Press edges with a fork. Use a knife to make 1 or 2 small slits in the top of each empanada. Lightly brush tops with glaze. Place on ungreased baking sheets. Repeat with remaining circles and filling. If desired, refrigerate until about 15 minutes before serving. Bake 10 to 12 minutes until golden brown. Serve with Sour-Cream Salsa or Avocado Dip. Makes 30 to 35 appetizers.

Sour-Cream Salsa:
Combine sour cream and salsa. Refrigerate 1 hour or longer to blend flavors.

 *tip*

If carrot curls, radish roses and green onion brushes are placed in ice water and refrigerated for a few hours, they will open and curl nicely.

Piroshki

These tiny Russian turnovers are often served with borscht.

Double-Crust Cream-Cheese Pastry, page 17
Egg Glaze, page 20
Meat Filling for Piroshki, page 44, or
    Cabbage Filling for Piroshki, below

1 cup dairy sour cream
1 tablespoon prepared horseradish

Prepare dough for pastry. Review Rolling Out, page 8. Preheat oven to 400F (205C). Cut dough into 2 equal portions. On a lightly floured board, roll out 1 portion 1/8 inch thick. Using a plastic lid or inverted bowl as a guide, cut into 3- to 3-1/2-inch circles. Stack circles, if desired. Lightly knead scraps and let rest 3 to 5 minutes. Continue rolling out and cutting circles until 1 portion of dough is used. Repeat with remaining dough. Place about half the circles on a flat surface. Prepare Egg Glaze. Lightly brush glaze on edges of circles to make 1/4-inch borders. Place a rounded teaspoonful of filling in center of each circle. Bring 2 opposite edges up over filling, making a boat shape. Pinch edges together to seal. Flute, if desired; see pages 10 and 11. Use a knife to make 1 or 2 small slits in the top of each Piroshki. If you are using both Meat Filling and Cabbage Filling, place meat-filled Piroshki seam side down so they can be easily identified. Repeat with remaining circles and filling. Brush filled Piroshki with glaze. If desired, refrigerate until about 20 minutes before serving. Bake 15 to 20 minutes until golden brown. Combine sour cream and horseradish. Serve with hot Piroshki. Makes 30 to 35 appetizers.

Cabbage Filling for Piroshki

Like many Russian savories, this one features hard-cooked eggs.

1/4 cup butter
3/4 cup chopped onion
4 cups shredded cabbage
1/2 teaspoon salt
1/4 teaspoon pepper

2 hard-cooked eggs, finely chopped
1 tablespoon snipped fresh dill or
    1 teaspoon dried dill weed, if desired
1/4 cup finely chopped ham, if desired

Melt butter in a medium skillet over medium heat. Add onion. Sauté until tender, stirring occasionally. Do not brown. Stir in cabbage, salt and pepper. Cover skillet and reduce heat to medium-low. Cook about 10 minutes until cabbage is tender, stirring twice. Stir in chopped eggs. Stir in dill and ham, if desired. Cool slightly. Makes filling for 30 to 35 Piroshki.

tip

For fresh-looking appetizer trays, refrigerate parsley sprigs in water. Use them to garnish appetizer trays just before serving.

Ham Pithiviers

Two circles of puff pastry enclosing a filling originated in Pithiviers, France.

2 cups Classic Puff Pastry, page 22, or
   Quick Puff Pastry, page 24
3/4 cup finely chopped cooked ham
1 tablespoon mayonnaise
1/4 teaspoon Worcestershire sauce

Dash pepper
1/4 cup grated Parmesan cheese (3/4 oz.)
2 tablespoons thinly sliced green onion
1 hard-cooked egg, chopped
Egg Glaze, page 20

Review Puff Pastry Techniques, page 21. Prepare dough for pastry. In a medium bowl, combine ham, mayonnaise, Worcestershire sauce and pepper. Stir in cheese, green onion and chopped egg. Set aside. Cut dough into 2 equal portions. On a lightly floured surface, roll out 1 portion to a 9-inch square. Using an 8-inch, round cake pan as a guide, cut an 8-inch circle from center of the square. Place circle on an ungreased baking sheet. Prepare Egg Glaze. Lightly brush glaze around edge of circle, making a 1-1/2-inch border and being careful not to let glaze drip over edge. Place ham mixture in center of circle and spread to inside edge of glazed border. Mound mixture slightly in center. Roll out remaining dough to a 9-inch square. Cut another 8-inch circle. Center circle over ham-topped circle, stretching as necessary to match edges and deflating any air pockets. Press edges firmly with your fingers to seal. Use the point of a knife to cut a small hole in center of top pastry. Brush top with Egg Glaze, being careful not to let glaze drip over edge. With a small sharp knife, make a design on pastry using 1/16-inch deep cuts. Do not cut all the way through dough. Long curved lines radiating from center are traditional, but any pattern may be used. Scallop edge with the back of a knife at 1/4-inch intervals. Refrigerate 30 minutes or longer. Preheat oven to 450F (230C). Bake Pithiviers 15 minutes. Reduce heat to 400F (205C). Bake 20 to 30 minutes longer until pastry is puffed and golden brown. Cool slightly. Serve warm. Makes 8 to 10 appetizer servings.

Meat Filling for Piroshki

Dill gives this filling a distinctive flavor. Piroshki are on page 43.

1 lb. lean ground beef
3/4 cup chopped onion
3 tablespoons dairy sour cream
1 teaspoon Worcestershire sauce
1 tablespoon snipped fresh dill or
   1 teaspoon dried dill weed

1/2 teaspoon salt
1/4 teaspoon pepper
2 hard-cooked eggs, finely chopped

Cook meat in a medium skillet over medium heat until no longer pink, breaking up with a spoon. Drain off all but 1 to 2 tablespoons drippings. Add onion. Sauté over medium heat until onion is tender. Stir in remaining ingredients. Cool slightly. Makes filling for 30 to 35 Piroshki.

How to Make Ham Pithiviers

1/Scallop edges with the back of a knife at 1/4-inch intervals.

2/Baked pastry will be puffed and golden. Cut into wedges to serve.

Appetizer Calzone

Miniature turnovers with an Italian influence.

1 cup Classic Puff Pastry, page 22, or
  Quick Puff Pastry, page 24
1 cup shredded mozzarella cheese (4 oz.)

2 oz. chopped salami or pepperoni
Egg Glaze, page 20
1 tablespoon grated Parmesan cheese

Review Puff Pastry Techniques, page 21. Prepare dough for pastry. Roll out dough 1/8 inch thick. Using a round cookie cutter, plastic lid or inverted bowl as a guide, cut into 2-1/2-inch circles. Stack circles, if desired. Lightly knead scraps and let rest 3 to 5 minutes. Continue rolling out and cutting circles until all dough is used. Combine mozzarella cheese and salami or pepperoni. Place about half the circles on a flat surface. Prepare Egg Glaze. Lightly brush glaze around edges of circles to make 1/4-inch borders. Place a teaspoon of cheese mixture on each circle. Fold circles in half over filling. Do not let filling go into glazed area or dough will not be securely sealed and filling will leak out during baking. Press edges together with a fork. Use a knife to make 1 or 2 small slits on the top of each turnover. Place on ungreased baking sheets. Lightly brush tops of turnovers with glaze. Sprinkle with Parmesan cheese. Repeat with remaining circles and filling. Refrigerate 15 minutes or longer. Preheat oven to 425F (220C). Bake 10 to 12 minutes until golden brown. Makes 20 to 24 appetizers.

Gougère

A cheese-flavored pastry ring with a soft chewy texture.

Choux Pastry made with 3 eggs, page 28　　　**2 tablespoons grated Parmesan cheese**
1/4 teaspoon salt
3/4 cup 1/4-inch sharp Cheddar
　cheese cubes (3 oz.)

Lightly grease and flour a 17" x 11" or 14-inch, round baking sheet. Using a plate as a guide, mark an 8-inch circle in the flour with your finger. Prepare dough for pastry, adding an additional 1/4 teaspoon salt. Stir in Cheddar cheese. Spoon dough in a ring just inside the marked circle, making the ring about 2 inches wide. Sprinkle with Parmesan cheese. At this point, Gougère may be refrigerated 3 to 5 hours. Preheat oven to 400F (205C). Bake Gougère 35 to 40 minutes until puffed and golden brown. Gougère will deflate slightly as it cools. Cut in wedges and serve warm. Makes 12 appetizer servings.

Ham Gougère

Wonderful as an appetizer or as a brunch main dish.

Choux Pastry made with 3 eggs, page 29　　**1 (2-1/4-oz.) can deviled ham**
1/4 teaspoon salt　　　　　　　　　　　　**3/4 cup 1/4-inch Swiss cheese or**
1/4 teaspoon dry mustard　　　　　　　　　**Cheddar cheese cubes**
2 dashes red (cayenne) pepper

Lightly grease and flour a 17" x 11" baking sheet. Using a plate as a guide, mark an 8-inch circle in the flour with your finger. Prepare dough for pastry, adding an additional 1/4 teaspoon salt. Stir in dry mustard, red pepper and deviled ham until mixed well. Stir in cheese. Spoon dough in a ring just inside the marked circle, making the ring about 2 inches wide. At this point, Gougère may be refrigerated 3 to 5 hours. Preheat oven to 400F (205C). Bake Gougère 35 to 40 minutes until puffed and golden brown. Gougère will deflate slightly as it cools. Cut in wedges and serve warm. Makes 12 appetizer servings.

tip

Soften chilled cream cheese by letting it stand at room temperature for 30 minutes or by mashing it with a fork.

Savory Turnovers

Miniature pies with meat, chicken or fish filling.

The word *savory* has been a commonplace word in English cuisine and is coming into worldwide use. It means flavorful and non-sweet. Savory foods are usually flavored with cheese, seafood or meat.

Savory turnovers are marvelous for busy families and provide a convenient meal for those eating away from home. We inherited the make-ahead, meal-in-one pastry from Cornish Pasties that are large turnovers filled with meat and potatoes. They were made by miners' wives in Cornwall, England, so their husbands could take a midday meal down into the mines. Turnovers are perfect for work and school lunches, biking and hiking snacks, brunches and midnight feasts, picnics and patio parties. They're not limited to a filling of meat and potatoes. Polynesian Tuna Filling, Sloppy Joe Filling and Sausage & Egg Filling are only a few turnover fillings you'll discover in this section.

Fillings are not the only variations you can explore with turnovers. Use different doughs for the pastry. Herb Pastry and Wheat Pastry are especially delicious with savory fillings.

Crescents, boats and triangles are the three basic turnover shapes. If you have a filling with excess sauce or gravy, the boat shape works best. Most of the seam is on top so there is less chance of the filling leaking out. For cutting circles to make crescents and boats, see page 57.

Turnovers can be frozen either before or after baking. Place them on a baking sheet and put the uncovered baking sheet in the coldest part of your freezer. The turnovers will be frozen through in 1 or 2 hours. Pack them in an airtight freezer container and label the container. Thaw frozen unbaked turnovers 30 minutes before baking and then bake them as directed in the recipe. Thaw baked turnovers and reheat them in a preheated 375F (190C) oven for about 5 minutes. When making turnovers to freeze, I make a different shape for each kind of filling. Then I know, for example, that Barbecue Meat Filling has a boat shape, that Curried Chicken Filling is a crescent, and that the triangles contain Sausage & Egg Filling.

Miniature turnovers are popular appetizers. Empanadas, Piroshki and Calzone are in Distinctive Appetizers. Although Potato Pockets, in Garden Favorites, are a different shape than triangles, crescents or boats, they are turnovers. Recipes for sweet turnovers are in The Bakery Shop.◆

Backpackers' Picnic
Polynesian Tuna Turnovers, pages 50, 51 and 56
Apples
Pecan Tarts, page 171

Sunday Supper
Reuben Turnovers, page 52
Pear Halves on Lettuce with
Poppy-Seed Dressing
Chocolate-Coconut Custard Pie, page 128

Cornish Pasties

Miners in England's Cornwall used to take these meal-in-one turnovers for their lunch.

Double-Crust Basic Pastry made with lard,
  page 14
3/4 lb. top sirloin
1 medium potato
1 small onion

1 small turnip, if desired
1 teaspoon Worcestershire sauce
3/4 teaspoon salt
1/4 teaspoon pepper
Egg Glaze, page 20

Prepare dough for pastry. Review Rolling Out, page 8. Trim fat from meat. Cut meat into 1/4-inch cubes. Peel potato and cut into 1/4-inch cubes. Chop onion. If desired, peel turnip and cut into 1/4-inch cubes. Place cubed meat and cut-up vegetables in a medium bowl. Sprinkle with Worcestershire sauce, salt and pepper. Toss to distribute seasonings. Lightly grease a 17'' x 11'' baking sheet. Preheat oven to 400F (205C). Divide dough into 8 equal portions. On a lightly floured surface, roll out each portion slightly larger than a 6-inch circle. Using a plastic lid or inverted bowl as a guide, cut a 6-inch circle from each portion. Prepare Egg Glaze. Lightly brush glaze around edge of each circle, making a 3/4-inch border. Place about 1/3 cup filling slightly off-center on each circle. Fold circle over filling, matching edges. Firmly press edges together with your fingers. Crimp with a fork, if desired. Place turnovers on prepared baking sheet. Lightly brush with glaze. Cut two 1-inch slits in top of each turnover. Bake 15 minutes. Reduce heat to 350F (175C). Bake about 30 minutes longer until golden brown. Serve warm. Makes 8 servings.

Calzone

Miniature Italian pastries are usually made with yeast dough. This version is quicker.

2 cups Quick Puff Pastry, page 24
2 cups shredded mozzarella cheese (8 oz.)
1/4 lb. salami or pepperoni, chopped

Egg Glaze, page 20
4 teaspoons olive oil
1 tablespoon grated Parmesan cheese

Review Puff Pastry Techniques, page 21. Prepare dough for pastry. Preheat oven to 425F (220C). Combine cheese and salami or pepperoni in a medium bowl. Divide dough into 8 equal portions. On a lightly floured surface, roll out each portion slightly larger than a 6-inch circle. Using a plastic lid or inverted bowl as a guide, cut a 6-inch circle from each portion. Prepare Egg Glaze. Lightly brush glaze around edge of each circle, making a 3/4-inch border. Brush center of each circle with 1/2 teaspoon olive oil. Place 1/8 of the cheese mixture slightly off-center on each circle. Fold circle over filling, matching edges. Press edges together with a fork. Place turnovers on a large ungreased baking sheet. Lightly brush each turnover with glaze. Cut two 1-inch slits on top of each turnover. Sprinkle with Parmesan cheese. Bake about 20 minutes until golden brown. Makes 8 servings.

Turnover Crescents

Miniature savory pies are most often made in this traditional turnover shape.

Desired filling, pages 54 to 56
Double-Crust Basic Pastry, page 14
Egg Glaze, page 20

Topping indicated in filling recipe,
  if desired

Prepare filling and dough for pastry. Review Rolling Out, pages 8 and 9. Lightly grease a 17" x 11" baking sheet. Preheat oven to 375F (190C). Divide dough into 8 equal portions. On a lightly floured surface, roll out each portion slightly larger than a 6-inch circle. Using a plastic lid or inverted bowl as a guide, cut a 6-inch circle from each portion. Prepare Egg Glaze. Lightly brush glaze around edge of each circle, making a 3/4-inch border. Place about 1/3 cup filling slightly off-center on each circle. Fold circle over filling, matching opposite sides. Firmly press edges together with your fingers. Crimp with a fork. Cut two 1-inch slits in the top of each crescent. Place crescents on prepared baking sheet. Brush lightly with glaze. Sprinkle with topping, if desired. Bake 40 to 45 minutes until golden brown. Makes 8 servings.

Variations

Substitute Cheddar Pastry, page 17, Cream-Cheese Pastry, page 17, or Process-Cheese Pastry, page 18, for the Basic Pastry.

Turnover Triangles   *Photo on page 53.*

Meat turnovers are especially flavorful with a cheese pastry. See the variations below.

Desired filling, pages 54 & 56
Double-Crust Basic Pastry, page 14, or
  Cheddar Pastry, page 17

Egg Glaze, page 20
Topping indicated in filling recipe,
  if desired

Prepare filling and dough for pastry. Review Rolling Out, pages 8 and 9. Lightly grease a 17" x 11" baking sheet. Preheat oven to 375F (190C). Divide dough into 2 equal portions. On a lightly floured surface, roll out each portion to a 12-inch square. Cut each square into four 6-inch squares. Prepare Egg Glaze. Lightly brush glaze around edge of each square, making a 3/4-inch border. Place about 1/3 cup filling slightly off-center on each square. Fold half of square over filling, matching opposite points and making a triangle. Firmly press edges together with your fingers. Crimp with a fork, if desired. Cut two 1-inch slits in the top of each triangle. Place triangles on prepared baking sheet. Lightly brush with glaze. Sprinkle with topping, if desired. Bake 40 to 45 minutes. Makes 8 servings.

Variations

Substitute Cheddar Pastry, page 17, Cream-Cheese Pastry, page 17, or Process-Cheese Pastry, page 18, for the Basic Pastry.

How to Make Turnovers

1/Shaping Turnover Crescents with Italian Sausage Filling.

2/Shaping Turnover Boats with Barbecue Meat Filling.

Turnover Boats   *Photo on page 53.*

Use this shape for fillings containing gravy or sauce.

Desired filling, pages 54 to 56
Double-Crust Basic Pastry, page 14
Egg Glaze, page 20

Topping indicated in filling recipe,
  if desired

Prepare filling and dough for pastry. Review Rolling Out, page 8. Lightly grease a 17" x 11" baking sheet. Preheat oven to 375F (190C). Divide dough into 8 equal portions. On a lightly floured surface, roll out each portion slightly larger than a 6-inch circle. Using a plastic lid or inverted bowl as a guide, cut a 6-inch circle from each portion. Prepare Egg Glaze. Lightly brush glaze around edge of each circle, making a 3/4-inch border. Place about 1/3 cup filling in center of each circle. Fold up opposite sides of circle to meet at the top. Firmly press edges together with your fingers. If desired, flute with Spiral or Rickrack Fluting, pages 10 and 11. Place boats on prepared baking sheet. Brush lightly with glaze. Sprinkle with topping, if desired. Bake 40 to 45 minutes until golden brown. Makes 8 servings.

Variations

Substitute Cheddar Pastry, page 17, Cream-Cheese Pastry, page 17, or Process-Cheese Pastry, page 18, for the Basic Pastry.

Reuben Turnovers

Tuck these in lunch boxes or backpacks.

2 cups Quick Puff Pastry, page 24
1 cup shredded fresh or canned corned beef
1/4 cup finely chopped onion
1 (8-oz.) can sauerkraut, drained

1 teaspoon caraway seeds
Egg Glaze, page 20
1 cup shredded Swiss cheese (4 oz.)
1 teaspoon caraway seeds

Review Puff Pastry Techniques, page 21. Prepare dough for pastry. Preheat oven to 425F (220C). Combine corned beef and onion in a small bowl. Combine sauerkraut and 1 teaspoon caraway seeds in another small bowl. On a lightly floured surface, roll out dough to an 18" x 12" rectangle. Cut into six 6-inch squares. Prepare Egg Glaze. Lightly brush glaze around edge of each square, making a 3/4-inch border. Place about 3 tablespoons corned-beef mixture slightly off-center on each square. Spread to inside edge of glazed border. Top beef with about 2 tablespoons sauerkraut mixture and about 2-1/2 tablespoons cheese. Fold half of square over filling, matching opposite points and making a triangle. Firmly press edges together with your fingers. Crimp with a fork, if desired. Make two 1-inch slits in the top of each turnover. Place on an ungreased baking sheet. Lightly brush turnovers with glaze. Sprinkle with 1 teaspoon caraway seeds. Bake about 20 minutes until golden brown. Makes 6 servings.

Puff Pastry Turnovers

Save puff pastry scraps in your freezer until you have 2 cups.

2 cups Quick Puff Pastry, page 24, or
   Classic Puff Pastry, page 22
Desired filling, pages 54 to 56

Egg Glaze, page 20
Topping indicated in filling recipe,
   if desired

Review Puff Pastry Techniques, page 21. Prepare filling and dough for pastry. Preheat oven to 425F (220C). Divide dough into 8 equal portions. On a lightly floured surface, roll out each portion slightly larger than a 6-inch circle or square. Using a plastic lid or inverted bowl as a guide, cut a 6-inch circle or 6-inch square from each portion. Prepare Egg Glaze. Lightly brush glaze around edge of each square, making a 3/4-inch border. Fill and shape as directed for Turnover Crescents or Turnover Triangles, page 50. Place on an ungreased 17" x 11" baking sheet. Prepare Egg Glaze. Lightly brush turnovers with glaze. Sprinkle with topping, if desired. Bake 20 minutes or until golden brown. Makes 8 servings.

Variation

To use 1 (10-ounce) package frozen patty shells, thaw patty shells. On a lightly floured surface, roll out each shell slightly larger than a 7-inch circle. Cut a 7-inch circle. Fill and shape according to above directions, dividing filling into 6 portions. Bake as directed above. Makes 6 servings.

Reuben Turnover Triangles, above and page 50. At the top, Reuben Turnover Boats, above and page 51.

Sausage & Egg Filling

A wonderful idea for brunch or a midnight snack.

1 lb. bulk pork sausage	1/4 teaspoon salt
1/4 cup finely chopped onion	1/8 teaspoon pepper
3 eggs	1 cup shredded Cheddar cheese (4 oz.)
2 tablespoons green chili salsa	2 teaspoons sesame seeds, if desired

Place sausage and onion in a medium skillet. Cook over medium heat until sausage is no longer pink, breaking up with a spoon. Drain excess drippings. Slightly beat eggs. Stir into sausage mixture. Cook and stir until egg is about half cooked. Remove from heat. Filling will continue to cook while turnovers are baking. Cool filling slightly. Stir in salsa, salt, pepper and cheese. Sprinkle turnovers with sesame seeds before baking, if desired. Makes filling for 8 turnovers.

Sloppy Joe Filling

Not as sloppy when enclosed in pastry as it is when mounded on a bun.

1 tablespoon vegetable oil	1/4 teaspoon dry mustard
1 lb. lean ground beef	2 tablespoons honey
1/4 cup finely chopped onion	1 teaspoon Worcestershire sauce
1/4 cup finely chopped green pepper	1/2 teaspoon salt
1 (8-oz.) can tomato sauce	1/4 teaspoon black pepper

Heat oil in a medium saucepan. Add meat. Cook over medium heat until no longer pink, breaking up with a spoon. Add onion and green pepper. Cook 3 minutes. Stir in remaining ingredients. Simmer 5 minutes. Cool before using. Makes filling for 8 turnovers.

Curried Filling

Serve your favorite chutney with these exotic turnovers.

2 tablespoons butter
1/4 cup chopped onion
1-1/2 to 2 teaspoons curry powder
1 tablespoon all-purpose flour
3/4 cup milk

2 cups chopped cooked chicken or turkey
1/2 cup chopped unpeeled tart apple
1/4 cup raisins
2 teaspoons sesame seeds, if desired

Melt butter in a medium saucepan. Add onion. Cook over medium heat 3 minutes. Stir in curry powder and flour. Cook 1 minute. Add milk. Stir constantly over medium heat until mixture comes to a full boil. Remove from heat. Stir in chicken, apple and raisins. Cool before using. Sprinkle turnovers with sesame seeds before baking, if desired. Makes filling for 8 turnovers.

Italian Sausage Filling

If you like really spicy food, use hot Italian sausages.

1 lb. sweet Italian sausages
2 tablespoons olive oil
1/3 cup chopped green pepper
1/3 cup chopped onion

1-1/2 cups thinly sliced fresh mushrooms
1/3 cup tomato sauce
2 tablespoons grated Parmesan cheese,
  if desired

Remove sausages from casings. Place sausage and olive oil in a medium skillet. Cook over medium heat until sausage is no longer pink, breaking up with a spoon. Add green pepper, onion and mushrooms. Cook 3 to 4 minutes. Remove from heat. Vegetables will be tender after turnovers are baked. Stir tomato sauce into vegetables. Cool before using. Sprinkle turnovers with Parmesan cheese before baking, if desired. Makes filling for 8 turnovers.

tip *If raisins have hardened during storage, cover them with hot water and let them stand 15 minutes. Drain off the water before using the raisins.*

Barbecue Meat Filling

Buy finely shaved meat, or slice leftover meat paper-thin.

1 lb. shaved cooked ham, beef or pork
1 cup barbecue sauce
1/4 cup finely chopped onion

2 tablespoons grated Parmesan cheese or
   1 teaspoon sesame seeds, if desired

Place meat, barbecue sauce and onion in a medium bowl. Stir and toss to coat meat with sauce and distribute onion. Sprinkle turnovers with cheese or sesame seeds before baking, if desired. Makes filling for 8 turnovers.

Polynesian Tuna Filling

Water chestnuts stay crisp even after cooking.

1 (12-1/2-oz.) can tuna, drained
1 (8-oz.) can crushed pineapple,
   drained (2/3 cup)
1/3 cup chopped green pepper
1/3 cup chopped water chestnuts

1/3 cup mayonnaise
1 green onion, finely chopped
1/2 teaspoon salt
1/8 teaspoon black pepper

Place tuna in a medium bowl. Flake with a fork. Add remaining ingredients. Mix well. Makes filling for 8 turnovers.

Individual Pork Pies

These little pies are best when the pastry is made with lard.

Double-Crust Basic Pastry, page 14
3/4 lb. boneless pork loin
1 small onion
1 large apple, cored, peeled
1 celery stalk
3/4 teaspoon salt

1/4 teaspoon pepper
1/4 teaspoon ground sage
1/8 teaspoon garlic powder
Egg Glaze, page 20
1 teaspoon sesame seeds

Prepare dough for pastry. Review Rolling Out, page 8. Trim fat from meat. Cut meat into 1/4-inch cubes. Coarsely chop onion, apple and celery. Place meat cubes, chopped vegetables and chopped apple in a medium bowl. Sprinkle with salt, pepper, sage and garlic powder. Toss to distribute seasonings. Lightly grease a 17" x 11" baking sheet. Preheat oven to 400F (205C). Divide dough into 8 equal portions. Roll out each portion slightly larger than a 6-inch circle. Using a plastic lid or inverted bowl as a guide, cut a 6-inch circle from each portion. Prepare Egg Glaze. Lightly brush glaze around edge of each circle, making a 3/4-inch border. Place about 1/3 cup meat mixture slightly off-center on each circle. Fold circle over filling, matching edges. Firmly press edges together with your fingers. Crimp with a fork, if desired. Place turnovers on prepared baking sheet. Brush lightly with glaze. Sprinkle with sesame seeds. Cut two 1-inch slits in top of each turnover. Bake 15 minutes. Reduce heat to 350F (175C). Bake about 30 minutes longer until golden brown. Serve warm. Makes 8 servings.

Cutting Circles of Pastry

Many recipes in this book call for cutting circles of pastry. For very small circles, use a biscuit cutter. For 8- or 9-inch circles, use an inverted cake pan or bowl. For 3- to 6-inch circles, use the plastic lids that come with some canned foods and refrigerated or frozen containers of food. Mark the lids with their sizes and store them with your other pastry tools.

Around the World in Pastry

Main dishes enclosed or layered in pastry.

Eating habits of nations vary tremendously. But many cultures have one food item in common: baked dough containing or enclosing whatever the tastes of the nation demand.

Classic Vol-au-Vent and Bouchées show how the French use puff pastry to enclose their richly sauced seafood fillings. English-Style Deep-Dish Pies may not be as elegant, but their convenience and robust flavors make them a favorite. The Greeks use filo dough to make their beloved spinach pie, Spanakopita. Russian Kulebiaka is salmon wrapped in puff pastry. And from United States farm country, come nostalgic Pot Pies with chicken, beef or pork filling.

Kulebiaka and Beef Wellingtons present opportunities to show your creativity in decorating with dough. Follow the suggestions on page 72 or make up your own designs. If you lack the confidence to try freehand cutouts, begin with hors d'oeuvre cutters. Your guests will be impressed with even the simplest designs.

English-Style Deep-Dish Pot Pie is made in a deep casserole with only a top crust. This recipe uses Quick Puff Pastry that is similar to the flaky pastry made by English cooks.

Novelty pies are made with a crust not containing the standard ingredients of flour and fat or liquid. In Italy, Sausage in Polenta Crust is a cornmeal shell filled with browned sausage, vegetables, herbs and cheese. Pork & Noodle Bake has a pasta crust. For a post-holiday pick-me-up, try curried turkey in a shell made from corn-bread stuffing.

See the recipe for Turkey in Corn-Bread Stuffing.

Unbaked pot pies—both top-crust and double-crust—are ideal for freezer storage. When you wrap and label the pot pies, write the oven temperatures and baking times on the labels. Be sure to use freezer-to-oven casseroles or metal pans.♦

Middle Eastern Dinner

Tomato & Cucumber Salad
Spanakopita, page 59
Shish Kabobs
Baklava, page 184
Turkish Coffee

Family Get-Together

Tossed Green Salad
Pork & Noodle Bake, page 74
Green Beans with Onion & Bacon
Apricot-Cheese Pie, page 151

Spanakopita

Spinach-and-cheese pie is popular in Greece and neighboring Mediterranean countries.

1 large bunch fresh spinach (about 10 oz.)
2 tablespoons olive oil
3/4 cup sliced green onions
4 eggs
1/2 cup milk
1/2 teaspoon salt

1/4 teaspoon pepper
1/4 cup chopped cilantro or parsley
1 tablespoon dried dill weed
1/2 lb. feta cheese
About 1/4 lb. butter, melted
1/2 lb. fresh or thawed frozen filo sheets

Review Filo Pastry Techniques, page 27. Wash spinach and shake dry. Cut off coarse stems. Chop leaves into 1-inch pieces. Heat olive oil in a medium skillet over medium heat. Add onion. Sauté until almost tender, stirring occasionally. Add chopped spinach. Cover and cook 5 minutes, stirring twice. Remove from heat. Beat eggs in a medium bowl. Stir in milk, salt, pepper, cilantro or parsley and dill. Crumble cheese. Stir spinach mixture and crumbled cheese into egg mixture. Lightly brush a 12" x 7" baking dish with melted butter. Place 1 filo sheet in buttered baking dish to cover bottom and sides. Fold so filo does not extend above rim. Brush lightly with butter. Repeat with half the filo, folding so filo does not extend up sides of dish. Lightly brush each sheet with butter. Spoon half the spinach mixture over stacked filo. Top with 2 or 3 filo sheets, lightly brushing each with butter. Spread with remaining spinach mixture. Top with remaining filo sheets, brushing each sheet with butter. Generously brush top sheet with butter. If necessary, melt more butter. Lightly score through top sheets to mark 8 servings. Preheat oven to 300F (150C). Bake pie 1 hour. Cool slightly before serving. Makes 8 servings.

Variation

Said's Meat & Spinach Pie: Brown 1 pound lean ground beef or lamb in the olive oil. Add green onion and proceed as directed above.

Bouchées

Fill these patty shells with your favorite creamed filling.

1 cup Classic Puff Pastry, page 22
Egg Glaze, page 20
Chicken-Liver Sauté, Bacon-Tomato Rarebit, or
    Crab & Shrimp in Mushroom Sauce, pages 60 and 61

Review Puff Pastry Techniques, page 21. Prepare dough for pastry. On a lightly floured surface, roll out dough 3/8 inch thick. Using a 3-inch fluted cutter, cut 6 circles. Do not cut within 3/4 inch of any folded edge. Place circles on an ungreased baking sheet. With a 2-inch plain or fluted cutter, make a smaller circle in center of each 3-inch circle without cutting all the way through dough. Carefully remove cutter, leaving circles intact. Refrigerate 15 minutes. Preheat oven to 425F (220C). Prepare Egg Glaze. Brush lightly on Bouchées, being careful not to let glaze drip over edges. Bake 15 to 20 minutes until golden brown and puffed. Cool slightly. Remove centers and any unbaked dough from inside shells. At this point, shells may be refrigerated until ready to serve. Prepare desired filling. Reheat shells in preheated 425F (220C) oven 3 to 5 minutes. Spoon filling into warm shells. Serve warm. Makes 6 servings.

Crab & Shrimp in Mushroom Sauce

A succulent seafood filling for crisp and flaky pastry shells.

1/2 lb. cooked fresh or frozen crabmeat
1/2 lb. cooked fresh or
  frozen shelled shrimp
1/4 cup butter
1/4 cup finely chopped onion
1 cup thinly sliced fresh mushrooms
1/4 cup all-purpose flour

1/2 teaspoon salt
1/4 teaspoon crushed dried leaf marjoram
1/2 cup chicken broth
1 cup half and half or whipping cream
2 tablespoons dry white wine
1 tablespoon chopped parsley

Rinse seafood. Melt butter in a medium saucepan over medium heat. Add onion and mushrooms. Sauté until onion is tender, stirring occasionally. Stir in flour, salt and marjoram. Add broth and half and half or cream all at once. Stir constantly over medium heat until mixture thickens and comes to a full boil. Stir and boil 1 minute. Stir in wine, parsley and seafood. Bring to serving temperature. Do not boil. Makes 4 to 6 servings.

Chicken-Liver Sauté

Fill a Vol-au-Vent, page 71, or Bouchées, page 59, with this gourmet favorite.

About 1/4 cup all-purpose flour
1/2 teaspoon salt
1/4 teaspoon pepper
1 lb. chicken livers
1/4 cup butter
1/2 teaspoon dry mustard
1/4 cup finely chopped onion

1/2 lb. thinly sliced fresh mushrooms
1 garlic clove, crushed
1 cup chicken broth
2 tablespoons dry white wine
1/2 teaspoon Worcestershire sauce
2 tablespoons finely chopped parsley

In a medium bowl, combine 1/4 cup flour, salt and pepper. Rinse and dry chicken livers. Cut into 1-inch pieces. Toss liver pieces in flour mixture. Melt 2 tablespoons butter in a medium skillet. Add about half the liver pieces. Sauté over medium heat until browned and cooked through, stirring occasionally. Remove from skillet. Sauté remaining liver pieces. Remove from skillet and set aside. Add remaining 2 tablespoons butter to drippings in skillet. Stir in dry mustard, onion, mushrooms and garlic. Sauté over medium heat until vegetables are tender, stirring occasionally. Stir in any leftover flour mixture plus flour to make 2 tablespoons. Add chicken broth. Stir constantly over medium heat until mixture comes to a full boil. Reduce heat amd simmer 1 minute. Stir in wine, Worcestershire sauce and parsley. Add cooked liver pieces. Heat to serving temperature. Makes filling for 1 Vol-au-Vent or 6 Bouchées.

Bacon-Tomato Rarebit

A royal version of a country dish.

Bouchées, page 59, or
  Main-Dish Pastry Puffs, below
1 tomato
8 bacon slices
2 tablespoons butter, if desired
2 tablespoons all-purpose flour
1/8 teaspoon dry mustard

1/2 cup beer or dry sherry
1/2 cup half and half or milk
1 teaspoon Worcestershire sauce
3 cups shredded Cheddar cheese (12 oz.)
2 to 3 drops hot pepper sauce, if desired
6 parsley sprigs

Prepare Bouchées or Main-Dish Pastry Puffs. Core tomato and cut into 1/2-inch cubes. Set aside. Cook bacon until crisp. Drain. While bacon is still pliable, cut 2 slices in half lengthwise and crosswise. Shape each piece into a curl. Set aside the 6 best curls for garnish. Crumble remaining bacon. Place 2 tablespoons bacon drippings or butter, if desired, in a medium saucepan over medium heat. Add flour and dry mustard. Stir until smooth. Stir in beer or sherry and half and half or milk. Stir constantly over medium heat until mixture thickens and comes to a full boil. Stir and boil 1 minute. Stir in Worcestershire sauce and cheese. Add hot pepper sauce, if desired. Reduce heat to medium-low. Stir and boil until cheese is melted. Stir in crumbled bacon and all but 12 tomato cubes. Cook 1 minute longer. Spoon into Individual Bouchées or over Main-Dish Pastry Puffs. Garnish with bacon curls, reserved tomato cubes and parsley sprigs. Serve hot. Makes 6 servings.

Main-Dish Pastry Puffs

Crisp puff pastry can take the place of toast or patty shells.

1 cup Classic Puff Pastry, page 22, or
  Quick Puff Pastry, page 24
Crab & Shrimp in Mushroom Sauce, page 60,
  or Bacon-Tomato Rarebit, above,
  or any pot-pie filling, pages 66 to 69

Egg Glaze, page 20

Review Puff Pastry Techniques, page 21. Prepare dough for pastry. Prepare desired topping. Set aside. On a lightly floured surface, roll out dough to a 13" x 11" rectangle. Trim each side to make a 12" x 10" rectangle. Cut into six 5" x 4" rectangles. Place on a baking sheet. With a fork, prick each rectangle at 1/2-inch intervals. Prepare Egg Glaze. Lightly brush rectangles with glaze. Refrigerate 15 minutes. Preheat oven to 425F (220C). Bake rectangles 15 to 20 minutes until crisp and golden brown. Cool slightly. If preparing ahead, reheat 3 minutes in preheated oven at 425F (220C). Serve with desired topping. Makes 6 servings.

Kulebiaka

This layered loaf of eggs, mushrooms, salmon and rice originated in Russia.

2 cups Classic Puff Pastry, page 22, or
    Quick Puff Pastry, page 24
1 cup water
1 cup dry white wine
1/2 cup coarsely chopped onion
1 celery stalk
1 small carrot, chopped
4 peppercorns

1-1/2 lbs. salmon steaks
Rice Layer, see below
Mushroom Layer, see below
3 hard-cooked eggs
Egg Glaze, page 20
Fresh dill or watercress, if desired
Dairy sour cream

Rice Layer:
2 tablespoons butter
1/2 cup chopped onion
1/2 cup long-grain rice, not converted

1 cup chicken broth
1/4 teaspoon salt
2 tablespoons chopped parsley

Mushroom Layer:
2 tablespoons butter
1/2 cup finely chopped onion

1/2 lb. thinly sliced fresh mushrooms

Review Puff Pastry Techniques, page 21. Prepare dough for pastry. Place water, wine, onion, celery, carrot and peppercorns in a medium skillet. Bring to a boil. Gently slide salmon steaks into liquid. Return to a boil. Reduce heat. Cover and simmer about 10 minutes until fish flakes when pierced with a fork. Remove fish from liquid with a metal spatula. Let cool. Remove and discard skin and bones. Flake salmon with a fork and set aside. Prepare Rice Layer. Cool. Prepare Mushroom Layer. Cool. Coarsely chop eggs. On a lightly floured surface, roll out dough to a 14-inch square. Place chopped eggs in center of square in a 9'' x 4'' strip. Place Mushroom Layer on top of eggs, shaping a rectangle with neat straight sides. Arrange flaked salmon over Mushroom Layer. Top with Rice Layer, keeping sides straight and patting layers down. Filling will be 3 to 4 inches high. Cut a 4'' x 2'' rectangle from each corner of square. Refrigerate scraps. Prepare Egg Glaze. Brush a 2-inch-wide strip at edge of one long side of dough with glaze. Fold unglazed long side over filling. Fold side with glazed edge to overlap unglazed side. Dough should fit snugly around filling. Brush short ends with glaze. Tuck in excess dough and fold ends up. Place an ungreased baking sheet next to loaf. Gently roll loaf onto baking sheet seam side down. Make a small hole in center of top. Brush top generously with glaze. Roll out chilled scraps about 1/8-inch thick. Cut decorations; see Decoration Ideas, page 72. Press onto loaf. Brush decorations with glaze. Refrigerate at least 30 minutes. One hour before serving, preheat oven to 400F (205C). Bake loaf 40 to 45 minutes until golden brown. Garnish with dill or watercress, if desired. Serve with sour cream. Makes 6 to 8 servings.

Rice Layer:
Melt butter in a small saucepan over medium heat. Add onion. Sauté until tender, stirring occasionally. Stir in rice until coated with butter. Add broth and salt. Bring to a boil. Reduce heat. Cover and simmer about 15 minutes until rice is tender and all liquid is absorbed. Stir in parsley.

Mushroom Layer:
Melt butter in a medium skillet over medium heat. Add onion and mushrooms. Stir occasionally until moisture from mushrooms is absorbed, about 5 minutes.

Kulebiaka

Quiche Lorraine

This famous quiche originated in the Lorraine and Alsace regions of France.

Single-Crust Rich Butter Pastry, page 19
1/2 lb. bacon
1 cup shredded Gruyère or
   natural Swiss cheese (4 oz.)
4 eggs
2 cups half and half or milk

1/2 teaspoon salt
1/8 teaspoon white pepper
Dash red (cayenne) pepper
Dash ground nutmeg
Parsley, if desired

Prepare dough for pastry. Review Unbaked Pie Shells, page 8. On a lightly floured surface, roll out dough to a 12-inch circle. Fit into a 9-inch quiche pan or pie pan. If using a quiche pan, fold dough edge under so it is even with rim of pan; press dough into scalloped sides of pan. If using a pie pan, fold dough under for a raised edge; make a high fluting. Cook bacon until crisp. Drain. While bacon is still pliable, cut 2 slices in half lengthwise and crosswise to make 8 pieces. Shape each piece into a curl. Set aside the 6 best curls for garnish. Preheat oven to 425F (220C). Crumble remaining bacon evenly over bottom of unbaked pie shell. Sprinkle cheese evenly over bacon. Place eggs, half and half or milk, salt, white pepper, red pepper and nutmeg in a medium bowl. Using a wire whip or rotary beater, mix until blended. Carefully pour over bacon and cheese. Bake 15 minutes. Reduce heat to 350F (175C). Bake 25 to 30 minutes longer until a knife inserted near center comes out clean. Let stand 5 to 10 minutes before serving. Garnish with bacon curls and parsley sprigs. Makes 6 servings.

Ham & Egg Pie

Sensational dish for brunch or midnight supper.

Single-Crust Wheat Pastry, page 16, or
   Cheddar Pastry, page 17
3 tablespoons butter
1/4 cup chopped green onion
3 tablespoons all-purpose flour
1/4 teaspoon pepper
1/4 teaspoon dry mustard

1/4 to 1/2 teaspoon salt
1-1/2 cups milk
2 cups 3/8-inch ham cubes
1 teaspoon Worcestershire sauce
6 eggs
1 tablespoon grated Parmesan cheese

Prepare dough for pastry. Review Rolling Out, page 8. Melt butter in a medium saucepan over medium heat. Add green onion. Sauté 2 minutes, stirring occasionally. Stir in flour, pepper and dry mustard until blended. Add 1/4 to 1/2 teaspoon salt, depending on saltiness of ham. Stir in milk. Stir constantly over medium heat until mixture thickens and comes to a boil. Remove from heat. Stir in ham and Worcestershire sauce. Pour into a shallow 1-1/2-quart casserole. Preheat oven to 425F (220C). On a lightly floured surface, roll out dough 1 inch larger than the casserole. Cut 6 slits radiating from center. With the back of a large spoon, make 6 evenly spaced indentations in ham mixture. Break an egg into each indentation as it is made. Cover with rolled out dough. Turn edge under and lightly press to casserole rim with a fork. Sprinkle with Parmesan cheese. Bake 20 to 25 minutes until lightly browned. Let stand 5 to 10 minutes before serving. Makes 4 to 6 servings.

Salmon Pie with Dill Sauce

A lattice top, pages 12 and 13, will show off the colorful filling.

Double-Crust Wheat Pastry, page 16
2 eggs
1/2 cup milk
1/2 teaspoon salt
1/4 teaspoon pepper
1/4 teaspoon dried dill weed

1 (16-oz.) can salmon
2 slices whole-wheat bread
3/4 cup thinly sliced celery
1/2 cup sliced ripe olives
1/2 cup sliced green onions
Creamy Dill Sauce, see below

Creamy Dill Sauce:
2 tablespoons butter
1/4 cup sliced green onion
2 tablespoons all-purpose flour
1 teaspoon dried dill weed

1/2 teaspoon salt
3/4 cup milk
1/2 cup dairy sour cream

Prepare dough for pastry. Review Double-Crust Pies, pages 9 and 10. In a small bowl, combine eggs, milk, salt, pepper and dill until smooth. Drain salmon and flake with a fork. Tear bread into 1/2-inch pieces. In a large bowl, place salmon, bread pieces, celery, olives and green onions. Add egg mixture. Stir gently to mix. Preheat oven to 375F (190C). Cut dough into 2 equal portions. On a lightly floured surface, roll out 1 portion to an 11-inch circle. Fit into a 9-inch pie pan. Spoon salmon mixture into unbaked pie shell. Trim edge of dough to rim of pan. Roll out remaining dough to a 12-inch circle. Cut slits as desired. Fit over filling. Fold top edge under bottom edge, making a raised edge. Flute as desired. Glaze or top as desired. Cover edge with foil. Bake 25 minutes. Remove foil. Bake 25 to 30 minutes longer until crust is golden brown. Let stand 5 to 10 minutes before serving. Prepare Creamy Dill Sauce. Serve sauce with pie. Makes 6 to 8 servings.

Creamy Dill Sauce:
Melt butter in a small saucepan over medium heat. Add green onion. Sauté 5 minutes, stirring occasionally. Add flour, dill and salt. Mix well. Add milk. Stir constantly over medium heat until mixture thickens and comes to a boil. Remove from heat. Stir in sour cream. Keep warm over very low heat.

Freezing Pot Pies

Stocking your freezer with homemade pot-pie fillings assures you of hot meals throughout busy winter months. Place the filling in desired freezer-to-oven casserole and cover it tightly. Or, line the casserole with foil and freeze as directed for Frozen-Fruit Pie Filling, page 111. Freeze up to 6 months. Remove cover or foil. Thaw filling in preheated oven 15 minutes while preparing desired crust. Top the pie with crust and bake as directed.

Pot Pies

Oh-so-good on a cold winter night!

Country-Style Filling, page 68,
   Pork Filling, page 67,
   Beef Filling, below, or
   Chicken Filling, page 69
Double-Crust Basic Pastry or Herb Pastry,
   page 14, or Cheddar Pastry, page 17

Egg Glaze, page 20
1 teaspoon sesame seeds,
   1/2 teaspoon poppy seeds or
   1 tablespoon grated Parmesan cheese

Prepare filling and dough for pastry. Review Rolling Out, page 8. If filling measures 4 to 5 cups, place it in a 10" x 6" baking pan or a shallow 1-1/2-quart casserole. If filling measures 6 to 7 cups, place it in a 12" x 7" baking pan or a 2-quart casserole. Or, divide filling between two 1-quart casseroles and bake one and freeze one. Preheat oven to 425F (220C). On a lightly floured surface, roll out dough slightly larger than top of casserole. Cut a 1/2-inch hole in center. Cut six to eight 2-inch slits evenly spaced around hole. Fold in half and place over filling. Fold edge of dough under so it is even with rim of pan or casserole. Crimp with a fork. Prepare Egg Glaze. Brush over top of pie. Sprinkle with seeds or cheese. Bake about 25 minutes until crust is golden brown. Makes 4 to 6 servings.

Variations

Cutout Crust: Roll out dough 1/4 inch thick and cut thirty-two 2-inch circles. Arrange circles on top of filling, overlapping slightly. Brush with glaze. Sprinkle with seeds or cheese. Bake about 30 minutes until crust is golden brown.

Lattice Crust: Roll out half the dough as long as the casserole and 5 inches wide. Cut into five 1-inch strips. Roll out remaining dough as wide as the casserole and about 7 inches long. Cut into seven 1-inch strips. Weave strips in a lattice pattern over filling, page 12. Brush with glaze. Sprinkle with seeds or cheese. Bake about 30 minutes until crust is golden brown.

Beef Filling for Pot Pies

Hearty, nourishing and full of flavor.

1 lb. lean chuck or stew beef
1 large onion
2 tablespoons vegetable oil
1-1/2 cups 1/4-inch peeled potato cubes
1 cup thinly sliced carrot
1 cup cut fresh, frozen or
   canned green beans

1 teaspoon salt
1/4 teaspoon pepper
1/8 teaspoon ground thyme
About 3 cups water
2 tablespoons cornstarch
1/4 cup water

Cut meat in 1/2-inch pieces. Coarsely chop onion. Heat oil in a large skillet. Add meat. Stir occasionally over high heat until meat is no longer pink and begins to brown. Add onion. Sauté 2 minutes. Reduce heat to medium. Add potato, carrot, green beans, salt, pepper, thyme and 3 cups water. Observe water level. It may be necessary to add water to maintain water level. Bring to a boil over medium heat. Reduce heat. Cover and simmer about 30 minutes until vegetables and meat are tender. If necessary, add water to bring up to original level. In a small bowl, mix cornstarch and 1/4 cup water. Add to meat and vegetables. Bring to a full boil over medium heat. Stir and boil 1 minute. Cool. Makes about 7 cups.

How to Make Pot Pies

1/Pot Pie with Chicken Filling is topped with Cutout Crust made from Herb Pastry.

2/Pot Pie with Beef Filling is topped with Lattice Crust made from Cheddar Pastry.

Pork Filling for Pot Pies

Use boneless shoulder or remove the bones from 2 pounds of pork loin chops.

1-1/2 lbs. boneless pork	**1 teaspoon salt**
1 medium onion	**1/4 teaspoon black pepper**
1 medium green pepper	**1/2 teaspoon ground sage**
1/4 cup bacon drippings or butter	**2 cups chicken broth**
1/4 cup all-purpose flour	**2 cups chopped peeled, cored apple**

Cut pork into 1/2-inch pieces. Coarsely chop onion and green pepper. Melt drippings or butter in a large skillet over medium heat. Add onion and green pepper. Sauté until onion is tender, stirring occasionally. Add meat pieces. Stir occasionally over high heat until meat is no longer pink. Stir in flour, salt, black pepper and sage until blended into drippings. Add broth. Stir constantly over medium heat until mixture thickens. Reduce heat. Cover and simmer about 40 minutes until pork is tender. Stir in apple. Remove from heat. Cool. Makes about 6 cups.

Individual Pot Pies

Cut slits in the crusts to make patterns according to the flavor of each pie.

Pork Filling, page 67,
  Beef Filling, page 66, or
  Chicken Filling, page 69

2 Double-Crust Basic Pastry, Herb Pastry,
  page 14, or Cheddar Pastry, page 17

Prepare filling and dough for pastry. Review Double-Crust Pies, pages 9 and 10; use measurements below. Preheat oven to 375F (190C). For 9 pies, cut dough into 18 portions. Shape each portion into a ball. On a lightly floured surface, roll out each ball to a 7-inch circle. Fit half the circles into 4-inch pie pans. Spoon in about 3/4 cup filling. Cut 4 slits in center of each remaining circle. Place over fillings. Fold top edge under bottom edge, making a raised edge. Flute as desired. Glaze and top as desired. Place pies on baking sheets. Bake 40 to 45 minutes until golden brown. If you are baking all pies at once, rearrange them in the oven after 20 minutes to allow even baking. Unbaked pies may be refrigerated 2 or 3 hours or quick-frozen. To quick-freeze, place unwrapped pies in freezer. As soon as pies are frozen, remove from freezer. Wrap each pie separately and store in freezer up to 6 months. To bake frozen pies, preheat oven to 425F (205C). Bake pies 40 to 45 minutes until golden brown. When using aluminum pie pans, bottom crusts will cook better if pies are placed slightly below center of oven. Makes 9 servings.

Variation

For Country-Style Filling, below, use 1 Single-Crust Standard Pastry and 1 Double-Crust Standard Pastry. Makes 6 servings.

Country-Style Filling for Pot Pies

Leftover roast and canned or cooked frozen vegetables make a quick, tasty meal.

1/4 cup butter
3/4 cup coarsely chopped onion
1 cup thickly sliced fresh mushrooms or
  1 (4-oz.) can sliced mushrooms
5 tablespoons all-purpose flour
1/2 teaspoon salt
1/4 teaspoon pepper

1-1/2 cups beef or chicken broth
1 cup milk
1/2 teaspoon Worcestershire sauce
2 cups chopped cooked beef, chicken or
  turkey
1-1/2 cups drained canned or
  cooked vegetables

Melt butter in a medium saucepan over medium heat. Add onion and mushrooms. Sauté until onions are tender, stirring occasionally. Stir in flour, salt and pepper. Stir in broth until blended. Add milk and Worcestershire sauce. Stir constantly over medium heat until mixture thickens and comes to a full boil. Stir and boil 1 minute. Add meat and vegetables. Makes about 5 cups.

Variations

Substitute 1 pound lean ground beef, seasoned and cooked, for the beef, chicken or turkey.

Substitute 3 (5- to 7-ounce) cans boneless chicken or ham for the beef, chicken or turkey.

Chicken Filling for Pot Pies

Browning the chicken adds rich flavor to the gravy.

1 (3-lb.) frying chicken
1 tablespoon vegetable oil
1 large onion
4 whole cloves
1 celery stalk, cut in 4 pieces
3 parsley sprigs
2 teaspoons salt
1/2 teaspoon pepper
1/4 teaspoon dried leaf thyme

4 to 5 cups water
1/4 cup butter, if desired
6 tablespoons all-purpose flour
1/2 teaspoon salt
1/4 teaspoon pepper
1/2 cup instant nonfat milk powder
1/2 teaspoon Worcestershire sauce
1 (10-oz.) pkg. frozen peas and carrots

Cut up chicken. Heat oil in a 3- to 4-quart pot. Cook meaty chicken pieces in oil over medium heat until golden brown on one side. Add remaining pieces of chicken. Cut onion in half crosswise. Stud stem half with cloves. Add to chicken. Set aside remaining onion half. Add celery, parsley, 2 teaspoons salt, 1/2 teaspoon pepper and thyme to chicken. Add water to cover. Bring to a boil and reduce heat. Cover and simmer about 1 hour until chicken is tender. Remove chicken. Strain broth. Skim fat from broth. Set aside fat and broth. Cool chicken slightly. Remove meat from bones. Cut meat into 3/4-inch pieces. Set aside. Chop reserved onion half. Place 1/4 cup reserved skimmed fat or butter in a medium saucepan. Add chopped onion. Sauté over medium heat until tender, stirring occasionally. Stir in flour, 1/2 teaspoon salt and 1/4 teaspoon pepper. Stir in 3 cups reserved broth, milk powder and Worcestershire sauce. Stir constantly over medium heat until mixture thickens and comes to a full boil. Stir and boil 1 minute. Add chicken pieces and peas and carrots. Reduce heat and simmer 10 minutes. Makes about 7 cups.

English-Style Deep-Dish Pie

Topping meat pie with puff pastry is traditionally English.

2 cups Quick Puff Pastry, page 24
Steak & Kidney Pie Filling, page 71, or
    Deep-Dish Carbonnade Filling, page 70

Egg Glaze, page 20

Review Puff Pastry Techniques, page 21. Prepare dough for pastry and filling. Preheat oven to 425F (220C). Place filling in a 1-1/2 quart casserole. If filling comes higher than 1/4 inch from top of casserole, remove excess gravy. Reserve for another use. On a lightly floured surface, roll out dough 3/8 inch thick and about 3 inches larger than casserole. Cut off a piece large enough to cover and slightly extend over edges of casserole. Set aside. Roll out remaining dough a little thinner than 3/8 inch. Cut enough 1/2-inch wide strips to go around rim of casserole. Lightly moisten casserole rim. Press dough strips around rim. Prepare Egg Glaze. Brush strips with glaze. Cover filling and strips with cut piece of dough. Do not stretch or dough may shrink while baking. With your fingers, firmly press dough cover to strips. Lift casserole in one hand. Hold a small knife at an angle and trim edge of dough even with rim of casserole. Scallop edge of dough using back of a knife blade; see Ham Pithiviers, page 44. Make a 1/2-inch hole in center. Brush top with glaze, being careful not to let glaze drip over edge. Roll out scraps about 1/8 inch thick. Cut decorations; see Decoration Ideas, page 72. Arrange on top of casserole. Brush with glaze. Bake pie 25 to 35 minutes until browned well. Makes 6 servings.

Vol-au-Vent

Serve this on your most elegant platter and enjoy the compliments.

2 cups Classic Puff Pastry, page 22
Egg Glaze, page 20
Chicken-Liver Sauté or Crab & Shrimp
   in Mushroom Sauce, page 60

Review Puff Pastry Techniques, page 21. Prepare dough for pastry. On a lightly floured surface, roll out dough to a 9-inch circle. Use a plastic lid or inverted bowl as a guide. Holding a knife slanting outward to make pastry wider at bottom, cut a 7-inch circle from center of dough. Turn circle upside-down on a baking sheet. Prepare Egg Glaze. Brush over circle, being careful not to let glaze drip over edge. Center a 5-inch plastic lid or inverted bowl on circle. Mark a circle 1/8 inch deep. With the back of a knife blade, mark lines between circles with V's or radiating lines. Mark inner circle with criss-cross lines to make a diamond pattern. Scallop outside edge of circle with back of the knife blade. Refrigerate 15 minutes. Preheat oven to 425F (220C). Bake circle 25 to 30 minutes or until puffed and browned. Cool. While still warm, cut around inner circle and remove. This will be the Vol-au-Vent lid. Set aside. Remove any unbaked dough from center of shell. Prepare desired filling. Place shell on a platter and fill with about 2 cups hot filling. Replace lid and serve immediately. Or, refrigerate unfilled shell until ready to serve. Reheat chilled unfilled shell and lid 10 minutes in 350F (175C) oven before filling and serving. Makes 4 servings.

Deep-Dish Carbonnade Filling

Especially for English-Style Deep-Dish Pie, page 69.

1/2 lb. thickly sliced bacon
1/4 cup all-purpose flour
1 teaspoon salt
1/4 teaspoon pepper
2 lbs. lean stew beef, cut in
   3/4-inch cubes
4 cups thinly sliced onions

1/4 cup butter
1 garlic clove, crushed
2 tablespoons chopped parsley
1/2 teaspoon dried leaf thyme
1 bay leaf
2 cups beef bouillon
1 (12-oz.) can beer (1-1/2 cups)

Cut bacon into 1-inch pieces. Cook in a large heavy skillet until crisp. Remove bacon and drippings, reserving about 1/4 cup drippings in skillet. Combine flour, salt and pepper. Toss beef cubes in flour mixture. Brown about a third of the beef cubes at a time in reserved bacon drippings. Set aside browned cubes. When all cubes are browned, return with bacon and any remaining seasoned flour to skillet. Melt butter in a medium skillet. Add onions. Cook over medium-low heat about 20 minutes until golden, stirring occasionally. Add to browned beef cubes with remaining ingredients. Bring to a boil. Reduce heat. Cover and simmer about 2 hours until meat is tender. Makes 5 to 6 cups.

Variation

Add 1-1/2 cups cooked vegetables to cooked beef mixture. Use as filling for Pot Pies, page 66.

How to Make Vol-au-Vent

1/Mark the inner circle with criss-cross lines to make a diamond pattern.

2/Baked Vol-au-Vent filled with Crab & Shrimp in Mushroom Sauce.

Steak & Kidney Pie Filling

A robust filling for English-Style Deep-Dish Pie, page 69.

1-1/2 lbs. top sirloin steak	1 cup coarsely chopped onion
1 lb. beef or veal kidneys	1-1/2 cups beef broth
1 teaspoon salt	1/2 teaspoon salt
1/2 teaspoon pepper	1/2 teaspoon crushed dried leaf thyme
1/4 cup all-purpose flour	1/4 teaspoon crushed dried leaf marjoram
1/4 cup butter	1/2 teaspoon Worcestershire sauce
1/4 lb. thickly sliced fresh mushrooms	

Cut steak into 1-inch cubes. Cut kidneys into 3/4-inch pieces, removing any fat from centers. If using beef kidneys, cover with water and soak 15 minutes. Combine 1 teaspoon salt, pepper and flour in a large plastic bag. If necessary, drain kidneys. Place kidney pieces and steak cubes in flour mixture in bag. Close top and shake to coat pieces. Melt 2 tablespoons butter in a medium skillet. Add half the meat and brown over medium heat. Remove from skillet and brown remaining meat. Remove from skillet. Add remaining 2 tablespoons butter to skillet. Add mushrooms and onion. Sauté over medium heat 3 minutes, stirring occasionally. Return meat to skillet. Stir in beef broth, 1/2 teaspoon salt, thyme, marjoram and Worcestershire sauce. Bring to a boil. Reduce heat. Cover and simmer 30 minutes. Cool. Makes 5 to 6 cups.

Beef Wellingtons

Decorate each Wellington with a different pastry shape.

**2 cups Classic Puff Pastry, page 22, or
   Quick Puff Pastry, page 24**
1 teaspoon vegetable oil
4 (6-oz.) beef fillets

Salt and pepper
Chopped-Mushroom Sauté, see below
Egg Glaze, page 20

Chopped-Mushroom Sauté:
Reserved drippings
2 tablespoons butter
1/4 lb. fresh mushrooms, finely chopped

1 green onion, chopped
1/8 teaspoon dry mustard

Review Puff Pastry Techniques, page 21. Prepare dough for pastry. Heat oil in a medium skillet over medium heat. Brown fillets about 1 minute on each side. Place on a plate. Salt and pepper both sides. Refrigerate. Reserve drippings in skillet. Prepare Chopped-Mushroom Sauté. Prepare Egg Glaze. Cut dough into 4 portions. On a lightly floured surface, roll out 1 portion to a 10-inch square. Place about 2 tablespoons Chopped-Mushroom Sautè in center of square and spread to size of beef fillets. Place 1 fillet on mushrooms. Cut a 2-inch square of dough from each corner. Refrigerate scraps. Fold one side of square up and at least halfway over fillet, keeping dough snug to fillet. If necessary, roll out 1 side of square a little thinner or cut off excess dough. Fold up opposite side, overlapping dough at least 1/2 inch. Brush end flaps with glaze. Fold ends up, tucking in dough to make neat corners. Turn over and place on a baking sheet. Repeat with remaining dough portions and fillets. Roll out chilled scraps about 1/8 inch thick. Cut decorations; see Decoration Ideas, below. Brush tops and sides of each Wellington with glaze. Press decorations onto Wellingtons and brush again with glaze. Refrigerate until 20 to 30 minutes before serving. Preheat oven to 425F (220C). Bake Wellingtons 15 minutes for rare and 18 minutes for medium-rare. Wellingtons will stay hot about 15 minutes. Makes 4 servings.

Chopped-Mushroom Sauté:
Melt butter in reserved drippings in skillet over medium heat. Add mushrooms and green onion. Sauté until green onion is tender and moisture is absorbed, stirring frequently. Stir in dry mustard. Cool.

Decoration Ideas

Puff pastry and standard pastry can be decorated with dough cutouts. Decorations made from puff pastry will rise significantly during baking. Those made from standard pastry will puff only slightly.

♦ Make a lattice with 1/2-inch-wide strips of dough. If pastry completely encloses filling, place strips across top and down sides.

♦ Place a twisted strip of dough or a braid around top edge of pastry.

♦ Garnish pastry with flat tulips, "mums" or daisies cut from dough with a knife or pastry cutter. Add appropriate leaf shapes.

♦ To make a pastry rose, cut a 9" x 1/2" strip of dough. Hold one end between the thumb and forefinger of your left hand. This will be the center of the rose. Wind strip around your thumb and finger. The strip will twist as you wrap. See the photo on page 62.

♦ Create decorative shapes relating to the theme of your dinner party. Cut shapes from dough freehand or use hors d'oeuvre cutters.

Chicken Sesame

Tender chicken is wrapped in layers of golden pastry and topped with a creamy sauce.

**1 cup Classic Puff Pastry, page 22, or
  Quick Puff Pastry, page 24**
1 tablespoon butter
4 halves boneless skinless chicken breasts
Salt and pepper
1 (3-oz.) pkg. cream cheese
1 teaspoon soy sauce

**2 tablespoons toasted sesame seeds,
  below**
**1 tablespoon chopped green onion,
  white part only**
Egg Glaze, page 20
1 teaspoon sesame seeds
Cream Sauce, see below

Cream Sauce:
1 tablespoon butter
1 tablespoon all-purpose flour
1/4 teaspoon salt

2/3 cup chicken broth
2/3 cup whipping cream
1/2 teaspoon soy sauce

Review Puff Pastry Techniques, page 21. Prepare dough for pastry. Lightly grease a baking sheet. Set aside. Melt butter in a medium skillet over medium heat. Sprinkle chicken with salt and pepper. Cook seasoned chicken in butter about 2 minutes on each side until lightly browned. Cool on a plate. In a small bowl, mix cream cheese and soy sauce until smooth. Stir in toasted sesame seeds and green onion. Spread an equal amount of cheese mixture on one side of each chicken breast. Prepare Egg Glaze, set aside. On a lightly floured surface, roll out dough to a 12-inch square. Cut into four 6-inch squares. Place a chicken breast, cheese side down, diagonally on each square. Wrap square around chicken, stretching as necessary to cover completely. Lightly brush Egg Glaze where edges of square overlap. Press lightly to seal. Place smooth side up on prepared baking sheet. Brush tops with Egg Glaze and sprinkle with sesame seeds. Refrigerate 30 minutes. Preheat oven to 425F (220C). Bake about 15 minutes until golden brown. Prepare Cream Sauce. Serve chicken packets with Cream Sauce. Makes 4 servings.

Cream Sauce:
Melt butter in a medium saucepan over medium heat. Stir in flour and salt until smooth. Stir in chicken broth and cream. Stir constantly until mixture thickens and comes to a full boil. Reduce heat. Simmer 1 minute, stirring occasionally. Stir in soy sauce. Serve hot.

How to Toast Sesame Seeds

Sesame seeds may be toasted in an oven or in a skillet. To toast them in an oven, spread the seeds in a pie pan. Place in an oven preheated to 350F (175C). Stir occasionally. After 10 to 15 minutes they will be golden brown. Or, place them in a skillet over medium heat. Stir frequently until golden brown.

Chicken Pie Suizas

Serve this Mexican-style pie with Avocado Dip, page 35, and a lettuce and tomato salad.

Double-Crust Basic Pastry, page 14
1 (10-3/4-oz.) can condensed cream of
  chicken soup
1/4 cup chopped green chilies
1/2 cup dairy sour cream
2 cups cubed cooked chicken or turkey

1/2 cup finely chopped onion
1/2 cup sliced ripe olives
1 cup shredded Cheddar cheese (4 oz.)
1/4 cup milk
1/4 cup dairy sour cream

Prepare dough for pastry. Review Double-Crust Pies, pages 9 and 10. Mix soup, chilies and 1/2 cup sour cream in a medium bowl. Remove 1/2 cup mixture and set aside. Add chicken or turkey, onion, olives and cheese to mixture remaining in bowl. Stir to mix well. Preheat oven to 375F (190C). Cut dough into 2 equal portions. On a lightly floured surface, roll out 1 portion to an 11-inch circle. Fit into a 9-inch pie pan. Spoon chicken mixture into unbaked pie shell. Trim edge of dough to rim of pan. Roll out remaining dough to a 12-inch circle. Cut slits as desired. Fit over filling. Fold top edge under bottom edge, making a raised edge. Flute as desired. Glaze and top as desired. Cover edge with foil. Bake 25 minutes. Remove foil. Bake 25 to 30 minutes longer until crust is golden brown. Stir milk and 1/4 cup sour cream into reserved soup mixture. Heat to serving temperature. Do not boil. Serve pie hot with sour cream sauce. Makes 8 servings.

Pork & Noodle Bake

Sour cream and pork in a crust made with cottage cheese and egg noodles.

Noodle Crust, see below
1 lb. ground pork
1/4 cup sliced green onion
1/4 cup green pepper slivers
1 cup sliced fresh mushrooms
2 tablespoons all-purpose flour
1/2 teaspoon salt

1/8 teaspoon garlic salt
1/8 teaspoon ground nutmeg
1 chicken bouillon cube, crushed
1/2 teaspoon Worcestershire sauce
1/2 cup water
1/2 cup dairy sour cream
1/2 cup shredded Cheddar cheese (2 oz.)

Noodle Crust:
3/4 cup cottage cheese (6 oz.)
1/2 cup dairy sour cream
1/2 teaspoon Worcestershire sauce

1/4 teaspoon garlic salt
1/4 cup sliced green onions
6 oz. medium egg noodles, cooked, drained

Preheat oven to 350F (175C). Prepare Noodle Crust. Brown pork in a medium skillet, breaking up with a spoon. Drain off all but 2 tablespoons drippings. Add green onion, green pepper and mushrooms. Cook over medium heat until vegetables are tender, stirring occasionally. Add flour, salt, garlic salt, nutmeg, bouillon cube and Worcestershire sauce. Blend well. Add water. Stir constantly over medium heat until mixture thickens. Remove from heat. Stir in sour cream. Spoon into crust. Bake 15 minutes. Sprinkle cheese around edge of filling. Bake 5 to 10 minutes longer until bubbly. Let stand 5 minutes. Makes 4 to 6 servings.

Noodle Crust:
Lightly grease a 9-inch pie pan. Combine all ingredients in a large bowl. Spoon into prepared pan. Using the back of a spoon, shape noodle mixture into a crust. Bake 10 minutes.

Turkey in Corn-Bread Stuffing

Here's a switch—the turkey's in the stuffing!

Stuffing Crust, see below
2 pork sausage links or
   1/4 cup bulk pork sausage
1/4 cup chopped onion
1/4 cup chopped green pepper
1/4 cup sliced celery
1 (10-3/4-oz.) can condensed cream of
   chicken soup

1/4 teaspoon curry powder
1/8 teaspoon black pepper
1/3 cup milk
2 cups cubed cooked turkey or chicken
1/4 cup sliced ripe olives
Celery leaves, if desired
6 whole pitted ripe olives, if desired

Stuffing Crust:
1/4 cup butter
1/4 cup chopped onion
1/4 cup thinly sliced celery

1 cup chicken broth or water
1 (6-oz.) pkg. seasoned
   corn-bread stuffing mix

Preheat oven to 375F (190C). Prepare Stuffing Crust. While crust is baking, break sausage into small pieces in a medium skillet. Cook over medium heat until lightly browned. Add onion, green pepper and celery. Reduce heat and cook about 5 minutes. Add condensed soup, curry powder and black pepper. Gradually add milk, stirring until mixture is smooth except for vegetables and sausage. Add turkey or chicken and olives. Stir to mix well. Pour into prepared crust. Bake 20 to 25 minutes until heated through. Let stand 5 minutes before serving. Garnish with celery leaves and ripe olives, if desired. Makes 6 servings.

Stuffing Crust:
Lightly butter a 9-inch pie pan. Set aside. Melt butter in a medium skillet over medium heat. Add onion and celery. Sauté until onion is tender, stirring occasionally. Stir in broth or water. If using a mix with a separate seasoning packet, add contents of packet and simmer 2 minutes. Add stuffing mix. Stir until all moisture is absorbed. Spoon stuffing mixture evenly into prepared pan. Use a custard cup to press stuffing against bottom and up side of pan, making a firm crust. Bake 15 minutes.

Spaghetti Crust

This crust and leftover turkey makes Turkey Tetrazzini, page 77, an economical dish.

6 oz. uncooked spaghetti
Salted boiling water
1 tablespoon butter

1 egg, slightly beaten
1/3 cup grated Parmesan cheese

Lightly grease a 9-inch pie pan. Set aside. Break spaghetti into 3-inch pieces. Cook in salted boiling water 10 to 12 minutes until tender. Drain. Immediately place hot cooked spaghetti in a medium bowl. Add butter. Toss until butter is melted. Add beaten egg and Parmesan cheese. Toss to coat spaghetti. Pour into prepared pan. Use a spoon to pat spaghetti into a pie shell, making shell edge slightly higher than rim of pan. Makes one 9-inch crust.

Sausage in Polenta Crust

Polenta, a cooked cornmeal mixture, is a basic food in northern Italy.

Polenta Crust, see below
1 lb. sweet Italian sausages
1/2 cup chopped green pepper
1/2 cup sliced onion
1 (8-oz.) can tomato sauce

1 teaspoon crushed dried leaf oregano
1/2 teaspoon crushed dried leaf basil
1/2 cup shredded mozzarella cheese (2 oz.)
2 tablespoons grated Parmesan cheese

Polenta Crust:
1-1/4 cups cornmeal
2-1/2 cups water
2 eggs
1-1/2 teaspoons salt

1/8 teaspoon white pepper
2 tablespoons olive oil
1/2 cup grated Parmesan cheese (1-1/2 oz.)

Preheat oven to 400F (205C). Prepare Polenta Crust. Remove sausages from casings and brown in a medium skillet, breaking up with a spoon. Add pepper and onion. Sauté until vegetables are tender, stirring occasionally. Drain off any drippings. Add tomato sauce, oregano and basil. Spoon into crust. Bake 25 minutes. Sprinkle with mozzarella cheese and Parmesan cheese. Bake about 5 minutes longer until bubbly. Let stand 10 minutes before serving. Makes 6 servings.

Polenta Crust:
Combine cornmeal and water in a medium saucepan. Bring to a full boil over medium heat, stirring frequently. Boil 5 minutes, stirring occasionally. Reduce heat if necessary. Generously grease a 9-inch pie pan. Sprinkle with dry cornmeal and set aside. Remove cooked cornmeal mixture from heat. Beat in eggs one at a time. Stir in salt, pepper, oil and cheese. Spread 1-1/2 cups mixture in bottom of prepared pan. Pipe or spoon remaining mixture around edge. Bake 10 minutes.

Turkey Tetrazzini

Freeze cubed leftover turkey in 1-1/2-cup amounts so you can make this any time of year.

Spaghetti Crust, page 75
3 tablespoons butter
1 cup thinly sliced fresh mushrooms
1/3 cup coarsely chopped green pepper
1/4 cup finely chopped onion
2 tablespoons all-purpose flour
1/2 teaspoon salt

1/4 teaspoon black pepper
1 cup half and half or milk
1 chicken bouillon cube, crushed
2 tablespoons chopped pimiento
1-1/2 cups cubed cooked turkey
1 tablespoon sherry
1/4 cup grated Parmesan cheese (3/4 oz.)

Prepare Spaghetti Crust. Preheat oven to 375F (190C). Melt butter in a medium saucepan over medium heat. Add mushrooms, green pepper and onion. Sauté until vegetables are tender, stirring occasionally. Stir in flour, salt and black pepper. Add half and half or milk and bouillon cube. Stir constantly over medium heat until mixture thickens and comes to a full boil. Stir and boil 1 minute. Stir in pimiento, turkey and sherry. Pour into Spaghetti Crust. Sprinkle with Parmesan cheese. Bake about 25 minutes until bubbly. Makes 6 servings.

Garden Favorites

Vegetable pies, quiches and strudels.

An advantage of serving the vegetable course in pastry is that it stays hot longer. This is a boon to buffet dining and outdoor barbecues. Potato Pockets, Scalloped Potato Pie and the three vegetable strudels are especially good for buffet or outdoor entertaining because they stay hot 15 to 20 minutes after being taken from the oven.

Hungarian housewives made strudel to use onions and cabbage that grew abundantly in the gardens of Eastern Europe. Vegetable strudel is especially convenient for an outdoor barbecue. While the meat is cooking over charcoal, the strudel can have the oven to itself.

Several dishes in this section were created with home gardens in mind. If you have several kinds of summer squash, but not many of any one variety, mix them in Zucchini Quiche. For a small broccoli harvest, Broccoli Pinwheel Puff stretches a little broccoli to several servings. Corn Custard does the same with two ears of corn. Ratatouille Pie is laden with wholesome eggplant, zucchini and tomato. And for an excess of green tomatoes, try the recipe for Green-Tomato Mince Pie in the fruit section, Bounties of the Seasons.

Custard is an indispensable base for vegetable pies. The cheese variation of custard is quiche. It combines hearty, high-protein foods such as eggs, milk and cheese with vegetables for a satisfying meatless main dish. Mushroom & Green Bean Quiche, Zucchini Quiche, Broccoli Pinwheel Puff and Onion Quiche are excellent main courses.

Whenever you have leftover vegetable pies, refrigerate them. Served cold, they are easy and nourishing breakfasts, snacks, lunches and midnight suppers. ◆

Light Luncheon

Bibb Lettuce with
Marinated Sliced Mushrooms
Zucchini Quiche, page 86
Pears Hélène

Patio Barbecue

Pissaladière, page 41
Barbecued Top Sirloin
Mushroom Strudel, page 89
Corn-on-the-Cob
Angelfood Pie, page 153

Dilled Mushroom Pie

Save time and effort by slicing the mushrooms in your food processor.

Single-Crust Wheat Pastry, page 16
1 lb. fresh mushrooms
3 tablespoons butter
1/4 cup chopped onion
1/3 cup chopped green pepper
3 tablespoons all-purpose flour
2 eggs

1/2 cup dairy sour cream
1 cup milk
3/4 teaspoon salt
1/8 teaspoon black pepper
1 teaspoon dried dill weed
2 tablespoons grated Parmesan cheese

Prepare dough for pastry. Review Unbaked Pie Shells, page 8. On a lightly floured surface, roll out dough to a 12-inch circle. Fit into a 9-inch pie pan. Fold dough edge under for a raised edge. Make a high fluting. Preheat oven to 350F (175C). Thinly slice mushrooms. Melt butter in a medium skillet over medium heat. Add sliced mushrooms, onion and green pepper. Sauté until vegetables are tender, stirring occasionally. Stir in flour until blended. Remove from heat. In a medium bowl, beat eggs and sour cream with a wire whip or rotary beater until smooth. Stir in milk, salt, black pepper and dill. Gradually stir egg mixture into mushroom mixture. Stir until mushrooms have separated from each other. Pour into unbaked pie shell. With a fork, rearrange mushrooms in mixture so attractive slices are on top. Bake 30 minutes. Sprinkle with Parmesan cheese. Bake 5 to 10 minutes longer or until filling is set. Let stand 5 to 10 minutes before serving. Makes 8 servings.

Ratatouille Pie

The vegetables are a traditional mixture in Provence, France.

Single-Crust Double-Wheat Pastry, page 16
Ratatouille, page 89
2 eggs
3/4 cup shredded Monterey Jack cheese
(3 oz.)

2 tablespoons wheat germ
1 tablespoon chopped fresh parsley

Prepare dough for pastry. Review Unbaked Pie Shells, page 8. Prepare Ratatouille. Preheat oven to 375F (190C). On a lightly floured surface, roll out dough to a 12-inch circle. Fit into a 9-inch pie pan. Fold dough edge under for a raised edge. Make a high fluting. Slightly beat eggs. Stir into cooled Ratatouille. Pour into unbaked pie shell. Bake 30 minutes. Remove from oven. Combine cheese, wheat germ and parsley. Sprinkle around edge of filling. Return pie to oven. Bake 5 to 10 minutes until cheese is melted and begins to bubble. Let stand 5 to 10 minutes before serving. Makes 8 servings.

Corn Pie

Crushed saltine crackers provide a different crust for the light corn filling.

Saltine Crust, see below:
2 tablespoons butter
1/2 cup finely chopped onion
2 tablespoons all-purpose flour
1/4 teaspoon salt
1/2 cup milk

1 (12-oz.) can whole-kernel corn,
    drained
2 tablespoons chopped green chilies,
    if desired
2 eggs

Saltine Crust:
36 small saltine cracker squares
1/3 cup butter, melted

Preheat oven to 350F (175C). Prepare Saltine Crust. Melt butter in a medium saucepan over medium heat. Add onion. Sauté until tender, stirring occasionally. Stir in flour and salt until blended. Add milk. Stir constantly over medium heat until mixture thickens and comes to a full boil. Stir and boil 1 minute. Stir in corn. Stir in chilies, if desired. Remove from heat. With an electric mixer, beat eggs until thick enough to mound slightly when dropped from a spoon, 5 to 8 minutes. Fold into corn mixture. Pour into crust. Sprinkle reserved crumb mixture over center of pie. Bake about 30 minutes until lightly browned. Let stand 5 to 10 minutes before serving. Makes 8 servings.

Saltine Crust:
Place saltine crackers in a plastic bag or between 2 sheets of waxed paper. Crush with a rolling pin to make small uniform crumbs. Or use a food processor or blender. Place crumbs in a small bowl. Add butter. Toss to distribute butter. Reserve 2 tablespoons crumb mixture. Spread remaining crumb mixture evenly over bottom of a 9-inch pie pan. Press against bottom and up side of pan to form a firm crust. Bake 5 minutes.

*tip*

Freeze bread ends and leftover toast in a food-storage bag. When you have the blender or food processor out, make breadcrumbs. Return the crumbs to the bag and freezer. Use them in strudels, meat loaves or as a casserole topping.

Corn Custard

Stretch a few ears of corn to feed a group. In winter, use canned or frozen whole-kernel corn.

Green Onion Curls, see below
Single-Crust Basic Pastry, page 14
4 bacon slices
2 medium ears fresh corn
1/4 cup sliced green onion
1/2 cup shredded mozzarella cheese or
   Monterey Jack cheese (2 oz.)

3 eggs
1 tablespoon all-purpose flour
1 teaspoon sugar
1 teaspoon salt
1/4 teaspoon pepper
2 cups milk

Green Onion Curls:
2 or 3 green onion tops

Prepare Green Onion Curls. Prepare dough for pastry. Review Unbaked Pie Shells, page 8. On a lightly floured surface, roll out dough to a 12-inch circle. Fit into a 9-inch pie pan. Fold dough edge under for a raised edge. Make a high fluting. Preheat oven to 425F (220C). Cook bacon until crisp. Drain. Crumble bacon into bottom of unbaked pie shell. To cut corn from the cob, break ears in half. With a sharp knife or corn cutter, cut off whole kernels, being careful not to include any hard fibrous cob. Cut corn should measure 1 rounded cup. Place in pie shell. Add green onion and cheese. Mix lightly with a fork, being careful not to puncture pastry. Place eggs, flour, sugar, salt and pepper in a medium bowl. Beat with a wire whip or rotary beater until smooth. Gradually stir in milk until blended. Pour over mixture in pie shell. Bake 15 minutes. Reduce heat to 350F (175C). Bake about 35 minutes longer until filling is set. Let stand 5 to 10 minutes before serving. Serve warm, garnished with Green Onion Curls. Makes 8 servings.

Green Onion Curls:
Cut green onion tops into 2-1/2-inch pieces. Slice lengthwise in 1/8-inch or smaller strips. Place in a bowl of ice water and refrigerate until ready to use. Drain before using.

Broccoli Pinwheel Puff

A delightful garden soufflé in a crisp pie shell.

Single-Crust Basic Pastry, page 14
3/4 lb. fresh broccoli or
  1 (10-oz.) pkg. frozen broccoli spears
Salted boiling water
3 tablespoons butter
1/4 cup finely minced onion
3 tablespoons all-purpose flour

1/4 teaspoon salt
1/8 teaspoon white pepper
1-1/3 cups milk
3 eggs, separated
1/2 cup shredded sharp Cheddar cheese
  (2 oz.)
1/2 cup grated Parmesan cheese (1-1/2 oz.)

Prepare dough for pastry. Review Baked Pie Shells, pages 8 and 9. On a lightly floured surface, roll out dough to a 12-inch circle. Fit into a 9-inch pie pan. Fold dough edge under for a raised edge. Make a high fluting. To bake blind, line shell with foil and fill with beans. Bake 7 minutes. Remove foil and beans. Set baked pie shell aside. Reduce oven temperature to 350F (175C). Separate broccoli into small spears about 3 inches long. Cook in salted boiling water until tender. Drain. Place on paper towels. Set aside 8 small uniform spears. Coarsely chop remaining cooked broccoli. Set aside. Melt butter in a small saucepan over medium heat. Add onion. Sauté until tender, stirring occasionally. Stir in flour, salt and white pepper until blended. In a small bowl, mix milk and egg yolks until smooth. Add to flour mixture. Stir constantly over medium heat until mixture thickens and comes to a full boil. Stir and boil 1 minute. Reduce heat. Add Cheddar cheese and 1/4 cup Parmesan cheese. Stir and boil until cheeses are melted. Stir in chopped cooked broccoli. Remove from heat. Beat egg whites until stiff peaks form. Fold into cheese mixture. Pour into baked pie shell. Arrange reserved broccoli spears pinwheel-fashion, with heads out, on cheese mixture. Press stem ends below surface of cheese mixture. Sprinkle with remaining 1/4 cup Parmesan cheese. Bake 40 to 45 minutes until puffed and golden brown. Serve hot. Soufflé will fall slightly while standing. Makes 8 servings.

How to Make Broccoli Pinwheel Puff

1/Fold stiffly beaten egg whites into cheese mixture.

2/Arrange broccoli pinwheel-fashion on filling.

Scalloped-Potato Pie

So good you'll want to finish it all—but it's even better warmed up the next day.

Double-Crust Basic Pastry, page 14	**1/2 teaspoon pepper**
5 medium potatoes	**1/4 teaspoon dry mustard**
1/3 cup butter	**3 tablespoons all-purpose flour**
1/2 cup thinly sliced green onions	**1-1/2 cups half and half or milk**
1 teaspoon salt	**1 cup shredded sharp Cheddar cheese (4 oz.)**

Prepare dough for pastry. Review Double Crust Pies, pages 9 and 10. Preheat oven to 375F (190C). Peel potatoes. Thinly slice enough to make 4 cups. Cover with water. Melt butter in a medium saucepan over medium heat. Add green onions. Sauté over medium heat until tender, stirring occasionally. Stir in salt, pepper, dry mustard and flour until blended. Stir in half and half or milk. Stir constantly over medium heat until sauce thickens and comes to a full boil. Stir and boil 1 minute. Remove from heat. Cut dough into 2 equal portions. Roll out 1 portion to an 11-inch circle. Fit into a 9-inch pie pan. Drain potatoes. Pat dry. Using a third of each ingredient, layer potatoes, cheese and sauce in unbaked pie shell. Repeat layers twice. Trim edge of dough to rim of pan. Roll out remaining dough to a 12-inch circle. Cut slits as desired. Fit circle over filling. Fold top edge under bottom edge, making a raised edge. Flute as desired. Glaze and top as desired. Cover edge with foil. Bake 25 minutes. Remove foil. Bake 30 to 35 minutes until golden brown and potatoes are tender. Makes 8 servings.

Potato Pockets

A marvelous make-ahead side dish for buffet dinners.

Double-Crust Cheddar Pastry, page 17
4 to 5 medium potatoes
1/3 cup butter
1/2 cup finely chopped onion
1 teaspoon salt

1/2 teaspoon pepper
1/4 teaspoon garlic salt
1/4 teaspoon dry mustard
2 tablespoons chopped parsley, if desired

Prepare dough for pastry. Review Rolling Out, page 8. Preheat oven to 375F (190C). Peel potatoes and coarsely shred to make 3-1/2 cups. Place shredded potatoes in a medium bowl. Cover with water. Melt butter in a small saucepan over medium heat. Add onion. Sauté until tender, stirring occasionally. Stir in salt, pepper, garlic salt and dry mustard. Add parsley, if desired. Drain potatoes. Pat with paper towels to absorb excess moisture. Return to bowl and add onion mixture. Toss lightly to coat potatoes. Cut dough into 8 equal portions. Shape each portion into a ball. On a lightly floured surface, roll out 1 ball to an 8-inch circle. Place about 1/3 cup potato mixture in center of circle. Pleat edge of circle, pulling pleats over filling to center. Twist pleats together. Carefully place pleat side up on an ungreased baking sheet. Repeat with remaining dough balls and potato mixture. Bake 40 minutes. Or refrigerate on baking sheet and bake chilled pockets 45 minutes. Baked pockets will stay hot 15 to 20 minutes. Makes 8 servings.

Onion Quiche

Onion slices can be complete circles or half circles.

Single-Crust Basic Pastry, page 14, or
   Rich Butter Pastry, page 19
3 to 4 bacon slices
3 cups thinly sliced onions
1/2 cup shredded Monterey Jack cheese or
   Swiss cheese (2 oz.)

1/4 cup grated Parmesan cheese (3/4 oz.)
3 eggs
1-1/2 cups half and half
1/2 teaspoon salt
1/8 teaspoon black pepper
Dash red (cayenne) pepper

Prepare dough for pastry. Review Unbaked Pie Shells, page 8. In a medium skillet, cook bacon until crisp. Drain and crumble. Add onions to bacon drippings. Stir occasionally over medium-low heat until onions are golden, about 20 minutes. On a lightly floured surface, roll out dough to a 12-inch circle. Fit into a 9-inch quiche pan or pie pan. If using a quiche pan, fold dough edge under so it is even with rim of pan; press dough into scalloped sides of pan. If using a pie pan, fold dough under for a raised edge; make a high fluting. Preheat oven to 425F (220C). Set aside 4 or 5 cooked onion slices and 1 teaspoon crumbled bacon for garnish. Spoon remaining cooked onion evenly into unbaked pie shell. Sprinkle with cheeses and remaining crumbled bacon. With a fork, gently lift some onion slices over cheese. In a medium bowl, combine eggs, half and half, salt, black pepper and red pepper. Mix until smooth. Pour over onion mixture. Bake 15 minutes. Reduce heat to 350F (175C). Bake 25 to 30 minutes longer until filling is set. Let stand 5 to 10 minutes before serving. Garnish with reserved onion slices and bacon. Makes 8 servings.

Mushroom & Green Bean Quiche

If you need a vegetarian dish, omit the bacon and sauté the vegetables in oil.

Single-Crust Basic Pastry, page 14
6 bacon slices
1 cup thinly sliced fresh mushrooms
1/2 cup chopped onion
1 (10-oz.) pkg. frozen French-cut
   green beans
Salted boiling water

1 cup shredded Swiss cheese (4 oz.)
4 eggs
2 cups half and half
1/2 teaspoon salt
1/8 teaspoon white pepper
1/16 teaspoon red (cayenne) pepper

Prepare dough for pastry. Review Unbaked Pie Shells, page 8. On a lightly floured surface, roll out dough to a 12-inch circle. Fit into a 9-inch quiche pan or pie pan. If using a quiche pan, fold dough edge under so it is even with rim of pan; press dough into scalloped sides of pan. If using a pie pan, fold dough under for a raised edge; make a high fluting. In a medium skillet, cook bacon until crisp. Drain and crumble. Reserve about 2 tablespoons drippings in skillet. Add mushrooms and onion. Sauté over medium heat until onion is tender, stirring occasionally. Place in a medium bowl. Cook green beans in salted boiling water according to package directions until tender. Drain. Add to mushroom mixture. Add crumbled bacon and cheese. Toss lightly. Preheat oven to 425F (220C). Spread mushroom mixture evenly in unbaked pie shell. Combine eggs, half and half, salt, white pepper and red pepper in a medium bowl. Beat with a wire whip or rotary beater until smooth. Carefully pour over vegetable mixture. Bake 15 minutes. Reduce heat to 350F (175C). Bake 25 to 30 minutes longer until filling is set. Let stand 5 to 10 minutes before serving. Makes 8 servings.

Zucchini Quiche

Use any combination of zucchini, yellow crookneck, patty pan or summer squash.

Single-Crust Basic Pastry, page 14, or
   Wheat Pastry, page 16
3-1/2 cups 1/4-inch zucchini slices
1/2 cup chopped onion
2 cups water
1 teaspoon salt
3 eggs
1 cup milk

1/2 teaspoon salt
1/2 teaspoon crushed dried leaf marjoram
   or oregano
1/8 teaspoon black pepper
Dash red (cayenne) pepper
2 cups shredded Monterey Jack cheese
   (8 oz.)
Tomato Topping, see below

Tomato Topping:
1 large tomato
4 small saltine cracker squares
1/4 teaspoon crushed dried leaf marjoram

1/4 cup shredded Monterey Jack cheese
   (1 oz.)

Prepare dough for pastry. Review Unbaked Pie Shells, page 9. Place zucchini, onion, water and 1 teaspoon salt in a medium saucepan. Bring to a boil. Reduce heat and simmer uncovered about 8 minutes until zucchini is tender. On a lightly floured surface, roll out dough to a 12-inch circle. Fit into a 9-inch quiche pan or pie pan. If using a quiche pan, fold dough edge under so it is even with rim of pan; press dough into scalloped sides of pan. If using a pie pan, fold dough under for a raised edge; make a high fluting. Preheat oven to 425F (220C). Drain cooked zucchini in a colander 5 minutes. Turn out onto paper towels to absorb any excess moisture. In a large bowl, combine eggs, milk, 1/2 teaspoon salt, marjoram or oregano, black pepper and red pepper. Beat with a wire whip or rotary beater until smooth. Add drained zucchini and cheese. Stir gently to mix. Pour into unbaked pie shell. Bake 15 minutes. Reduce heat to 350F (175C) and bake 25 minutes longer. While quiche is baking, prepare Tomato Topping. Remove quiche from oven. Arrange tomato slices from Tomato Topping in a circle on top of filling. Sprinkle tomatoes with cracker mixture. Return quiche to oven and bake about 5 minutes until cheese is melted. Let stand 5 to 10 minutes before serving. Makes 6 to 8 servings.

Tomato Topping:
Peel and core tomato. Cut in half lengthwise. Place halves cut side down on a board. Cut in 1/4-inch slices. Set aside. With the back of a spoon, finely crush saltine crackers in a small bowl. Add marjoram and cheese. Toss lightly.

Zucchini Quiche made with Wheat Pastry, page 16.

Cabbage Strudel

Although this recipe calls for shredded cabbage, chopped cabbage will give the same result.

Strudel Pastry, page 26	1/2 teaspoon pepper
6 tablespoons butter	2 teaspoons caraway seeds, if desired
1 cup chopped onion	1/2 cup finely chopped ham
8 cups shredded cabbage (1 medium cabbage)	6 tablespoons butter, melted
1 teaspoon salt	3/4 cup fresh breadcrumbs

Review Strudel Pastry Techniques, page 25. Begin preparing dough for pastry. While dough is resting, melt 6 tablespoons butter in a large skillet over medium heat. Add onion. Sauté until almost tender, stirring occasionally. Stir in cabbage, salt and pepper. Add caraway seeds, if desired. Cover skillet. Reduce heat to medium-low. Cook about 10 minutes until cabbage is tender, stirring occasionally. Stir in ham. Remove from heat. Stretch dough as directed. Let stand to dry 10 minutes. While dough is drying, butter a 17" x 11" baking sheet. Preheat oven to 425F (220C). Brush dough with 5 tablespoons melted butter. Sprinkle with breadcrumbs. Place cabbage mixture on dough in a strip about 3 inches from one long edge and to within 2 inches of each short edge. Fold the 3-inch edge of dough over filling. Lift up cloth at that edge and use to roll up strudel jelly-roll fashion. Place seam side down in a horseshoe shape on prepared baking sheet. Brush with remaining 1 tablespoon butter. Bake 10 minutes. Reduce heat to 400F (205C). Bake about 20 minutes longer until strudel is crisp and browned. Cool slightly before serving. Makes 10 to 12 servings.

Onion Strudel

Cut this savory treat into 12 pieces and serve it as an appetizer.

Strudel Pastry, page 26	1/4 teaspoon crushed dried leaf thyme
1/4 cup butter	Dash pepper
4 to 5 cups thinly sliced onions	1 egg, slightly beaten
1 (8-oz.) pkg. cream cheese	6 tablespoons butter, melted
1/2 cup finely chopped ham	3/4 cup fresh breadcrumbs
1/4 teaspoon salt	

Review Strudel Pastry Techniques, page 25. Begin preparing dough for pastry. While dough is resting, melt 1/4 cup butter in a large skillet. Add onions. Stir occasionally over medium-low heat until onions are golden, about 20 minutes. Stretch dough as directed. Let stand to dry 10 minutes. While dough is drying, butter a 17" x 11" baking sheet. Preheat oven to 425F (220C). Add cream cheese and ham to onions in skillet. Use a large spoon to mash cheese into mixture over low heat until evenly distributed. Remove from heat. Add salt, thyme, pepper and egg. Mix well. Brush dough with 5 tablespoons butter. Sprinkle evenly with breadcrumbs. Place onion mixture on dough in a long strip about 3 inches from one long edge and to within 2 inches of each short edge. Fold the 3-inch edge of dough over filling. Lift up cloth at that edge and use to roll up strudel jelly-roll fashion. Place seam side down in a horseshoe shape on prepared baking sheet. Brush with remaining 1 tablespoon butter. Bake 10 minutes. Reduce heat to 400F (205C). Bake about 20 minutes longer until strudel is crisp and browned. Makes 8 to 10 servings.

Mushroom Strudel

If your baking sheet is too small for a single large strudel, make 2 smaller ones. See page 114.

Strudel Pastry, page 26
6 tablespoons butter
1/2 cup finely chopped onion
1/2 cup chopped green pepper
2 lbs. fresh mushrooms, thinly sliced
1 teaspoon salt

1/4 teaspoon black pepper
1 egg
1/2 cup dairy sour cream
1/2 teaspoon ground nutmeg
6 tablespoons butter, melted
3/4 cup fresh breadcrumbs

Review Strudel Pastry Techniques, page 25. Begin preparing dough for pastry. While dough is resting, melt 6 tablespoons butter in a large skillet over medium heat. Add onion and green pepper. Sauté 3 minutes, stirring occasionally. Add mushrooms. Sauté until vegetables are tender and moisture is absorbed. Stir in salt, black pepper, egg, sour cream and nutmeg. Mix well. Remove from heat. Stretch dough as directed. Let stand to dry 10 minutes. While dough is drying, butter a 17" x 11" baking sheet. Preheat oven to 425F (220C). Brush dough with 5 tablespoons butter. Sprinkle with breadcrumbs. Place mushroom mixture on dough in a long strip about 3 inches from one edge and to within 2 inches of adjoining ends. Fold the 3-inch edge of dough over filling. Lift up cloth at that edge and use to roll up strudel jelly-roll fashion. Place seam side down in a horseshoe shape on prepared baking sheet. Tuck ends under. Brush with remaining 1 tablespoon butter. Bake 10 minutes. Reduce heat to 400F (205C). Bake about 20 minutes longer until strudel is crisp and browned. Cool slightly before serving. Makes 10 to 12 servings.

Ratatouille

Use this to make Ratatouille Pie, page 79.

1 medium unpeeled eggplant (about 1 lb.)
2 small zucchini
1/4 cup olive oil
1 cup coarsely chopped onion
1 garlic clove, crushed
1/2 cup diced green pepper
1 (16-oz.) can tomatoes or
   2 medium, fresh tomatoes

1 teaspoon salt
1/2 teaspoon crushed dried leaf oregano
1/2 teaspoon crushed dried leaf thyme
1/2 teaspoon crushed dried leaf basil
1/4 teaspoon black pepper

Remove and discard ends from eggplant and zucchini. Cut eggplant into 1/2-inch cubes. Cut zucchini into 1/4-inch slices. Heat olive oil in a medium skillet over medium heat. Add onion and garlic. Sauté until onion is tender, stirring occasionally. Add eggplant cubes, zucchini slices and green pepper. Sauté 10 minutes, stirring occasionally. Drain canned tomatoes and cut in 1-inch pieces. Or peel and core fresh tomatoes and cut in 3/4-inch pieces. Add to eggplant mixture. Add salt, oregano, thyme, basil and black pepper. Mix well. Cook about 10 minutes until zucchini is tender, stirring occasionally. Cool. Makes about 4 cups.

Bounties of the Seasons

Fruit pies, tarts and strudels.

Glorious fruit in open-face pies can be traced back to fruit-filled tarts enjoyed for centuries in France and England. For an authentic French tart, use a flan pan with a removable bottom. See the photo on page 107. But don't avoid these recipes because you lack a special pan. Place the dough circle on a pizza pan, roll the edge under and make a high fluting. Or, use a pie pan. This will give a high tart with a thick crust. For a variation of French open-face tarts, see Glazed Fruit Tartlets in The Bakery Shop.

Frozen-Fruit Pie made with Frozen-Fruit Pie Filling will provide summer flavor in mid-January. If you live in a fruit-growing area or have a fruit tree in your yard, freeze fillings for several pies during the height of the season. For double convenience, store Multi-Crust Basic Pastry in your freezer, too.

To freeze double-crust unbaked fresh-fruit pies, prepare the bottom crust in a freezer-to-oven baking dish. Fill and top as directed. Place the unbaked pie on the coldest shelf of your freezer for about 2 hours until it's frozen. Wrap the frozen pie securely with foil and place it in a freezer bag. When you're ready to bake the pie, remove the bag and wrapping. Be sure the slits in the top of the pie are open to let steam escape. Cover the edge with foil to prevent overbrowning. Place the pie in a preheated 425F (220C) oven. Bake it for 40 to 60 minutes, removing the foil after the first 30 minutes. The center of a frozen pie is always the last to thaw and bake. Baking the pie on a pizza pan will help distribute heat to the pie's center and hasten thawing and baking.

Apple pie is the pie-lover's favorite. In this section there are six entirely different apple pies! Grandma's Apple Pie is old-fashioned apple pie as my Grandma Switzer made it. Tarte Tatin is a traditional French apple pie. Cheddar-Apple Pie is an English blend of mild apples and sharp Cheddar cheese. Apple Strudel is from the home kitchens and pastry shops of Vienna. Cranberry-Apple Relish Pie honors the holiday season. The spicy nut topping on Apple Streusel Pie is drizzled with icing.

Golden Delicious apples are sweet, store well and are available year round. They are usually sweet enough so you can use the smaller amount of sugar called for in the recipe. If you like a sweet-tart flavor, try Newtown Pippins, Winesap or Jonathan apples. The tarter the apple, the more sugar you'll need to use. ◆

Alpine Dinner

Pork Roast with Potato Dumplings
Buttered Carrots
Cabbage Strudel, page 88
Apple Streusel Pie, page 93

Country Feast for a Crowd

Fruit Salad with Whipped Cream
Chicken-Fried Steak with Gravy
Green Beans with Tomatoes
Mashed Potatoes
Berry Pie, page 102
Ginger Peachy Pie, page 98

Cheddar-Apple Pie   *Photo on cover.*

Make the pastry for this pie with the sharpest Cheddar you can find.

Double-Crust Cheddar Pastry, page 17
3/4 cup sugar
2 tablespoons all-purpose flour
1/4 teaspoon ground cinnamon
1/4 teaspoon salt

1/8 teaspoon ground nutmeg
2 tablespoons butter
6 to 7 cups thinly sliced, peeled apples
  (about 3 lbs.)

Prepare dough for pastry. Review Double-Crust Pies, pages 9 and 10. Combine sugar, flour, cinnamon, salt and nutmeg. Cut in butter until pieces are the size of large peas. Place apple slices in a large bowl. Add sugar mixture. Toss to coat apple slices with sugar mixture. Preheat oven to 375F (190C). Divide dough into 2 equal portions. On a lightly floured surface, roll out 1 portion to an 11-inch circle. Fit into a 9-inch pie pan. Spoon apple mixture into unbaked pie shell. Trim edge of dough to rim of pan. Roll out remaining dough to a 12-inch circle. Cut slits as desired. Fit circle over filling. Fold top edge under bottom edge, making a raised edge. Flute as desired. Glaze and top as desired. Cover edge with foil. Bake 25 minutes. Remove foil. Bake 25 to 30 minutes longer until crust is golden brown, apples are tender and juices are bubbly. Serve warm. Makes 8 servings.

Variation

Add 1/3 cup seedless raisins or 1/3 cup chopped walnuts or pecans to apples with sugar mixture.

Cranberry-Apple Relish Pie   *Photo on pages 2 and 3.*

A whole fresh orange with tender skin gives this pie special zest.

Double-Crust Basic Pastry, page 14
1 cup sugar
2 teaspoons all-purpose flour
1/2 teaspoon ground cinnamon

1/4 teaspoon salt
1 small fresh orange
1-1/2 cups fresh or frozen cranberries
4 cups sliced peeled apples (about 2 lbs.)

Prepare dough for pastry. Review Double-Crust Pies, pages 9 and 10, and Quick Lattice, page 13. Combine sugar, flour, cinnamon and salt in a medium bowl. Cut orange in 8 pieces and remove any seeds and hard core. Place in blender with 1/2 cup cranberries. Process until orange is coarsely chopped. Add to sugar mixture. Add apples and remaining 1 cup cranberries. Toss lightly to coat apple slices. Preheat oven to 375F (190C). Cut dough into 2 equal portions. On a lightly floured surface, roll out 1 portion to an 11-inch circle. Fit into a 9-inch pie pan. Spoon apple mixture into unbaked pie shell. Trim edge of dough to rim of pan. Roll out remaining dough to a 12-inch circle. Make a Quick Lattice, cutting leaves and berries with hors d'oeuvre cutters. Fit lattice over filling. Fold top edge under bottom edge, making a raised edge. Flute with cutouts or as desired. Glaze and top as desired. Cover edge with foil. Bake 25 minutes. Remove foil. Bake 25 to 30 minutes longer until crust is golden brown and fruit is tender. Makes 8 servings.

Grandma's Apple Pie

The name says it all—homemade, warm and fragrant.

Double-Crust Basic Pastry, page 14
1/2 cup granulated sugar
1/3 cup packed brown sugar
2 tablespoons all-purpose flour
1/2 teaspoon ground cinnamon
1/4 teaspoon ground nutmeg
1/4 teaspoon salt

2 tablespoons butter
6 to 7 cups thinly sliced peeled apples
  (about 3 lbs.)
1 tablespoon granulated sugar
Dash of ground cinnamon
Vanilla ice cream, if desired

Prepare dough for pastry. Review Double-Crust Pies, pages 9 and 10. Combine 1/2 cup granulated sugar, brown sugar, flour, 1/2 teaspoon cinnamon, nutmeg and salt in a small bowl. Cut in butter until pieces are the size of large peas. Place apple slices in a large bowl. Add sugar mixture. Toss to coat apple slices with sugar mixture. Preheat oven to 375F (190C). Cut dough into 2 equal portions. On a lightly floured surface, roll out 1 portion to an 11-inch circle. Fit into a 9-inch pie pan. Spoon apple mixture into unbaked pie shell. Trim edge of dough to rim of pan. Roll out remaining dough to a 12-inch circle. Cut slits as desired. Fit circle over filling. Fold top edge under bottom edge, making a raised edge. Flute as desired. Glaze as desired. Combine 1 tablespoon sugar and dash of cinnamon. Sprinkle over pie. Cover edge with foil. Bake 25 minutes. Remove foil. Bake 25 to 30 minutes longer until crust is golden brown, apples are tender and juices are bubbly. Serve warm with vanilla ice cream, if desired. Makes 8 servings.

Variation

Add 1/3 cup seedless raisins or 1/3 cup chopped walnuts or pecans to apples with sugar mixture.

Tarte Tatin

Golden Delicious apples are best for this easy French pie, but use whatever apples you have.

1 cup Classic Puff Pastry, page 22, or
  Quick Puff Pastry, page 24
5 large Golden Delicious apples

1/2 cup sugar
3 tablespoons butter

Review Puff Pastry Techniques, page 21. Prepare dough for pastry. Peel and core apples. Cut in half. Thinly slice lengthwise into even slices. Lightly butter a 1-1/2-quart shallow baking dish or cast-iron skillet. Place 6 tablespoons sugar and 1 tablespoon butter in a small saucepan. Stir occasionally over medium-low heat until sugar melts and starts to turn golden. Immediately pour into prepared baking dish or skillet. Arrange a layer of apple slices over melted sugar in a daisy pattern. Fill the center or edges as necessary. After half the apple slices have been used, sprinkle with 1 tablespoon sugar. Arrange remaining apple slices in concentric circles or in even rows. Sprinkle with remaining sugar and dot with remaining butter. Preheat oven to 425F (220C). On a lightly floured surface, roll out dough slightly larger than the baking dish or skillet. Place on top of apples and tuck in edge. Make a 1/2-inch hole in the center. Bake 15 minutes. Reduce heat to 375F (190C). Bake about 45 minutes longer until pie is golden brown and apples are tender. Remove from oven and cool about 1 hour. Place a platter over pie. Invert pie and platter. Remove baking dish or skillet and serve pie. Makes 8 servings.

Apple Streusel Pie

Fresh breadcrumbs make a crunchy topping.

Single-Crust Basic Pastry, page 14
2/3 cup sugar
2 tablespoons all-purpose flour
1/2 teaspoon ground cinnamon
1/4 teaspoon ground nutmeg

1/4 teaspoon salt
6 cups thinly sliced peeled apples
  (about 3 lbs.)
Streusel Topping, see below
Drizzle Icing, see below

Streusel Topping:
1 cup fresh breadcrumbs
3/4 cup all-purpose flour
1/3 cup packed brown sugar
1/4 teaspoon ground cinnamon

1/4 teaspoon ground nutmeg
1/3 cup finely chopped walnuts, pecans or
  almonds
1/4 cup butter, melted

Prepare dough for pastry. Review Unbaked Pie Shells, page 8. On a lightly floured surface, roll out dough to a 12-inch circle. Fit into a 10-inch pie pan. Fold dough under, making a raised edge. Flute as desired. Preheat oven to 375F (190C). Combine sugar, flour, cinnamon, nutmeg and salt in a medium bowl. Add apple slices. Toss to coat with sugar mixture. Spoon into unbaked pie shell. Cover edge with foil. Bake 40 minutes. While pie is baking, prepare Streusel Topping. Remove foil from pie. Sprinkle topping evenly over apples. Bake 25 to 30 minutes longer until topping is lightly browned and filling starts to bubble around edge. Cool 1 hour. Prepare Drizzle Icing. Drizzle 1 spoonful at a time over browned topping. Serve warm or cooled. Makes 8 servings.

Streusel Topping:
Combine breadcrumbs, flour, brown sugar, cinnamon, nutmeg and nuts in a medium bowl. Add melted butter. Toss until mixed well.

Drizzle Icing

The finishing touch for Apple Streusel Pie, above.

1/2 cup powdered sugar
2 to 2-1/2 teaspoons milk

Combine powdered sugar and 2 teaspoons milk in a small bowl. Mix until smooth. Add remaining milk a few drops at a time until mixture pours in a thick ribbon when dropped from a spoon.

Piled-High Strawberry Pie

Celebrate the arrival of summer with this glorious fruit pie.

1 (9-inch) baked pie shell, pages 8 and 9,
    made with Basic Pastry, page 14
3 (1-pint) baskets fresh ripe strawberries
    (about 8 cups)
1/4 cup sugar

2 tablespoons cornstarch or arrowroot
1-1/4 cups water
1/3 cup red currant jelly or strawberry jelly
6 drops red food coloring
Sweetened Whipped Cream, page 185

Prepare baked pie shell and set aside to cool. Wash, hull and dry berries. Invert a 9-inch pie pan. On the inverted pan, arrange the most-attractive berries as desired for top of pie. If berries vary in size, place largest in center and smaller ones around edge. In a small saucepan, combine sugar and cornstarch or arrowroot. Gradually stir in water. Stir constantly over medium heat until mixture thickens and comes to a full boil. Stir and boil 1 minute. Add jelly and food coloring. Stir until smooth. Let glaze cool while filling pie shell, stirring occasionally. Arrange less-attractive berries in bottom of shell. Spoon about 1/2 cup glaze over berries. Use berries on inverted pie pan for the top, repeating the same order. Spoon and brush remaining glaze over berries. Refrigerate 2 hours or longer until ready to serve. Before serving, prepare Sweetened Whipped Cream. Pipe or spoon around edge of pie filling. Makes 8 servings.

Strawberry-Rhubarb Pie

Add 10 minutes to the baking time if you use partially thawed, frozen unsweetened fruit.

Double-Crust Basic Pastry, page 14
3/4 cup sugar
1/3 cup all-purpose flour

1/4 teaspoon salt
2-1/2 cups fresh strawberries
2-1/2 cups 1/2-inch fresh rhubarb pieces

Prepare dough for pastry. Review Double-Crust Pies, pages 9 and 10, and Lattice Tops, pages 12 and 13. Combine sugar, flour and salt in a medium bowl. Add strawberries and rhubarb. Toss lightly to coat with sugar mixture. Preheat oven to 375F (190C). Cut dough into 2 equal portions. On a lightly floured surface, roll out 1 portion to an 11-inch circle. Fit into a 9-inch pie pan. Spoon filling into unbaked pie shell. Make a lattice top or top crust. Flute as desired. Glaze and top as desired. Cover edge with foil. Bake 25 minutes. Remove foil. Bake 25 to 30 minutes longer until crust is golden brown, rhubarb is tender and juices are bubbly. Serve warm. Makes 8 servings.

Piled-High Strawberry Pie with Flower-Petal Fluting, page 11.

Strawberry Tart a l'Orange

To make a tart shell without a pan, place dough circle on a pizza pan, fold edge under and flute.

Sweet Butter Pastry, page 19
1/4 cup sugar
1 (8-oz.) pkg. cream cheese
1/4 cup orange marmalade

1 qt. fresh strawberries
Marmalade Topping, see below
Orange peel twists or orange slices,
   if desired

Marmalade Topping:
1 tablespoon sugar
1 tablespoon cornstarch
1/2 cup water

1/2 cup orange marmalade
2 tablespoons Triple Sec or
   other orange liqueur

Prepare dough for pastry. Review Baked Pie Shells, pages 8 and 9. Preheat oven to 400F (205C). On a lightly floured surface, roll out dough to a 13-inch circle. Fit into an 11-inch flan pan with a removable bottom or a 9- or 10-inch quiche pan or pie pan. If using a flan pan, roll a rolling pin across the top to trim edge of dough to top of pan. If using a quiche pan, fold dough edge under so it is even with rim of pan; press dough into scalloped sides of pan. If using a pie pan, fold dough under for a raised edge; make a high fluting. With a fork, prick bottom of unbaked pie shell at 1/2-inch intervals. To bake blind, line shell with foil and fill with beans. Bake 10 minutes. Remove foil and beans. Bake 10 to 12 minutes longer until crust is golden brown. Prick with a fork to deflate any large bubbles. Glaze as directed for Baked Pie Shells. Cool. In a small bowl, cream sugar and cream cheese until smooth. Stir in marmalade. Spread in bottom of glazed pie shell. Wash, hull and dry berries. Arrange stem ends down on cheese mixture in concentric circles, placing smaller berries in center. Cut large berries in half and place cut side down. Refrigerate while preparing Marmalade Topping. Spoon cooled topping over berries. Refrigerate pie until ready to serve. If baked in a flan pan, place on a can or bowl to remove rim; place tart on a large plate. Garnish with orange peel twists or orange slices, if desired. Makes 10 to 12 servings.

Marmalade Topping:
Combine sugar and cornstarch in a small saucepan. Add water and marmalade. Stir frequently over medium heat until mixture thickens and boils. Continue to boil 1 minute. Stir in Triple Sec or other orange liqueur. Cool slightly.

Taste fruit before making a fruit filling. If the fruit is not sweet, slice it thinner than usual. This will increase the surface area for absorbing sugar.

Medley Fruit Pie

Mix and match until you find your favorite fruit combination.

5 cups any combination of the following
  fresh or drained canned fruit:
  quartered apricots or plums;
  seedless grapes; peeled and sliced
  nectarines, peaches or pears;
  orange wedges; 3/4-inch pineapple cubes
Double-Crust Basic Pastry, page 14, or
  Almond Pastry, page 20

3/4 to 1 cup sugar
1-1/2 tablespoons quick-cooking tapioca
1/4 teaspoon salt
1/4 teaspoon ground nutmeg
2 tablespoons brandy or Amaretto, if desired

Prepare fruit. Prepare dough for pastry. Review Double-Crust Pies, pages 9 and 10. Combine sugar, tapioca, salt and nutmeg in a medium bowl. Add fruit. Add brandy or Amaretto, if desired. Toss to coat fruit with sugar mixture. Preheat oven to 375F (190C). Cut dough into 2 equal portions. On a floured surface, roll out 1 portion to an 11-inch circle. Fit into a 9-inch pie pan. Spoon fruit mixture into unbaked pie shell. Trim edge of dough to rim of pan. Roll out remaining dough to a 12-inch circle. Cut slits as desired. Fit circle over filling. Fold top edge under bottom edge. Flute as desired. Glaze and top as desired. Cover edge with foil. Bake 25 minutes. Remove foil. Bake 20 to 25 minutes longer until crust is golden brown, fruit is tender and juices are bubbly. For best flavor, serve warm. Makes 8 servings.

Fresh-Rhubarb Lattice Pie

Rhubarb is seasonal and more common in home gardens than in supermarkets.

Double-Crust Basic Pastry, page 14
1/2 cup granulated sugar
1/2 cup packed brown sugar

1/3 cup all-purpose flour
1/4 teaspoon salt
4 to 5 cups 1/2-inch fresh rhubarb pieces

Prepare dough for pastry. Review Double-Crust Pies, pages 9 and 10, and Lattice Tops, pages 12 and 13. Combine granulated sugar, brown sugar, flour and salt in a medium bowl. Add rhubarb. Toss to coat with sugar mixture. Preheat oven to 375F (190C). Divide dough into 2 equal portions. On a lightly floured surface, roll out 1 portion to an 11-inch circle. Fit into a 9-inch pie pan. Spoon rhubarb mixture into unbaked pie shell. Roll out remaining dough and prepare lattice. Flute as desired. Glaze and top as desired. Cover edge with foil. Bake 25 minutes. Remove foil. Bake 25 to 30 minutes longer until crust is golden brown, rhubarb is tender and juices are bubbly. Makes 8 servings.

Ginger Peachy Pie

Crushed gingersnaps and chopped pecans make a quick crunchy topping.

Single-Crust Basic Pastry, page 14
1/2 cup sugar
1 tablespoon all-purpose flour
1/2 teaspoon ground nutmeg
4 cups sliced peeled fresh or
   thawed frozen unsweetened peaches

Ginger Topping, see below
Sweetened Whipped Cream, page 185
1 to 2 tablespoons crushed gingersnaps

Ginger Topping:
1 cup crushed gingersnaps
1/2 cup chopped pecans

1/4 cup butter, melted

Prepare dough for pastry. Review Unbaked Pie Shells, page 8. Combine sugar, flour and nutmeg in a medium bowl. Add peaches. Toss to coat with sugar mixture. Preheat oven to 375F (190C). On a lightly floured surface, roll out dough to an 11-inch circle. Fit into a 9-inch pie pan. Fold dough under, making a raised edge. Flute as desired. Spoon peach mixture evenly into unbaked pie shell. Cover edge with foil. Bake 30 minutes. While pie is baking, prepare Ginger Topping. Remove foil. Sprinkle topping evenly over peaches. Bake 15 minutes longer until topping is lightly browned and peaches are tender. Prepare Sweetened Whipped Cream. Serve pie topped with Sweetened Whipped Cream. Garnish with a sprinkling of crushed gingersnaps. Makes 8 servings.

Ginger Topping:

Combine all ingredients in a medium bowl. Mix well.

Variation

Substitute 2 (16-ounce) cans drained sliced peaches or apricot halves for the fresh peaches. Reduce sugar to 1/4 cup.

*tip*

Freeze dough scraps in a small container or food-storage bag. If you don't have fresh leftover dough scraps for decorating a finished pie, use thawed frozen scraps.

Fresh Peach Pie *Photo on pages 100 and 101.*

Pretty as a summer picture when topped with a lattice.

Double-Crust Basic Pastry, page 14, or
  Almond Pastry, page 20
3/4 to 1 cup sugar
1-1/2 tablespoons quick-cooking tapioca
1/4 teaspoon salt
1/4 teaspoon ground cinnamon

1/4 teaspoon ground nutmeg
5 cups peeled fresh peach slices
1 teaspoon lemon juice
2 tablespoons butter, if desired
Spicy Thickened Cream, page 180, if desired

Prepare dough for pastry. Review Double-Crust Pies, pages 9 and 10, and Lattice Tops, pages 12 and 13. Combine sugar, tapioca, salt, cinnamon and nutmeg in a medium bowl. Add peaches and lemon juice. Toss to coat peaches with sugar mixture. Preheat oven to 375F (190C). Cut dough into 2 equal portions. On a lightly floured surface, roll out 1 portion to an 11-inch circle. Fit into a 9-inch pie pan. Spoon peach mixture into unbaked pie shell. Dot with butter, if desired. Make a lattice top or top crust. For both a lattice top or top crust, flute as desired. Glaze and top as desired. Cover edge with foil. Bake 25 minutes. Remove foil. Bake 20 to 25 minutes longer until crust is golden brown, peaches are tender and juices are bubbly. Serve warm. Top with Spicy Thickened Cream, if desired. Makes 8 servings.

Variation

Frozen Peach Pie: Substitute 1 (20-ounce) package thawed, frozen unsweetened sliced peaches for the fresh peaches.

Blueberry Pie

Be sure to remove all stems from fresh or frozen berries.

Double-Crust Basic Pastry, page 14
3/4 cup sugar
2 tablespoons quick-cooking tapioca

1/4 teaspoon salt
1 teaspoon finely shredded lemon peel
4 cups fresh or thawed frozen blueberries

Prepare dough for pastry. Review Double-Crust Pies, pages 9 and 10. Combine sugar, tapioca and salt in a medium bowl. Add lemon peel and blueberries. Toss to coat berries with sugar mixture. Preheat oven to 375F (190C). Cut dough into 2 equal portions. On a lightly floured surface, roll out 1 portion to an 11-inch circle. Fit into a 9-inch pie pan. Spoon blueberry mixture into unbaked pie shell. Trim edge of dough to rim of pan. Roll out remaining dough to a 12-inch circle. Cut slits as desired. Fit circle over filling. Fold top edge under bottom edge, making a raised edge. Flute as desired. Glaze and top as desired. Cover edge with foil. Bake 25 minutes. Remove foil. Bake 20 to 25 minutes longer until crust is golden brown and juices are bubbly. Serve warm. Makes 8 servings.

On the following pages, Fresh Peach Pie with Woven Lattice Method 1, page 13, and Flower-Petal Fluting, page 11.

Peaches & Cream Pie

A mellow creamy flavor.

Double-Crust Basic Pastry, page 14
2 (16-oz.) cans sliced peaches
1 egg
3/4 cup whipping cream
2 tablespoons all-purpose flour

1/3 cup sugar
1/4 teaspoon salt
1/2 teaspoon ground nutmeg
1/4 teaspoon ground cinnamon

Prepare dough for pastry. Review Double-Crust Pies, pages 9 and 10. Drain peaches. Cut any large slices in half lengthwise. In a medium bowl, combine remaining ingredients. Beat with a wire whip or rotary beater until smooth. Preheat oven to 375F (190C). Cut dough into 2 equal portions. On a lightly floured surface, roll out 1 portion to an 11-inch circle. Fit into a 9-inch pie pan. Arrange drained peaches evenly in unbaked pie shell. Trim edge of dough to rim of pan. Pour cream mixture over peaches. Roll out remaining dough to a 12-inch circle. Cut slits as desired. Fit circle over filling. Fold top edge under bottom edge, making a raised edge. Flute as desired. Glaze and top as desired. Cover edge with foil. Bake 25 minutes. Remove foil. Bake 20 to 25 minutes longer until crust is golden brown. Cool. Refrigerate until ready to serve. Makes 8 servings.

Variation

Creamy Apple Pie: Substitute 4 cups sliced peeled apples (about 2 pounds) for canned peaches and increase sugar to 2/3 cup. If necessary, increase baking time 5 to 10 minutes until apples are tender.

Berry Pie

A Quick Lattice helps prevent the filling from boiling over in the oven.

Double-Crust Basic Pastry, page 14
1 cup sugar
1/4 cup all-purpose flour

1/4 teaspoon salt
4 cups fresh blackberries, boysenberries or
   loganberries

Prepare dough for pastry. Review Double-Crust Pies, pages 9 and 10, and Quick Lattice, page 13. Combine sugar, flour and salt in a medium bowl. Add berries and toss gently. Preheat oven to 375F (190C). Cut dough into 2 equal portions. On a lightly floured surface, roll out 1 portion to an 11-inch circle. Fit into a 9-inch pie pan. Spoon berry mixture into unbaked pie shell. Roll out remaining dough to a 12-inch circle and make a Quick Lattice. Fit lattice over filling. Fold top edge under bottom edge. Flute as desired. Glaze and top as desired. Cover edge with foil. Bake 25 minutes. Remove foil. Bake 25 to 30 minutes longer until crust is golden brown and juices are bubbly. Serve warm. Makes 8 servings.

Variation

Substitute 1 (16- to 20-ounce) bag partially thawed, frozen unsweetened berries for the fresh berries. Increase first baking time to 35 minutes.

Deep-Dish Apricot Pie

The extra spoonful of lemon juice brings out the ripe-fruit flavor.

Single-Crust Almond Pastry, page 20
6 cups fresh apricot halves
  (about 2-1/2 lbs.)
1/2 cup granulated sugar
1/4 cup packed brown sugar
3 tablespoons all-purpose flour

1/4 teaspoon ground nutmeg
1/8 teaspoon ground allspice
1/8 teaspoon salt
1 to 2 tablespoons lemon juice
Half and half or vanilla ice cream

Prepare dough for pastry. Review Rolling Out, page 8. Cut large pieces of fruit into quarters. Combine granulated sugar, brown sugar, flour, nutmeg, allspice and salt in a medium bowl. Add fruit. Toss lightly to coat with sugar mixture. Spoon into a deep 1-1/2-quart casserole. Sprinkle with 1 tablespoon lemon juice. If fruit is very ripe, add 1 more tablespoon lemon juice. Preheat oven to 375F (190C). On a lightly floured surface, roll out dough about 1 inch larger than the casserole. Cut four 1-inch slits radiating from center of dough. Fit dough over fruit. Roll edge under and crimp to edge of casserole with fork tines. Cut a piece of foil slightly larger than the casserole. Place over crust. Bake 25 minutes. Remove foil. Bake 30 to 35 minutes longer until crust is lightly browned and fruit is tender. Serve warm with half and half or ice cream. Makes 6 to 8 servings.

Variations

Deep-Dish Plum Pie: Substitute 6 cups sweet plum halves for the apricots.
Deep-Dish Peach Pie: Substitute 6 cups thickly sliced, peeled peaches for the apricots.

Cherry Pie

For Valentine's Day, use a heart-shape cookie cutter to make a Quick Lattice, page 13.

Double-Crust Almond Pastry, page 20,
  or Basic Pastry, page 14
2 (16-oz.) cans pitted tart cherries
1-1/2 cups sugar
3 tablespoons cornstarch
2 tablespoons all-purpose flour

1/8 teaspoon salt
10 drops red food coloring, if desired
1/8 teaspoon almond extract, if desired
1 tablespoon butter
1 tablespoon finely shredded lemon peel

Prepare dough for pastry. Review Double-Crust Pies, pages 9 and 10. Drain cherries, reserving 3/4 cup juice. Combine sugar, cornstarch, flour and salt in a medium saucepan. Gradually stir in drained cherries, reserved liquid and food coloring. Stir constantly over medium heat until mixture thickens and comes to a full boil. Stir and boil 1 minute. Stir in almond extract, butter and lemon peel. Let cool while rolling out dough. Preheat oven to 375F (190C). Cut dough into 2 equal portions. On a lightly floured surface, roll out 1 portion to an 11-inch circle. Fit into a 9-inch pie pan. Pour cherry mixture into unbaked pie shell. Trim edge of dough to rim of pan. Roll out remaining dough to a 12-inch circle. Cut slits as desired. Place circle over filling. Fold top edge under bottom edge, making a raised edge. Flute as desired. Glaze and top as desired. Cover edge with foil. Bake 25 minutes. Remove foil. Bake 25 to 30 minutes longer until golden brown. Makes 8 servings.

Cherry-Almond Tart

Remove stones from cherries with your fingers or a cherry pitter.

Sweet Butter Pastry, page 19
2 lbs. fresh sweet cherries

2 tablespoons sugar
Almond-Coconut Topping, see below

Almond-Coconut Topping:
3/4 cup all-purpose flour
1/2 cup sugar
1/2 cup butter, slightly softened

3/4 cup flaked or shredded coconut
1/2 cup sliced almonds

Prepare dough for pastry. Cover and set aside. Review Rolling Out, page 8. Wash cherries and remove stones. Preheat oven to 400F (205C). On a lightly floured surface, roll out dough to a 13-inch circle. Fit into an 11-inch flan pan with a removable bottom. Trim edge of dough to top of pan. Arrange cherries evenly in unbaked pie shell. Sprinkle with sugar. Bake 20 minutes. While pie is baking, prepare Almond-Coconut Topping. Sprinkle topping evenly over cherries. Bake 25 to 30 minutes longer until topping is golden brown. Cool. Place on a can or bowl to remove pan rim. Place tart on a large round platter. Serve warm. Makes 10 to 12 servings.

Almond-Coconut Topping:
Combine flour and sugar in a medium bowl. Blend in butter with a fork. Stir in coconut and almonds.

Variation
Substitute 2 (1-pound) and 1 (8-ounce) can well-drained, pitted dark or light sweet cherries for the fresh cherries. Reduce first baking time to 15 minutes.

French Puff Tart *Photo on cover.*

Make this tart in the traditional rectangle or in one of the shapes given below.

Cream Filling, see below
2 cups Classic Puff Pastry, page 22, or
  Quick Puff Pastry, page 24
Apple Glaze, page 169
Egg Glaze, page 20

2 to 3 cups any combination of the following
  fruit: orange segments or slices;
  grapes, pear, peach or apricot slices;
  blueberries or raspberries; banana slices,
  strawberries; peeled kiwi or apple slices

Cream Filling:
1/4 cup sugar
1 tablespoon cornstarch
1/8 teaspoon salt

2 egg yolks
1 cup milk
1/4 teaspoon vanilla extract

Prepare Cream Filling. Review Puff Pastry Techniques, page 21. Prepare dough for pastry. Tart may be a rectangle, an 11-inch square, a 12-inch circle or a 12-inch heart. To make a rectangle, roll out dough on a lightly floured surface to a 16" x 10" rectangle. Measuring carefully, trim to a 14" x 8" rectangle. Cut a 3/4-inch strip from both sides and both ends of rectangle. Prepare Egg Glaze. Brush rectangle with glaze. Place the 3/4-inch strips flat around top surface of rectangle about 1/16th inch in from edge. Trim off edges of strips as necessary. With the back of a knife blade, scallop edges of rectangle at 1/4-inch intervals. Use the back of the knife blade to make a zigzag design around stripping. Brush stripping with glaze, being careful not to let glaze drip over edges. Cut out leaves or other decorations from trimmings and place at corners and on strips as desired. Lightly brush decorations with glaze. With a fork, prick bottom of pastry at 1/4-inch intervals. Refrigerate 15 minutes. Preheat oven to 425F (220C). Bake tart 15 to 20 minutes until golden brown and puffed. Lightly press on center with a metal spatula to deflate puff. Cool completely. Prepare Apple Glaze. Spread Cream Filling in center of pastry. Top with fruit as desired. Spoon or brush Apple Glaze over fruit as necessary. Makes 6 to 8 servings.

Cream Filling:
Combine sugar, cornstarch and salt in a medium saucepan. Beat egg yolks and milk until smooth. Gradually stir into sugar mixture. Stir constantly over medium heat until mixture comes to a full boil. Stir and boil 1 minute. Stir in vanilla. Pour into a small bowl. Place plastic wrap on surface to prevent a film from forming. Refrigerate 2 hours.

Fruit for French Puff Tart
- For Christmas, use kiwi, strawberries and pears.
- For Valentine's Day, use canned cherry pie filling.
- For a spring buffet, make a rainbow of kiwi, pineapple, peach, orange and strawberries.
- For Fourth of July, use strawberries, blueberries and pears or apples.

Raspberry Tart

Cream Custard and Sweet Butter Pastry enhance raspberries or your favorite fruit.

Sweet Butter Pastry, page 19
Cream Custard, see below
3 cups fresh raspberries

1/2 cup red currant jelly
Mint leaves, if desired

Cream Custard:
3/4 cup sugar
1/4 cup all-purpose flour
1-1/2 cups milk
3 egg yolks

1 teaspoon vanilla extract
2 tablespoons kirsch or other cherry brandy,
** if desired**

Prepare dough for pastry. Review Baked Pie Shells, pages 8 and 9. Preheat oven to 400F (205C). On a lightly floured surface, roll out dough to a 13-inch circle. Fit into an 11-inch flan pan with a removable bottom or a 9- or 10-inch quiche pan or pie pan. If using a flan pan, roll a rolling pin across the top to trim edge of dough even with top of pan. If using a quiche pan, fold dough edge under so it is even with rim of pan; press dough into scalloped sides of pan. If using a pie pan, fold dough under for a raised edge; make a high fluting. With a fork, prick bottom of unbaked pie shell at 1/2-inch intervals. To bake blind, line pie shell with foil and fill with beans. Bake 10 minutes. Remove foil and beans. Bake 10 minutes longer. Prick with a fork to deflate any large bubbles. Glaze as directed for Baked Pie Shells. Cool. Prepare Cream Custard. Spread in bottom of glazed pie shell. Place plastic wrap on surface of pie filling to prevent a film from forming. Refrigerate. About 2 hours before serving, remove plastic wrap. Arrange raspberries over filling. Stir jelly in a small saucepan. Bring to a boil, stirring frequently to break up jelly. Brush immediately over berries. Refrigerate pie until ready to serve. If baked in a flan pan, place on a can or bowl to remove rim; place tart on a large platter. Garnish with mint leaves, if desired. Makes 10 to 12 servings.

Cream Custard:
Combine sugar and flour in a small saucepan. In a small bowl, mix milk and egg yolks until smooth. Gradually stir into sugar mixture in saucepan. Stir constantly over medium heat until mixture comes to a full boil. Boil 1 minute. Remove from heat. Stir in vanilla and kirsch or other cherry brandy. Cool 10 minutes, stirring frequently.

How to Make Raspberry Tart

1/If using a flan pan, trim edge of the shell with a rolling pin.

2/Place the flan pan on a can or a bowl to remove the rim.

Fresh Pineapple Pie

For a tropical flavor, add 2 tablespoons chopped candied ginger to the filling.

Double-Crust Basic Pastry, page 14
3/4 cup sugar
2 tablespoons quick-cooking tapioca

1/4 teaspoon salt
4 to 5 cups 3/4-inch fresh pineapple pieces,
** undrained**

Prepare dough for pastry. Review Double-Crust Pies, pages 9 and 10. Combine sugar, tapioca and salt in a medium bowl. Add pineapple. Toss to coat with sugar mixture. Preheat oven to 375F (190C). Cut dough into 2 equal portions. On a lightly floured surface, roll out 1 portion to an 11-inch circle. Fit into a 9-inch pie pan. Spoon pineapple mixture into unbaked pie shell. Trim edge of dough to rim of pan. Roll out remaining dough to a 12-inch circle. Cut slits as desired. Fit circle over filling. Fold top edge under bottom edge, making a raised edge. Flute as desired. Glaze and top as desired. Cover edge with foil. Bake 25 minutes. Remove foil. Bake 20 to 25 minutes longer until crust is golden brown, pineapple is tender and juices are bubbly. Serve warm. Makes 8 servings.

Tropical Banana Pie

If you prefer topping without coconut, use the Ginger Topping from Ginger Peachy Pie, page 98.

Single-Crust Basic Pastry, page 14
3/4 cup sugar
4 teaspoons quick-cooking tapioca
1/4 teaspoon salt
1 (20-oz.) can crushed pineapple

3 large or 4 medium bananas
Coconut-Ginger Topping, see below
Ice cream or Sweetened Whipped Cream,
   page 185

Coconut-Ginger Topping:
2/3 cup all-purpose flour
1/2 cup sugar
1/8 teaspoon ground ginger
1/8 teaspoon ground cinnamon

3/4 cup flaked or shredded coconut
1/4 cup butter, melted
1/2 cup chopped macadamia nuts or pecans

Prepare dough for pastry. Review Unbaked Pie Shells, page 8. Combine sugar, tapioca and salt in a medium bowl. Drain pineapple. Stir into sugar mixture. Peel bananas. Slice in half lengthwise and cut into 1/4-inch pieces. Stir into pineapple mixture. Preheat oven to 375F (190C). On a lightly floured surface, roll out dough to a 12-inch circle. Fit into a 9-inch pie pan. Fold edge under, making a raised edge. Flute as desired. Spoon fruit mixture into unbaked pie shell. Cover edge with foil. Bake 30 minutes. Prepare Coconut-Ginger Topping. Remove foil. Sprinkle topping evenly over fruit. Bake 15 to 20 minutes longer until topping is lightly browned. Serve with ice cream or Sweetened Whipped Cream. Makes 8 servings.

Coconut-Ginger Topping:
Combine flour, sugar, ginger and cinnamon in a medium bowl. Add coconut and melted butter. Toss to mix well. Stir in nuts.

tip

Pie a la mode is always a special treat. Instead of topping a pie wedge with ice cream, spoon on a dollop of Sweetened Whipped Cream, page 185; Spicy Thickened Cream, page 180; Spiced Topping, page 130; or Maple Topping, page 131.

Fruit for Frozen-Fruit Pie Fillings, page 110
(Makes 4 to 5 cups)

Fruit	Purchase	How to Prepare
Apricots	2 lbs. (12 to 16)	Quarter and pit.
Blueberries	2 baskets (4 cups)	Wash and remove stems.
Blackberries	3 small baskets (4 cups)	Wash.
Boysenberries	3 small baskets (4 cups)	Wash.
Peaches	2 lbs. (6 to 8)	Peel, pit and slice.
Plums	2 lbs. (12 to 16)	Pit and cut each plum into 6 pieces.
Rhubarb	4 to 8 stalks	Cut into 1/2-inch slices.
Strawberries	2 baskets (4 cups)	Hull and halve.
Strawberry-Rhubarb	2-1/2 cups each	Hull and halve strawberries. Cut rhubarb into 1/2-inch slices.

How to Prepare Fresh Fruit

Peaches, Plums, Nectarines and Cherries—Insert a small paring knife in the seam at the stem end and cut along the seam around the fruit through to the pit. Then hold one side of the fruit in each hand and turn your hands in opposite directions. The halves of fruit will separate. Remove the pit with a fruit pitter, melon baller, grapefruit spoon or a small paring knife.

Apricots—Place both your thumbs at the stem end and pull apart at the seam. The pit usually comes out easily with no cutting.

Apples and Pears—Insert a corer through the stem end of the fruit, making a round cut through the center and removing seeds, hard fibers and stem. If you don't have a corer and sliced fruit is required for the recipe, cut the fruit lengthwise in quarters and then cut out the core with a paring knife. If you need the fruit left whole, use a steak knife or other knife with a long thin blade to cut a 3/4-inch hole through the center of the fruit.

Peel fruit after pitting or coring. If you toss just-sliced fruit with sugar and other filling ingredients, the fruit will not become brown. If you're not using peeled apples, pears, peaches or nectarines immediately, toss them with a solution made from half lemon juice and half water. Fruit for 1 pie can be tossed with 1/4 cup lemon juice and water.

Frozen-Fruit Pie Filling

For homemade convenience, keep a stack of foil-wrapped pie fillings in your freezer.

3/4 to 1 cup sugar
2 tablespoons quick-cooking tapioca
1/4 teaspoon salt
1/2 teaspoon ground nutmeg, if desired

4 to 5 cups Fruit for Frozen-Fruit Pie Filling,
  page 109
2 tablespoons water
1 teaspoon lemon juice

Combine sugar, tapioca and salt in a medium bowl. Add nutmeg, if desired. Add fruit, water and lemon juice. Toss to coat fruit with sugar mixture. Let stand 10 minutes. Toss again. Center a 24'' x 12'' piece of aluminum foil over a 9-inch pie pan. Press to mold to curve of pan. Spoon in fruit mixture, mounding slightly in center. Bring long sides of foil to center and fold over twice. Roll ends of foil under and press to seal. Place in freezer on a fast-freeze shelf, if possible. Freeze overnight. Remove pie pan. Label foil packet with date and fruit. Return to freezer. May be frozen up to 6 months. Makes filling for one 9-inch pie.

How to Make Frozen-Fruit Pie Filling

Place fruit mixture in foil-lined pie pan. Wrap in foil and freeze. Remove from pan for storage.

Frozen-Fruit Pie

Now you can have summer flavors all year round!

Frozen-Fruit Pie Filling, page 111
Double-Crust Basic Pastry, page 14

Prepare and freeze Frozen-Fruit Pie Filling. Review Double-Crust Pies, pages 9 and 10. Preheat oven to 425F (220C). Cut dough into 2 equal portions. Roll out 1 portion to an 11-inch circle. Fit into a 9-inch pie pan. Remove Frozen-Fruit Pie Filling from freezer and remove foil. Place filling in unbaked pie shell. Trim edge of dough to rim of pan. Roll out remaining dough to a 12-inch circle. Cut slits as desired. Fit circle over filling. Fold top edge under bottom edge. Flute as desired. Glaze and top as desired. Cover edge with foil. Bake 30 minutes. Remove foil. Bake 25 to 30 minutes longer until crust is golden brown, fruit is tender and juices are bubbly. Serve warm. Makes 8 servings.

Variation

Open-House Deep-Dish Fruit Pie: Prepare a double recipe of Frozen-Fruit Pie Filling. Do not place in pie pan. Line a 13" x 9" x 2" baking pan with a 30-inch piece of foil. Pour in fruit filling. Fold foil over and press edges together. Label and freeze. Remove baking pan. Store foil packet in freezer up to 6 months. To bake, prepare dough for Double-Crust Basic Pastry. Roll out about 1/4 inch thick and cut into thirty-two 2-inch circles. Preheat oven to 425F (220C). Remove foil from filling and place in baking pan with above measurements. Slightly overlap circles in 3 rows on filling. Or, roll out dough and cut to fit baking pan; cut slits as desired and place dough over filling. Top or glaze as desired. Bake 45 to 50 minutes until crust is golden brown, fruit is tender and filling is bubbly. Serve warm or cooled. Makes 16 servings.

How to Make Frozen-Fruit Pies

Remove foil from Frozen-Fruit Pie Filling. Place frozen filling in unbaked pie shell.

Pear-Mince Pie

Crisp winter pears blend with raisins and currants in this spicy mince variation.

Pear-Mince Filling, see below   **Ice cream**
Double-Crust Basic Pastry, page 14

Pear-Mince Filling:
6 cups 1/4-inch peeled pear cubes   **1-1/2 teaspoons ground cinnamon**
1-1/2 cups raisins   **1-1/2 teaspoons ground nutmeg**
1/2 cup currants   **1 teaspoon ground cloves**
3/4 cup packed brown sugar   **1/2 teaspoon salt**
1 cup chopped candied lemon peel   **1 cup apple cider or apple juice**

Prepare Pear-Mince Filling up to 1 week ahead if it is to be refrigerated, or up to 6 months ahead if it is to be frozen. Prepare dough for pastry. Review Double-Crust Pies, pages 9 and 10. Preheat oven to 375F (190C). Cut dough into 2 equal portions. On a lightly floured surface, roll out 1 portion to an 11-inch circle. Fit into a 9-inch pie pan. Spoon Pear-Mince Filling into unbaked pie shell. Trim edge of dough to rim of pan. Roll out remaining dough to a 12-inch circle. Cut slits as desired. Fit circle over filling. Fold top edge under bottom edge. Flute as desired. Glaze and top as desired. Cover edge with foil. If filling is frozen, increase oven temperature to 425F (220C). Bake 25 minutes. Remove foil. Bake 25 to 30 minutes longer until crust is golden brown. Serve warm. Top each serving with ice cream. Makes 8 servings.

Pear-Mince Filling:
In a 3-quart or larger saucepan, combine all ingredients. Stir occasionally over medium heat 1 to 1-1/2 hours until pears are tender and sauce is syrupy. If necessary, add water to prevent mixture from becoming completely dry. If desired, freeze according to directions for Frozen-Fruit Pie Filling, page 110.

Pear Strudel

Also delightful with canned apricot halves, peach slices, or mixed apricots, peaches and pears.

Strudel Pastry, page 26   **6 tablespoons butter, melted**
1/2 cup granulated sugar   **3/4 cup fresh breadcrumbs**
1 tablespoon finely shredded orange peel   **3 (1-lb.) cans drained sliced pears (4 cups)**
1/2 cup finely chopped blanched almonds or   **Powdered sugar**
  pecans

Review Strudel Pastry Techniques, page 25. Begin preparing dough for pastry. While dough is resting, combine granulated sugar, orange peel and nuts. Stretch dough as directed. Let stand to dry 10 minutes. Preheat oven to 425F (220C). Butter a 17'' x 11'' baking sheet. Set aside. Generously brush stretched dough with 5 tablespoons melted butter. Sprinkle evenly with breadcrumbs. Place pears on dough in a long strip about 3 inches from one edge and to within 2 inches of adjoining ends. Sprinkle pears with sugar mixture. Fold the 3-inch edge of dough over filling. Lift up cloth at that edge and use to roll up strudel jelly-roll fashion. Place seam side down in a horseshoe shape on prepared baking sheet. Tuck ends under. Brush with 1 tablespoon melted butter. Bake 10 minutes. Reduce heat to 400F (205C). Bake about 20 minutes longer until strudel is crisp and browned. Cool. Sprinkle generously with powdered sugar. Makes 8 to 10 servings.

Apple Strudel

The most traditional of all strudels.

Strudel Pastry, page 26
3/4 cup granulated sugar
1 teaspoon ground cinnamon
2 teaspoons finely shredded lemon peel
7 to 8 cups thickly sliced, peeled apples
 (about 3-1/2 lbs.)

1/2 cup ground or finely chopped almonds,
 pecans or walnuts
1/2 cup seedless golden raisins
6 tablespoons butter, melted
3/4 cup fresh breadcrumbs
Powdered sugar

Review Strudel Pastry Techniques, page 25. Begin preparing dough for pastry. While dough is resting, combine granulated sugar, cinnamon and lemon peel. In a large bowl, combine apples, nuts and raisins. Stretch dough as directed. Let stand to dry 10 minutes. Preheat oven to 425F (220C). Butter a 17" x 11" baking sheet. Set aside. Add sugar mixture to apples. Toss to coat apples with sugar mixture. Generously brush stretched dough with 5 tablespoons melted butter. Sprinkle evenly with breadcrumbs. Place apple mixture on dough in a long strip about 3 inches from one edge and to within 2 inches of adjoining ends. Fold the 3-inch edge of dough over filling. Lift up cloth at that edge and use to roll up strudel jelly-roll fashion. Place seam side down in a horseshoe shape on prepared baking sheet. Tuck ends under. Brush with 1 tablespoon melted butter. Bake 10 minutes. Reduce heat to 400F (205C). Bake about 20 minutes longer until strudel is crisp and browned. Cool. Sprinkle generously with powdered sugar. Makes 8 to 10 servings.

Variations

Cheese Strudel: Omit cinnamon, lemon peel, apples and nuts. Decrease granulated sugar to 1/2 cup. Beat sugar with 1 (8-ounce) package cream cheese and 1 egg yolk until smooth. Stir in raisins, 1 tablespoon finely shredded orange peel and 1 teaspoon vanilla extract. Fill, roll and bake strudel as directed.

Poppy Seed Strudel: Omit cinnamon, apples and nuts. Decrease granulated sugar to 1/2 cup. Decrease lemon peel to 1-1/2 teaspoons. Combine sugar, 1 cup poppy seeds, 1/4 cup honey and 1/2 cup milk in a small saucepan. Stir over medium heat until boiling. Remove from heat. Stir in raisins, lemon peel and 1 shredded, peeled tart apple. Fill, roll and bake strudel as directed.

Cherry Strudel

A special treat with afternoon tea or coffee.

Strudel Pastry, page 26
1 cup granulated sugar
2 teaspoons grated lemon peel
1/2 cup finely chopped blanched almonds
6 tablespoons butter, melted

3/4 cup fresh breadcrumbs
3 (1-lb.) cans drained pitted tart cherries
  (4 cups)
Powdered sugar

Review Strudel Pastry Techniques, page 25. Begin preparing dough for pastry. While dough is resting, combine granulated sugar, lemon peel and almonds. Stretch dough as directed. Let stand to dry 10 minutes. Preheat oven to 425F (220C). Butter a 17" x 11" baking sheet. Set aside. Generously brush stretched dough with 5 tablespoons melted butter. Sprinkle evenly with breadcrumbs. Place cherries on dough in a long strip about 3 inches from one edge and to within 2 inches of adjoining ends. Sprinkle cherries with sugar mixture. Fold the 3-inch edge of dough over filling. Lift up cloth at that edge and use to roll up strudel jelly-roll fashion. Place seam side down in a horseshoe shape on prepared baking sheet. Tuck ends under. Brush with 1 tablespoon melted butter. Bake 10 minutes. Reduce heat to 400F (205C). Bake about 20 minutes longer until strudel is crisp and browned. Cool. Sprinkle generously with powdered sugar. Makes 8 to 10 servings.

Variation

For a richer strudel, substitute dark sweet cherries for the tart cherries. Reduce granulated sugar to 1/2 cup.

How to Make Two Small Strudels

If your baking sheet is not large enough to accommodate a horseshoe-shape strudel, make 2 smaller strudels. When placing the filling on the stretched dough, leave a gap of about 3 inches in the center. In the gap, cut a slit about 12 inches long toward the center of the dough. Fold the newly cut edges over the filling. Then roll up as directed above. Cut through the pastry at center of roll so you have 2 equal halves. Place halves, seam side down and about 2 inches apart, on prepared baking sheet and tuck ends under. Brush with butter and bake as directed.

How to Make Cherry Strudel

1/Place cherries on dough in a long strip. Sprinkle with sugar mixture.

2/Fold dough over filling. Use cloth to roll up strudel jelly-roll fashion.

3/Sprinkle baked strudel with powdered sugar and cut into slices.

Traditional Mince Pie

The filling will make two pies—one for Thanksgiving, the other for Christmas.

Traditional Mince Filling, see below   **Vanilla ice cream**
Double-Crust Basic Pastry, page 14

Traditional Mince Filling:

1 small orange	4 cups raisins
6 cups 1/4-inch peeled apple cubes	2 cups apple cider or apple juice
(about 3 lbs.)	1 cup packed brown sugar
2 cups fruit-cake mix or a combination of	1 teaspoon ground allspice
chopped candied citron, pineapple,	1 teaspoon ground cinnamon
lemon peel or orange peel	1/2 teaspoon ground nutmeg
1/2 cup currants	1/2 teaspoon salt

Prepare Traditional Mince Filling up to 1 week ahead if it is to be refrigerated, or up to 6 months ahead if it is to be frozen. Prepare dough for pastry. Review Double-Crust Pies, pages 9 and 10, and Lattice Tops, pages 12 and 13, if desired. Preheat oven to 375F (190C). Cut dough into 2 equal portions. On a lightly floured surface, roll out 1 portion to an 11-inch circle. Fit into a 9-inch pie pan. Spoon 1 portion mince mixture into unbaked pie shell. Make a lattice top or top crust. Flute as desired. Glaze and top as desired. Cover edge with foil. If filling is frozen, increase oven temperature to 425F (220C). Bake 25 minutes. Remove foil. Bake 25 to 30 minutes longer until crust is golden brown. Serve warm with vanilla ice cream. Makes 8 servings.

Traditional Mince Filling:

Cut orange in 8 pieces. Remove seeds. Process orange in blender until coarsely chopped. In a 3-quart or larger saucepan, combine chopped orange and remaining ingredients. Stir occasionally over medium heat 1 to 1-1/2 hours until apples are tender and sauce is syrupy. If necessary, add water to prevent mixture from becoming completely dry. Cool. Divide mince mixture into 2 equal portions (about 4 cups each). Place each portion in a separate storage container. Refrigerate or freeze until ready to use. If desired, freeze according to directions for Frozen-Fruit Pie Filling, page 110.

Variation

For Christmas, stir 1 cup chopped red and green candied cherries into mince before preparing pie.

Green-Tomato Mince Pie

An imaginative way to use those last green tomatoes that never seem to ripen.

Green-Tomato Mince Filling, see below　　　　Ice cream
Double-Crust Basic Pastry, page 14

Green-Tomato Mince Filling:

4 cups 1/4-inch green tomato cubes	1 tablespoon lemon juice
3 cups 1/4-inch peeled apple cubes	1/2 teaspoon salt
(about 1-1/2 lbs.)	1 teaspoon ground cinnamon
1 cup raisins	1/4 teaspoon ground cloves
1/2 cup packed brown sugar	1/8 teaspoon ground ginger

Prepare Green-Tomato Mince Filling up to 1 week ahead if it is to be refrigerated, or up to 6 months ahead if it is to be frozen. Prepare dough for pastry. Review Double-Crust Pies, pages 9 and 10. Prepare dough for pastry. Preheat oven to 375F (190C). Divide dough into 2 equal portions. On a lightly floured surface, roll out 1 portion to an 11-inch circle. Fit into a 9-inch pie pan. Spoon Green-Tomato Mince Filling into unbaked pie shell. Trim edge of dough to rim of pan. Roll out remaining dough to a 12-inch circle. Cut slits as desired. Fit circle over filling. Fold top edge under bottom edge, making a raised edge. Flute as desired. Glaze and top as desired. Cover edge with foil. If filling is frozen when put into unbaked pie shell, increase oven temperature to 425F (220C). Bake 25 minutes. Remove foil. Bake 25 to 30 minutes longer or until crust is golden brown. Serve warm with ice cream. Makes 8 servings.

Green-Tomato Mince Filling:
In a 3-quart or larger saucepan, combine all ingredients. Cover and place over medium heat. Bring to a boil. Reduce heat. Simmer about 30 minutes, stirring occasionally, until apples are tender and sauce is syrupy. Cool slightly. If desired, freeze according to directions for Frozen-Fruit Pie Filling, page 110.

Nostalgic Delights

Regional custard pies.

Custard pie may be defined as a mixture of egg and liquid baked in a crust. Recipes in this section are for the sweet custards that were standard fare in our childhoods. Quiche Lorraine in the main-dish section, Around the World in Pastry, and some of the pies in Garden Favorites are also custard pies.

American favorites take the spotlight in custards. Spicy Shoofly Pie is traditional in Pennsylvania-Dutch country. Rhubarb Custard Pie and Raisin & Sour Cream Pie are popular in the Midwest. Chess Pie and Pecan Pie are Southern specialties.

A common complaint with milk-based custard pies is a soggy crust on the bottom of the pie. Here are two solutions to choose from: First, use heavy freezer-to-oven glass baking dishes. They retain the heat longer than metal does and give a brown, well-cooked bottom crust. The second method is to bake the unfilled crust for about 5 minutes. Do not prick the crust before baking it, and cool it for 15 minutes before adding the filling. After the crust has been filled, bake the pie as directed in the recipe. It may be necessary to cover the edge with foil to prevent overbrowning.

It's sometimes said that the test of a good cook is the quality of a finished custard. If custard fillings are not watched carefully and overcook, they will be watery or even tough. I use the jiggle test. Holding the edge of the pie pan or baking dish with a pot holder, gently shake the pie back and forth. If it's difficult to grasp, shake the oven shelf. If the 1-inch area in the center of the pie has a rolling wave rather than a sharp liquid wave, remove the pie from the oven.

The filling will continue to cook as the pie stands. You can see the difference between the liquid wave and the rolling wave if you jiggle the pie at least 15 minutes before the end of the specified cooking time. The wave you see then will be the liquid wave.

A more-accurate method is to insert a knife slightly off-center in the pie. This leaves a mark in the custard. But if the knife comes out clean, the pie is done. If there is some liquid on the knife, let the pie bake a few more minutes. If small pieces of cooked filling appear on the knife, the custard is overcooked. If this happens, refrigerate the pie immediately to stop the cooking process. Overcooked custard will have small bubbles near the bottom of the filling. When the custard is cut, it will leak a watery syrup, or whey. Very overcooked custard will be tough.

Because custard pies contain eggs and milk, they should be eaten within a few hours or refrigerated. ◆

After-the-Holiday Supper

Waldorf Salad
Turkey in Corn-Bread Stuffing, page 75
Glazed Carrots
Almond-Peach Custard Pie, page 126

Harvest Dinner

Molded Fruit Salad
Roast Chicken
Sautéed Zucchini & Onions
Scalloped-Potato Pie, page 83
Date-Nut Pie, page 126

Chess Pie

Similar to pecan pie but with the added richness of cream.

Single-Crust Basic Pastry, page 14
1/4 cup butter
1 cup packed brown sugar
1 tablespoon all-purpose flour
1/2 teaspoon salt
2 eggs

1/2 pint whipping cream or half and half
   (1 cup)
1 teaspoon vanilla extract
1-1/2 cups chopped pecans or walnuts
1/2 cup chopped dates or raisins,
   if desired

Prepare dough for pastry. Review Unbaked Pie Shells, page 8. On a lightly floured surface, roll out dough to a 12-inch circle. Fit into a 9-inch pie pan. Fold dough under for a raised edge. Flute as desired. Preheat oven to 375F (190C). In a medium bowl, cream butter and brown sugar until smooth. Add flour, salt and eggs. Beat until almost smooth. Beat 2 minutes longer. Stir in whipping cream or half and half and vanilla until mixed well. Stir in nuts. Add dates or raisins, if desired. Pour into unbaked pie shell. Bake 40 to 45 minutes until top of filling is dark golden brown. Cool slightly. Serve warm or cooled. Refrigerate cooled pie. Makes 8 servings.

Spicy Shoofly Pie

A traditional Pennsylvania-Dutch dessert.

Single-Crust Basic Pastry, page 14
1-1/2 cups all-purpose flour
1/2 cup packed brown sugar
1/2 teaspoon ground ginger
1/2 teaspoon salt
1/4 teaspoon ground cinnamon
1/8 teaspoon ground cloves

1/4 cup butter
3/4 cup molasses
3/4 cup hot water
1/2 teaspoon baking soda
Vanilla ice cream or Spicy Thickened Cream,
   page 180

Prepare dough for pastry. Review Unbaked Pie Shells, page 8. On a lightly floured surface, roll out dough to a 12-inch circle. Fit into a 9-inch pie pan. Fold dough under for a raised edge. Make a high fluting. Preheat oven to 375F (190C). In a medium bowl, combine flour, brown sugar, ginger, salt, cinnamon and cloves. Add butter. Cut in with a pastry blender or fork until mixture resembles cornmeal. Set aside. Mix molasses and hot water until blended. Stir in baking soda. Mixture will foam slightly. Pour about a third of the molasses mixture into unbaked pie shell. Sprinkle with a third of the flour mixture. Repeat layers twice, ending with flour mixture. Bake about 35 minutes until top of filling is lightly browned. Cool slightly. Serve warm. Top with vanilla ice cream or Spicy Thickened Cream. Refrigerate cooled pie. Makes 8 servings.

Buttermilk Pie

A refreshing treat on a hot summer day.

Single-Crust Basic Pastry, page 14
1/3 cup butter
1 cup sugar
3 eggs
2 tablespoons all-purpose flour

1/4 teaspoon salt
1 teaspoon finely shredded lemon peel
1 teaspoon lemon juice
1-1/2 cups buttermilk

Prepare dough for pastry. Review Unbaked Pie Shells, page 8. On a lightly floured surface, roll out dough to a 12-inch circle. Fit into a 9-inch pie pan. Fold dough under for a raised edge. Flute as desired. Preheat oven to 375F (190C). In a large bowl, cream butter and sugar until smooth. Add eggs, flour and salt. Beat until almost smooth. Beat 2 minutes longer. Stir in lemon peel, lemon juice and buttermilk. Mix well. Pour into unbaked pie shell. Bake 40 to 45 minutes until top of filling is dark golden brown. Cool slightly. Serve warm or cooled. Refrigerate cooled pie. Makes 8 servings.

Raisin & Sour Cream Pie

Raisin pudding with a meringue topping and flaky crust.

Single-Crust Basic Pastry, page 14
2 cups raisins
Hot water for soaking raisins
2/3 cup sugar
2 tablespoons all-purpose flour
1 teaspoon ground cinnamon

1/4 teaspoon ground nutmeg
1/4 teaspoon ground cloves
1 teaspoon finely shredded lemon peel
2 cups dairy sour cream
4 egg yolks
Meringue Topping, page 134

Prepare dough for pastry. Review Unbaked Pie Shells, page 8. Place raisins in a small bowl. Cover with hot water. Set aside. On a lightly floured surface, roll out dough to a 12-inch circle. Fit into a 9-inch pie pan. Fold dough under for a raised edge. Flute as desired. Preheat oven to 425F (220C). In a medium bowl, combine sugar, flour, cinnamon, nutmeg, cloves and lemon peel. Mix well. Add sour cream and egg yolks. Beat with a wire whip or rotary beater until smooth. Drain raisins. Stir into sour cream mixture. Pour into unbaked pie shell. Bake 10 minutes. Reduce heat to 350F (175C). Bake 30 to 35 minutes longer until filling is set. Prepare Meringue Topping. Bake as directed. Cool pie slightly. Serve warm or cooled. Refrigerate cooled pie. Makes 8 servings.

Variation

Omit Meringue Topping. Top each serving with a dollop of dairy sour cream.

Spicy Walnut Pie

If you like sugar-spice nuts, you'll adore this pie!

Single-Crust Basic Pastry, page 14, or
 Rich Butter Pastry, page 19
2 tablespoons butter, melted
3 eggs
3/4 cup sugar
1 teaspoon ground nutmeg
1/2 teaspoon ground cinnamon

1/4 teaspoon ground cloves
1/2 teaspoon salt
1/2 teaspoon vanilla extract
1 cup light corn syrup
1-1/2 cups walnut pieces
Sweetened Whipped Cream, page 185, or
 vanilla ice cream

Prepare dough for pastry. Review Unbaked Pie Shells, page 8. On a lightly floured surface, roll out dough to a 12-inch circle. Fit into a 9-inch pie pan. Fold dough under for a raised edge. Flute as desired. Preheat oven to 375F (190C). In a medium bowl, combine butter, eggs, sugar, nutmeg, cinnamon, cloves, salt, vanilla and corn syrup. Beat with a wire whip or rotary beater until smooth. Stir in walnuts. Pour into unbaked pie shell. Bake 40 to 45 minutes until filling is set. Cool slightly. Serve warm or cooled. Top each serving with Sweetened Whipped Cream or vanilla ice cream. Refrigerate cooled pie. Makes 8 to 10 servings.

Denny's Pecan Pie

Christmas at our house is not complete without my husband's favorite pie.

Single-Crust Basic Pastry, page 14
1/3 cup butter, melted
3 eggs
1 cup packed light brown sugar
1/2 teaspoon salt

1 teaspoon vanilla extract
1 cup light corn syrup
1-1/3 cups pecan halves and pieces
Vanilla ice cream

Prepare dough for pastry. Review Unbaked Pie Shells, page 8. On a lightly floured surface, roll out dough to a 12-inch circle. Fit into a 9-inch pie pan. Fold dough under for a raised edge. Flute as desired. Preheat oven to 375F (190C). In a medium bowl, combine butter, eggs, brown sugar, salt and vanilla. Beat with a wire whip or rotary beater until smooth. Stir in corn syrup until blended, making as little foam as possible. Fold in pecans. Pour into unbaked pie shell. Use the blade of a knife to arrange pecan halves rounded side up. Bake 40 to 45 minutes until filling is set. Cool slightly. Serve warm or cooled. Top with vanilla ice cream. Refrigerate cooled pie. Makes 8 servings.

Variations

Nut Pie: Substitute any unsalted nuts for the pecans.
Chocolate Pecan Pie: Stir 3 ounces melted semisweet chocolate into butter-egg mixture before adding corn syrup.

Praline Sweet-Potato Pie

Sweet-potato pie has a different texture than pumpkin pie but the flavor is similar.

Single-Crust Basic Pastry, page 14
2 eggs
1/2 cup granulated sugar
1/4 cup packed brown sugar
1/2 teaspoon ground cinnamon
1/2 teaspoon ground nutmeg
1/4 teaspoon ground cloves

1/2 teaspoon salt
1 (24-oz.) can sweet potatoes, drained, mashed (2 cups)
1-1/2 cups half and half or evaporated milk
Praline Topping, see below
Sugar & Cream Topping, page 141, if desired

Praline Topping:
1/3 cup granulated sugar
1/3 cup packed brown sugar
3 tablespoons half and half or evaporated milk

1/2 cup chopped pecans

Prepare dough for pastry. Review Unbaked Pie Shells, page 8. On a lightly floured surface, roll out dough to a 12-inch circle. Fit into a 9-inch pie pan. Fold dough under for a raised edge. Make a high fluting. Preheat oven to 425F (220C). In a medium bowl, combine eggs, granulated sugar, brown sugar, cinnamon, nutmeg, cloves and salt. Beat with a wire whip or rotary beater until smooth. Add sweet potatoes and mix well. Gradually stir in half and half or evaporated milk, making as little foam as possible. Pour into unbaked pie shell. Bake 15 minutes. Reduce heat to 350F (175C). Bake 40 to 45 minutes longer until filling is set. Cool about 5 minutes. Prepare Praline Topping. Spread topping over pie. Preheat oven to broil and place rack so top of pie will be about 5 inches from heat source. Cover edge of pie with foil. Broil about 1 minute until topping is bubbly and begins to brown. Cool slightly. Serve warm or cooled. Top with Sugar & Cream Topping, if desired. Refrigerate cooled pie. Makes 8 servings.

Praline Topping:
Combine granulated sugar, brown sugar and half and half or evaporated milk in a small bowl. Mix well. Stir in pecans.

tip

Custard filling may spill over as you place the pie in the oven. To prevent this, pull out the oven rack and place the unfilled pie shell on it. Pour in the filling. Gently slide the rack back into the oven.

Praline Sweet-Potato Pie with Star Fluting, page 11, and Sugar & Cream Topping.

Rhubarb Custard Pie

Establish your own summer tradition. You can use fresh or thawed frozen rhubarb.

Single-Crust Basic Pastry, page 14
1/4 cup granulated sugar
2 tablespoons all-purpose flour
1/4 teaspoon ground cinnamon
1/8 teaspoon ground cloves
4 cups 1/2-inch rhubarb slices
1/4 cup granulated sugar

2 tablespoons all-purpose flour
1/2 cup packed brown sugar
1/2 teaspoon salt
2 eggs
1/2 cup milk
1/2 cup dairy sour cream
1 tablespoon brown sugar

Prepare dough for pastry. Review Unbaked Pie Shells, page 8. Roll out dough to a 12-inch circle. Fit into a 9-inch pie pan. Fold dough under for a raised edge. Make a high fluting. Preheat oven to 375F (190C). In a medium bowl, combine 1/4 cup granulated sugar, 2 tablespoons flour, cinnamon and cloves. Add rhubarb. Toss to coat with sugar mixture. Spread evenly in unbaked pie shell. Cover edge with foil. Bake 35 minutes. While pie is baking, combine 1/4 cup granulated sugar, 2 tablespoons flour, 1/2 cup brown sugar and salt in a medium bowl. Add eggs, milk and sour cream. Beat with a wire whip or rotary beater until smooth. Remove partially baked pie from oven. Remove foil. Pour egg mixture over rhubarb. Bake 20 to 25 minutes until filling is set. Sprinkle with 1 tablespoon brown sugar. Bake 5 minutes longer. Cool slightly. Serve warm or cooled. Refrigerate cooled pie. Makes 8 servings.

Vanilla Custard Pie

If the pie is chilled, serve it with slices of fresh fruit.

Single-Crust Basic Pastry, page 14
2-2/3 cups milk
4 eggs
1/2 cup sugar

1/4 teaspoon salt
1 teaspoon vanilla extract
1/4 teaspoon ground nutmeg

Prepare dough for pastry. Review Unbaked Pie Shells, page 8. On a lightly floured surface, roll out dough to a 12-inch circle. Fit into a 9-inch pie pan. Fold dough under for a raised edge. Make a high fluting. Preheat oven to 425F (220C). In a medium saucepan, heat milk to scalding or just below boiling, about 180F (80C). In a medium bowl, combine eggs, sugar, salt and vanilla. Beat with a wire whip or rotary beater until smooth. Gradually stir in hot milk. Mix until blended. Pour into unbaked pie shell. Sprinkle with nutmeg. Carefully place in oven. Bake 15 minutes. Reduce heat to 350F (175C). Bake about 35 minutes longer until filling is set. Cool slightly. Serve warm or cooled. Refrigerate cooled pie. Makes 8 servings.

tip

Recipes in this book were developed with whole milk. Non-fat milk or low-fat milk may be substituted. The result will be a slight change in flavor and texture of the finished dish.

Nesselrode Pie

Classic Nesselrode is rich custard with fruit.

Double-Crust Basic Pastry, page 14
1 (8-oz.) pkg. cream cheese
1 lb. cottage cheese (2 cups)
2 eggs
2/3 cup sugar
3 tablespoons all-purpose flour
1 tablespoon finely shredded orange peel

1 teaspoon vanilla extract or rum extract
1/4 cup each of 3 of the following:
 raisins, semisweet chocolate pieces,
 and chopped candied fruit such as
 cherries, lemon peel, orange peel,
 pineapple or citron

Prepare dough for pastry. Review Double-Crust Pies, pages 9 and 10, and Quick Lattice, page 13. In a medium bowl, beat cream cheese and cottage cheese with electric mixer until mixed well; mixture will not be smooth. Add eggs, sugar, flour, shredded orange peel and vanilla or rum extract. Beat until mixed well. Stir in remaining ingredients. Preheat oven to 375F (190C). Divide dough into 2 equal portions. On a lightly floured surface, roll out 1 portion to an 11-inch circle. Fit into a 9-inch pie pan. Pour cheese mixture into unbaked pie shell. Trim edge of dough to rim of pan. Roll out remaining dough and top pie with Quick Lattice. Glaze and top as desired. Cover edge of pie with foil. Bake 25 minutes. Remove foil. Bake 25 to 30 minutes longer until crust is golden brown. Cool slightly. Serve warm or cooled. Refrigerate cooled pie. Makes 8 servings.

Variation

Christmas Cheese Pie: Substitute 1/3 cup chopped red maraschino cherries or candied cherries and 1/3 cup chopped green candied cherries or candied pineapple for the 3/4 cup chopped fruits.

Sliced-Lemon Pie

Don't pass up this recipe!

Single-Crust Basic Pastry, page 14
2 large lemons
2 cups sugar
4 eggs

3 tablespoons all-purpose flour
Sweetened Whipped Cream, page 185
8 wafer-thin lemon slices for garnish

Prepare dough for pastry. Review Unbaked Pie Shells, page 8. On a lightly floured surface, roll out dough to a 12-inch circle. Fit into a 9-inch pie pan. Fold dough under for a raised edge. Flute as desired. Preheat oven to 350F (175C). Finely shred peel of lemons, being careful not to include white pith. Measure 1 tablespoon shredded peel and set aside. Remove all peel and all outer white membrane from lemons. Cut lemons into slices about 1/8 inch thick, removing seeds as you slice. Combine 1/8-inch thick lemon slices and 1 cup sugar in a small bowl. In a medium bowl, lightly beat eggs, flour and remaining 1 cup sugar until smooth. Gently stir in lemon mixture and reserved shredded peel. Pour into unbaked pie shell. Bake about 45 minutes until top of filling is golden brown. Cool. Refrigerate until ready to serve. Top each serving with Sweetened Whipped Cream and a thin lemon slice. Refrigerate cooled pie. Makes 8 servings.

Almond-Peach Custard Pie

Plan your dinner preparation so the pie can be served warm.

Single-Crust Basic Pastry, page 14
1 (16-oz.) can sliced peaches
2 tablespoons butter, melted
3 eggs
1/2 cup sugar
1/2 teaspoon salt

1/4 teaspoon ground nutmeg
1/2 teaspoon vanilla extract
1/4 teaspoon almond extract, if desired
1/2 cup light corn syrup
2/3 cup evaporated milk or half and half
1 (2-oz.) pkg. sliced almonds (1/2 cup)

Prepare dough for pastry. Review Unbaked Pie Shells, page 8. On a lightly floured surface, roll out dough to a 12-inch circle. Fit into a 9-inch pie pan. Fold dough under for a raised edge. Make a high fluting. Preheat oven to 375F (190C). Drain peaches. Place butter, eggs, sugar, salt, nutmeg and vanilla in a medium bowl. Add almond extract, if desired. Beat with a wire whip or rotary beater until smooth. Gradually stir in corn syrup and evaporated milk or half and half until blended. Stir in drained peaches and almonds. Pour into unbaked pie shell. Use a fork to arrange peach slices in a pinwheel pattern. Bake 35 to 40 minutes until filling is set. Cool slightly. Serve warm or cooled. Refrigerate cooled pie. Makes 8 servings.

Date-Nut Pie

A chewy pie that's so rich it's best served in small slices.

Single-Crust Basic Pastry, page 14
1/4 cup butter, melted
4 eggs
1/2 cup granulated sugar
1/2 cup packed brown sugar
1/4 teaspoon salt
1/4 teaspoon ground cinnamon

1/4 teaspoon ground nutmeg
1 teaspoon vanilla extract
1-1/2 cups chopped dates
1 cup chopped walnuts
Vanilla ice cream or Spicy Thickened Cream,
  page 180

Prepare dough for pastry. Review Unbaked Pie Shells, page 8. On a lightly floured surface, roll out dough to a 12-inch circle. Fit into a 9-inch pie pan. Fold dough under for a raised edge. Flute as desired. Preheat oven to 375F (190C). In a medium bowl, combine butter, eggs, granulated sugar, brown sugar, salt, cinnamon, nutmeg and vanilla. Beat with a wire whip or rotary beater until smooth. Stir in dates and walnuts. Pour into unbaked pie shell. Bake 40 to 45 minutes until filling is set. Cool slightly. Serve warm or cooled. Top with vanilla ice cream or Spicy Thickened Cream. Refrigerate cooled pie. Makes 10 to 12 servings.

How to Make Almond-Peach Pie

1/Use a fork to arrange peach slices in a pinwheel pattern.

2/Bake pie until filling is firm. Serve warm or cooled.

Valencia Custard Pie

Orange and cinnamon are typical flavorings in the province of Valencia on the coast of Spain.

Single-Crust Basic Pastry, page 14
1 medium orange
2-2/3 cups milk
1 (3-inch) piece cinnamon stick
4 eggs

1/2 cup sugar
1/4 teaspoon salt
1 teaspoon vanilla extract
Mint leaves, if desired

Prepare dough for pastry. Review Unbaked Pie Shells, page 8. On a lightly floured surface, roll out dough to a 12-inch circle. Fit into a 9-inch pie pan. Fold dough under for a raised edge. Make a high fluting. Finely shred peel of orange, being careful not to include white pith. Set aside shredded peel. Peel and section orange. Wrap and refrigerate orange sections. Preheat oven to 425F (220C). Pour milk into a medium saucepan. Break cinnamon stick into several pieces and drop into milk. Heat to scalding or just below boiling, about 180F (80C). In a medium bowl, combine eggs, sugar, salt, vanilla and shredded orange peel. Beat with a wire whip or rotary beater until smooth. Pour about half the hot milk through a strainer into egg mixture. Mix well. Add remaining milk through strainer. Mix well. Pour into unbaked pie shell. Bake 15 minutes. Reduce heat to 350F (175C). Bake 35 minutes longer until filling is set. Cool slightly. Serve warm or cooled. Garnish with reserved orange sections and mint leaves, if desired. Refrigerate cooled pie. Makes 8 servings.

Coconut Custard Pie

For a nuttier flavor, toast the coconut in a 325F (165C) oven for 10 minutes.

Single-Crust Basic Pastry, page 14
2-1/2 cups milk
4 eggs
1/3 cup sugar

1/4 teaspoon salt
1 teaspoon vanilla extract
1 cup flaked or shredded coconut

Prepare dough for pastry. Review Unbaked Pie Shells, page 8. On a lightly floured surface, roll out dough to a 12-inch circle. Fit into a 9-inch pie pan. Fold dough under for a raised edge. Make a high fluting. Preheat oven to 425F (220C). In a medium saucepan, heat milk to scalding or just below boiling, about 180F (80C). In a medium bowl, combine eggs, sugar, salt and vanilla. Beat with a wire whip or rotary beater until smooth. Gradually stir in hot milk. Stir in coconut. Mix until blended. Pour egg mixture into unbaked pie shell. Carefully place pie in oven. Bake 15 minutes. Reduce heat to 350F (175C). Bake about 35 minutes longer until filling is set. Cool slightly. Serve warm or cooled. Refrigerate cooled pie. Makes 8 servings.

Chocolate-Coconut Custard Pie

Gradually add liquid to melted chocolate or the mixture will be lumpy.

Single-Crust Basic Pastry, page 14
4 (1-oz.) squares semisweet chocolate
2-1/2 cups milk
4 eggs

1/3 cup sugar
1/4 teaspoon salt
1 teaspoon vanilla extract
1 cup flaked or shredded coconut

Prepare dough for pastry. Review Unbaked Pie Shells, page 8. On a lightly floured surface, roll out dough to a 12-inch circle. Fit into a 9-inch pie pan. Fold dough under for a raised edge. Make a high fluting. Preheat oven to 425F (220C). In a medium saucepan, melt chocolate over low heat. In another medium saucepan, heat milk to scalding or just below boiling, about 180F (80C). In a medium bowl, combine eggs, sugar, salt and vanilla. Beat with a wire whip or rotary beater until smooth. Add hot milk 1/2 cup at a time to melted chocolate, stirring after each addition until smooth. Gradually pour chocolate mixture into egg mixture. Stir in coconut. Pour into unbaked pie shell. Bake 15 minutes. Reduce heat to 350F (175C). Bake about 35 minutes longer until filling is set. Cool slightly. Serve warm or cooled. Refrigerate cooled pie. Makes 8 servings.

Variation

Chocolate Custard: Omit coconut.
German Chocolate-Coconut Custard: Substitute sweet cooking chocolate for the semisweet chocolate. Stir in 1/2 cup chopped pecans with the coconut.

Pumpkin Pie

If you don't make the Pumpkin Cutouts, sprinkle the whipped cream with nutmeg.

Single-Crust Basic Pastry, page 14
Pumpkin Cutouts, if desired, see below
2 eggs
3/4 cup sugar
1 teaspoon ground cinnamon
1/2 teaspoon ground nutmeg

1/2 teaspoon salt
1/4 teaspoon ground cloves
1/4 teaspoon ground ginger
1 (16-oz.) can pumpkin (2 cups)
1-2/3 cups half and half or evaporated milk
Sweetened Whipped Cream, page 185

Pumpkin Cutouts:
Reserved pastry
1 teaspoon sugar

Dash ground cinnamon

Prepare dough for pastry. If making Pumpkin Cutouts, pinch off 1/8 of the dough, wrap and set aside. Review Unbaked Pie Shells, page 8. On a lightly floured surface, roll out remaining dough or all dough to a 12-inch circle. Fit into a 9-inch pie pan. Fold dough under for a raised edge. Make a high fluting. Preheat oven to 425F (220C). In a medium bowl, combine eggs, sugar, cinnamon, nutmeg, salt, cloves and ginger. Beat with a wire whip or rotary beater until smooth. Add pumpkin. Mix well. Gradually stir in half and half or evaporated milk. Pour into unbaked pie shell. Bake 15 minutes. Reduce heat to 350F (175C). Bake 40 to 45 minutes longer until filling is set. Cool slightly. Prepare Pumpkin Cutouts, if desired. Serve warm or cooled. Top with Sweetened Whipped Cream and Pumpkin Cutouts, if desired. Refrigerate cooled pie. Makes 8 servings.

Pumpkin Cutouts:
Roll out reserved dough very thin and cut out six 2-inch circles. Roll out scraps and cut 2 more 2-inch circles. Preheat oven to 350F (175C). With your fingers, lightly push in 2 opposite sides of each circle to make top and base of pumpkin. Use scraps to make 3/4-inch stems. Lightly brush bottom of each stem with water and press onto top indentation of a pumpkin. Turn pumpkins over. With the back of a knife blade, make long curved grooves in each pumpkin. Place on a baking sheet. Combine sugar and cinnamon. Sprinkle generously over pumpkins. Bake 12 to 15 minutes until golden brown. Cool.

 *tip*

When making a pie, mashed cooked sweet potatoes or yams may be substituted for mashed cooked or canned pumpkin.

Fresh Pumpkin Pie

At last—a pie made with uncooked fresh pumpkin or squash!

Single-Crust Basic Pastry, page 14
1-1/2 lbs. fresh pumpkin or winter squash
2 eggs
3/4 cup packed brown sugar
2 tablespoons all-purpose flour
1 teaspoon ground cinnamon

1/2 teaspoon ground nutmeg
1/2 teaspoon salt
1/4 teaspoon ground cloves
1-2/3 cups half and half or evaporated milk
Spiced Topping, see below

Spiced Topping:
1 cup dairy sour cream
2 tablespoons brown sugar

1/8 teaspoon ground cinnamon
1/8 teaspoon ground nutmeg

Prepare dough for pastry. Review Unbaked Pie Shells, page 8. On a lightly floured surface, roll out dough to a 12-inch circle. Fit into a 9-inch pie pan. Fold dough under for a raised edge. Make a high fluting. Preheat oven to 425F (220C). Peel pumpkin or squash. Shred using large holes of a shredder to make 2 packed cups. Spread evenly but loosely in unbaked pie shell. In a medium bowl, combine eggs, brown sugar, flour, cinnamon, nutmeg, salt and cloves. Beat with a wire whip or rotary beater until smooth. Gradually stir in half and half or evaporated milk. Slowly pour mixture over shredded pumpkin or squash. Bake 15 minutes. Reduce heat to 350F (175C). Bake 40 to 45 minutes longer until filling is set. Cool slightly. Prepare Spiced Topping. Serve pie warm or cooled. Top with Spiced Topping. Refrigerate cooled pie. Makes 8 servings.

Spiced Topping:
Mix all ingredients in a small bowl. Refrigerate until ready to serve.

Pumpkin & Sour Cream Pie

A rich variation of a traditional holiday dessert.

Single-Crust Basic Pastry, page 14
2 eggs
1 cup packed brown sugar
1/2 teaspoon ground cinnamon
1/2 teaspoon ground nutmeg
1/2 teaspoon salt

1/4 teaspoon ground cloves
1 (16-oz.) can pumpkin (2 cups)
2 cups dairy sour cream
1/2 cup raisins
Sweetened Whipped Cream, page 185,
    if desired

Prepare dough for pastry. Review Unbaked Pie Shells, page 8. On a lightly floured surface, roll out dough to a 12-inch circle. Fit into a 9-inch pie pan. Fold dough under for a raised edge. Make a high fluting. Preheat oven to 425F (220C). In a medium bowl, combine eggs, brown sugar, cinnamon, nutmeg, salt and cloves. Beat with a wire whip or rotary beater until smooth. Add pumpkin. Mix well. Add sour cream and raisins. Mix well. Pour into unbaked pie shell. Bake 15 minutes. Reduce heat to 350F (175C). Bake 40 to 45 minutes longer until filling is set. Cool slightly. Serve warm or cooled. Top with Sweetened Whipped Cream, if desired. Refrigerate cooled pie. Makes 8 servings.

Maple Pumpkin Pie

Enjoy traditional New England flavors in a rich and spicy pie.

Single-Crust Basic Pastry, page 14
2 eggs
1/4 cup sugar
1/2 teaspoon salt
1/2 teaspoon ground cinnamon
1/4 teaspoon ground cloves
1/4 teaspoon ground nutmeg

1 (16-oz.) can pumpkin (2 cups)
3/4 cup maple-flavored syrup
1 cup evaporated milk or half and half
1/2 cup chopped pecans, if desired
Maple Topping, see below
Pecan halves for garnish

Maple Topping:
1/2 pint whipping cream (1 cup)
2 tablespoons maple-flavored syrup

Prepare dough for pastry. Review Unbaked Pie Shells, page 8. On a lightly floured surface, roll out dough to a 12-inch circle. Fit into a 9-inch pie pan. Fold dough under for a raised edge. Make a high fluting. Preheat oven to 425F (220C). In a medium bowl, combine eggs, sugar, salt, cinnamon, cloves and nutmeg. Beat with a wire whip or rotary beater until smooth. Add pumpkin and mix well. Gradually stir in syrup and evaporated milk or half and half until mixed well. Stir in pecans, if desired. Pour into unbaked pie shell. Bake 15 minutes. Reduce heat to 350F (175C). Bake 40 to 45 minutes longer until filling is set. Cool slightly. Prepare Maple Topping. Serve pie warm or cooled. Top with Maple Topping and garnish with pecan halves. Refrigerate cooled pie. Makes 8 servings.

Maple Topping:
Whip cream until stiff peaks form. Fold in maple syrup. Refrigerate until ready to serve.

 **tip**

To avoid bubbles on the surface of pumpkin pie or custard pie, beat the filling mixture only until it is mixed well. Do not beat so hard that the mixture becomes foamy.

Smooth & Sweet

Easy to elegant cream pies.

The word *cream* in cream pies describes the satin-smooth pudding filling rather than cream as an ingredient or topping.

Cream pies have a reputation of being difficult to make, and even some experienced cooks shy away from making them. This reputation is not deserved. If you stir as directed in the recipe and have a heavy saucepan, the result will be a lovely pudding filling. If you don't own a heavy saucepan, follow the Alternate Method for Cream Fillings, page 133.

Sometimes the filling will become lumpy as it thickens. If the heat is not too high and the egg mixture is blended well, the custard will smooth out with constant stirring and continued cooking. Constant stirring is important because it assures even distribution of heat throughout the mixture. This promotes even thickening, discourages lumps and prevents scorching.

Give your cream pies a final creative touch with a whipped-cream garnish. Work with a pastry tube and a star tip for a professional look. If a recipe has whipped cream and 8 pieces of garnish, pipe the cream in 8 curved shapes, leaves or large rosettes. Place a garnish in the center of each shape. If the directions suggest spreading the whipped cream over the pie, pipe a lattice or spiral design instead. Don't be afraid to experiment. If you don't like the finished design, spread the whipped cream over the pie with a spatula and top the pie with grated chocolate, chopped nuts or whatever garnish is appropriate for that pie.

One recipe of Sweetened Whipped Cream will generously cover a 9-inch pie. A pastry tube can also be used for topping a pie with meringue.

To be sure a cream pie is always fresh, refrigerate it as soon as the filling is cool. Keep any leftover cream pie in the refrigerator. ◆

Cook's Night Out

Sliced Apple & Orange Salad
with
French Dressing
Frozen Individual Pot Pies, page 68
Tropical Sunshine Pie, page 143

Lunch for the Younger Set

Banana-Pineapple Salad
Sloppy Joe Turnovers, pages 50, 51 and 54
Chocolate & Peanut Butter Swirl, page 142
Milk

Alternate Method for Cream Fillings

If you are consistently having problems making cream fillings, your saucepan may not be heavy enough or your heating element may not be as predictable as it should be. In either case, use this method:

In a medium saucepan, combine sugar, flour or cornstarch, salt and any other dry ingredients listed with these in the recipe directions. Gradually stir in milk. Stir constantly over medium heat until mixture thickens and comes to a full boil. Reduce heat. Place egg yolks in a small bowl. Stir in about 1 cup hot mixture. Mix thoroughly. Gradually stir yolk mixture into pudding in saucepan. Cook and stir 1 minute. Proceed with the recipe.

Chocolate Cream Pie

A creamy chocolate delight you'll make again and again.

1 (9-inch) Baked Pie Shell, pages 8 and 9, made with Basic Pastry, page 14	4 egg yolks
1-1/4 cups sugar	3 (1-oz.) squares unsweetened chocolate
2 tablespoons all-purpose flour	1 tablespoon butter
2 tablespoons cornstarch	1 teaspoon vanilla extract
1/4 teaspoon salt	Sweetened Whipped Cream, page 185
2-1/2 cups milk	Chocolate Curls, page 187, or
	chocolate candy sprinkles

Prepare baked pie shell and set aside. In a medium saucepan, combine sugar, flour, cornstarch and salt. In a medium bowl, beat milk and egg yolks until smooth. Gradually stir into sugar mixture. Stir constantly over medium heat until mixture thickens and comes to a full boil. Stir and boil 1 minute. Remove from heat. Break chocolate squares in half. Add broken chocolate, butter and vanilla to hot mixture. Stir until chocolate is melted. Pour into baked pie shell. Place plastic wrap on surface of filling to prevent a film from forming. Refrigerate 3 hours or longer. Prepare Sweetened Whipped Cream. Prepare Chocolate Curls, if desired. Remove plastic wrap from pie. Spoon or pipe Sweetened Whipped Cream over filling. Garnish with Chocolate Curls or sprinkles. Refrigerate until ready to serve. Refrigerate leftover pie. Makes 8 servings.

Variation

Chocolate Meringue Pie: Do not cover filling with plastic wrap. Immediately after pouring filling into shell, prepare Meringue Topping or Chocolate-Topped Meringue, page 134, and top pie as directed. Bake as directed. Refrigerate until ready to serve. Makes 8 servings.

Lemon Meringue Pie

Classic elegance with the traditional sweet-but-tart blend.

1 (9-inch) Baked Pie Shell, pages 8 and 9,
  made with Basic Pastry, page 14
1-3/4 cups sugar
6 tablespoons cornstarch
2 tablespoons all-purpose flour
1/4 teaspoon salt

4 egg yolks
1-3/4 cups water
1 tablespoon butter
1 tablespoon finely shredded lemon peel
1/2 cup lemon juice
Meringue Topping, below

Prepare baked pie shell and set aside. In a medium saucepan, combine sugar, cornstarch, flour and salt. In a medium bowl, beat egg yolks and water until smooth. Gradually stir into sugar mixture. Stir constantly over medium heat until mixture thickens and comes to a full boil. Stir and boil 1 minute. Remove from heat. Stir in butter, lemon peel and lemon juice. Pour into baked pie shell. Immediately prepare Meringue Topping and top pie as directed. Bake as directed. Cool 2 hours. Refrigerate until ready to serve. Refrigerate leftover pie. Makes 8 servings.

Variation

Lemon Cream Pie: Omit Meringue Topping. Place plastic wrap on surface of pie filling to prevent a film from forming while pie is cooling. Spread, pipe or spoon Sweetened Whipped Cream, page 185, over cooled filling. Refrigerate until ready to serve.

Meringue Topping

A light and pretty topping to contrast with rich cream fillings.

4 egg whites
1/4 teaspoon cream of tartar

1/2 cup superfine or granulated sugar

Review Working with Egg Whites, opposite. Preheat oven to 400F (205C). Combine egg whites and cream of tartar in a small bowl. Beat with electric mixer on medium speed until soft peaks form, about 1 minute. Increase speed to high and gradually add sugar 1 tablespoon at a time. Beat until stiff peaks form and sugar is dissolved. Total beating time on high speed should be 3 to 4 minutes. Immediately spoon meringue carefully around edge and in center of hot pie filling. Spread over filling. With a narrow spatula or knife, seal meringue to rim of pie shell or crumb crust. This helps prevent shrinkage of topping during baking. Use the knife or spatula to swirl meringue slightly but do not make high peaks. Or, spoon meringue into a pastry bag fitted with a star tube. Pipe stars or rosettes over entire surface of filling or pipe a lattice pattern. Bake about 5 minutes until golden brown. Makes topping for one 9-inch pie.

Variations

Coconut Meringue Topping: Sprinkle 1/4 cup flaked or shredded coconut over meringue before baking.
Nut-Topped Meringue: Sprinkle 1 tablespoon finely chopped nuts over meringue before baking.
Chocolate-Topped Meringue: Sprinkle 2 teaspoons chocolate candy sprinkles over meringue before baking.

How to Make Meringue Topping

1/Beat egg whites and cream of tartar until soft peaks form.

2/Use a spatula or a knife to seal meringue to rim of pie shell.

Working with Egg Whites

♦ Separate eggs one at a time while cold.

♦ If separating more than one egg, place each egg white in a custard cup and then transfer it to a common bowl for storage or beating. This avoids accidently dropping some yolk into the bowl of whites. If even a drop of yolk is present in egg whites, they will not beat to the desired stiffness.

♦ For best volume, egg whites should be brought to room temperature before beating. If you do not have time to let this happen naturally, place the bowl containing the egg whites in another bowl containing about 1 inch of warm water. Swirl egg whites occasionally with a spoon until they are at room temperature.

♦ Be sure beaters and bowl are completely clean. Oil of any kind will interfere with the forming of peaks.

♦ Use a small deep bowl for beating up to 4 egg whites. Use a larger bowl for beating more egg whites.

Lime & Sour Cream Pie

If you can't find fresh limes, use reconstituted lime juice

1 (9-inch) Baked Pie Shell, pages 8 and 9,
  made with Basic Pastry, page 14
1-1/4 cups sugar
1/4 cup cornstarch
2 tablespoons all-purpose flour
1/4 teaspoon salt
1-3/4 cups water
4 egg yolks

1 tablespoon butter
2 teaspoons finely shredded lime peel
1/4 cup lime juice
3 drops green food coloring and
  1 drop yellow food coloring, if desired
1/2 cup dairy sour cream
Meringue Topping, page 134, or 1 cup
  dairy sour cream and 8 thin lime slices

Prepare baked pie shell and set aside. In a medium saucepan, combine sugar, cornstarch, flour and salt. In a medium bowl, beat water and egg yolks until smooth. Gradually stir into sugar mixture. Stir constantly over medium heat until mixture thickens and comes to a full boil. Stir and boil 1 minute. Remove from heat. Add butter, lime peel and lime juice. Add food coloring, if desired. Stir until butter is melted. Stir in sour cream until blended. Pour into baked pie shell. If using Meringue Topping, prepare immediately and top pie as directed. Bake as directed. Refrigerate 2 hours or longer before serving. If not using Meringue Topping, refrigerate 1 hour or longer and serve topped with sour cream and lime slices. Refrigerate leftover pie. Makes 8 servings.

Orange Meringue Pie

Freshly squeezed orange juice gives the sweetest flavor.

1 (9-inch) Baked Pie Shell, pages 8 and 9,
  made with Basic Pastry, page 14
2/3 cup sugar
5 tablespoons cornstarch
1/4 teaspoon salt
1-1/2 cups orange juice

4 egg yolks
1 cup water
1 tablespoon butter
1 tablespoon lemon juice
1 tablespoon finely shredded orange peel
Meringue Topping, page 134

Prepare baked pie shell and set aside. In a medium saucepan, combine sugar, cornstarch and salt. Stir in orange juice. In a small bowl, beat egg yolks and water until smooth. Gradually stir into sugar mixture. Stir constantly over medium heat until mixture thickens and comes to a full boil. Stir and boil 1 minute. Remove from heat. Stir in butter, lemon juice and orange peel. Pour into baked pie shell. Immediately prepare Meringue Topping and top pie as directed. Bake as directed. Cool 2 hours. Refrigerate until ready to serve. Refrigerate leftover pie. Makes 8 servings.

*tip*

When cutting a meringue-topped pie, dipping the knife in water will prevent the meringue from sticking to the knife.

Vanilla Cream Pie

This basic cream filling has variations for coconut, banana, butterscotch and fruit, see below.

1 (9-inch) Baked Pie Shell, pages 8 and 9,
   made with Basic Pastry, page 14, or
   Chocolate Pastry, page 19
3/4 cup sugar
2 tablespoons all-purpose flour
2 tablespoons cornstarch

1/4 teaspoon salt
2-1/2 cups milk
4 egg yolks
1 tablespoon butter
1 teaspoon vanilla extract
Sweetened Whipped Cream, page 185

Prepare baked pie shell and set aside. In a medium saucepan, combine sugar, flour, cornstarch and salt. In a medium bowl, beat milk and egg yolks until smooth. Stir into sugar mixture. Stir constantly over medium heat until mixture thickens and comes to a full boil. Stir and boil 1 minute. Remove from heat. Stir in butter and vanilla. Pour hot mixture into baked pie shell. Place plastic wrap on surface of pie filling to prevent a film from forming. Refrigerate 2 hours or longer. Prepare Sweetened Whipped Cream. Remove plastic wrap from pie. Spread, spoon or pipe Sweetened Whipped Cream over filling. Refrigerate until ready to serve. Refrigerate leftover pie. Makes 8 servings.

Variations

Vanilla Meringue Pie: Do not cover filling with plastic wrap. Immediately after pouring filling into baked pie shell, prepare Meringue Topping, page 134, and top pie as directed. Bake as directed. Refrigerate pie until ready to serve.

Coconut Cream Pie or Coconut Meringue Pie: Stir 1 cup flaked or shredded coconut into filling with butter and vanilla. Top pie with Sweetened Whipped Cream or Coconut Meringue Topping, page 134.

Banana Cream Pie or Banana Meringue Pie: Thinly slice 2 bananas into bottom of baked pie shell before pouring in filling. Top with Sweetened Whipped Cream, Meringue Topping, page 134, or Nut-Topped Meringue, page 134.

Butterscotch Cream Pie: Substitute 3/4 cup packed brown sugar for granulated sugar.

Fruit Cream Pie: Place 1 to 1-1/2 cups soft fruit in baked pie shell before pouring in filling. Choose sliced fresh or thoroughly drained and blotted canned fruit. Top with Sweetened Whipped Cream or Meringue Topping, page 134.

Microwave Directions for Cream Fillings

In a 1-1/2-quart bowl, combine sugar, flour or cornstarch, salt and any other dry ingredients listed with these in the recipe directions. Combine milk or water and egg yolks as directed. Gradually stir the egg mixture into the flour mixture until thoroughly blended. Cook uncovered at 100% (HIGH) 4 minutes. Stir thoroughly. Cook at 100% (HIGH) 4 to 6 minutes longer, stirring after each minute, until mixture is thickened. Cook 1 minute longer at 100% (HIGH). Proceed with the recipe.

German Chocolate Cream Pie

A luscious flavor blend of chocolate, coconut and pecans.

1 (9-inch) Baked Pie Shell, pages 8 and 9,
  made with Basic Pastry, page 14
1/2 cup sugar
2 tablespoons cornstarch
1 tablespoon all-purpose flour
1/4 teaspoon salt
2-1/2 cups milk

4 egg yolks
4 oz. sweet cooking chocolate
1 teaspoon vanilla extract
2/3 cup flaked or shredded coconut
2/3 cup chopped pecans
Sweetened Whipped Cream, page 185

Prepare baked pie shell and set aside. In a medium saucepan, combine sugar, cornstarch, flour and salt. In a medium bowl, beat milk and egg yolks until smooth. Gradually stir into sugar mixture. Stir constantly over medium heat until mixture thickens and comes to a full boil. Stir and boil 1 minute. Remove from heat. Break chocolate into several pieces. Add broken chocolate and vanilla to thickened mixture. Stir until chocolate is melted. Set aside 2 tablespoons each of coconut and pecans. Stir remaining coconut and pecans into chocolate mixture. Pour into baked pie shell. Place plastic wrap on surface of pie filling to prevent a film from forming. Refrigerate 3 hours or longer. Preheat oven to 375F (190C). Spread reserved coconut in a pie pan and toast in oven 3 to 4 minutes, stirring 2 or 3 times. Prepare Sweetened Whipped Cream. Remove plastic wrap from pie. Spread, spoon or pipe Sweetened Whipped Cream over chilled pie filling. Sprinkle with toasted coconut and pecans. Refrigerate until ready to serve. Refrigerate leftover pie. Makes 8 servings.

Variation

German Chocolate Meringue Pie: Immediately after pouring filling into shell, prepare Meringue Topping, page 134, and top pie as directed. Sprinkle with reserved untoasted coconut and pecans. Bake as directed. Makes 8 servings.

 *tip*

For neater wedges when cutting cream pies, wipe off the knife frequently with a damp paper towel.

German Chocolate Cream Pie

Ribbon Cream Pie

Spur-of-the-moment pie uses canned pie filling and instant pudding to create a ribbon effect.

1 (9-inch) Baked Pie Shell, pages 8 and 9,
    made with Basic Pastry, page 14, or
    Graham-Cracker Crust, page 31
1 (21-oz.) can blueberry, cherry or
    pineapple pie filling
1 cup dairy sour cream

1/2 cup milk
1 (3-3/4-oz.) pkg. vanilla or
    fruit-flavor instant pudding mix
Sweetened Whipped Cream, page 185
1/4 cup sliced almonds

Prepare baked pie shell or crumb crust and set aside. Spread 1 cup pie filling in pie shell or crust. Combine sour cream and milk in a medium bowl. Add pudding mix. Beat with a wire whip or rotary beater until blended, about 1 minute. Spread over pie filling. Spoon remaining fruit filling over pudding as evenly as possible. Refrigerate while preparing Sweetened Whipped Cream. Place whipped cream in a pastry tube fitted with a star tip. Pipe rosettes of cream over pie, completely covering filling. Place an almond slice upright in center of each rosette. Refrigerate 1 hour or longer. Refrigerate leftover pie. Makes 8 servings.

Praline Eggnog Pie

There's a surprise in the bottom of this pie—a crunchy nut layer.

Single-Crust Basic Pastry, page 14
1/4 cup butter
1/3 cup packed brown sugar
1/2 cup chopped pecans
3/4 cup granulated sugar
2 tablespoons all-purpose flour
2 tablespoons cornstarch
1/4 teaspoon salt

2-1/2 cups milk
4 egg yolks
1 tablespoon butter
1/2 teaspoon rum extract
1/4 teaspoon ground nutmeg
Sugar & Cream Topping, page 141
Ground nutmeg
Pecan halves

Prepare dough for pastry. Review Unbaked Pie Shells, page 8. On a lightly floured surface, roll out dough to a 12-inch circle. Fit into a 9-inch pie pan. Fold dough under for a raised edge. Flute as desired. Use a fork to prick sides and bottom of unbaked pie shell at 1/2-inch intervals. Preheat oven to 475F (245C). Mix 1/4 cup butter and brown sugar until smooth. Stir in pecans. Sprinkle evenly over bottom of pricked pie shell. Bake 8 to 10 minutes until pie shell is browned and butter mixture is bubbly. In a medium saucepan, combine granulated sugar, flour, cornstarch and salt. In a medium bowl, beat milk and egg yolks until smooth. Stir into sugar mixture. Stir constantly over medium heat until mixture thickens and comes to a full boil. Stir and boil 1 minute. Remove from heat. Stir in 1 tablespoon butter, rum extract and 1/4 teaspoon nutmeg. Pour hot mixture into baked pie shell. Place plastic wrap on surface of pie filling to prevent a film from forming. Refrigerate 3 hours or longer. Prepare Sugar & Cream Topping. Remove plastic wrap from pie. Spread, spoon or pipe topping over filling. Sprinkle with nutmeg and garnish with pecan halves. Refrigerate until ready to serve. Refrigerate leftover pie. Makes 8 to 10 servings.

Maple Nut Pie

Pecans and maple are a traditional flavor duo, but cashews add an original touch.

1 (9-inch) Baked Pie Shell, pages 8 and 9,
    made with Basic Pastry, page 14
Nut Crunch Topping, see below
1/4 cup sugar
2 tablespoons all-purpose flour
2 tablespoons cornstarch
1/4 teaspoon salt

1-3/4 cups milk
4 egg yolks
3/4 cup maple syrup
1 tablespoon butter
Maple Topping, page 131
8 whole pecans or cashews, if desired

Nut Crunch Topping:
1/3 cup sugar
1/3 cup all-purpose flour

3 tablespoons butter
1/2 cup chopped pecans or cashews

Prepare baked pie shell and set aside. Prepare Nut Crunch Topping. Cool. In a medium saucepan, combine sugar, flour, cornstarch and salt. In a medium bowl, beat milk and egg yolks until smooth. Stir milk mixture and maple syrup into sugar mixture. Stir constantly over medium heat until mixture thickens and comes to a full boil. Stir and boil 1 minute. Remove from heat. Stir in butter. Pour hot mixture into baked pie shell. Sprinkle with Nut Crunch Topping. Refrigerate 3 hours or longer. Prepare Maple Topping and spoon around edge of pie filling. Garnish with whole nuts, if desired. Refrigerate until ready to serve. Refrigerate leftover pie. Makes 8 servings.

Nut Crunch Topping:
Preheat oven to 400F (205C). Combine sugar and flour in a small bowl. Cut in butter until mixture resembles coarse meal. Stir in chopped nuts. Spread on an ungreased baking sheet. Bake 5 minutes, stirring twice. Remove from oven.

Sugar & Cream Topping   *Photo on page 122.*

Especially for Praline Eggnog Pie, opposite, and Praline Sweet-Potato Pie, page 123.

1/2 pint whipping cream (1 cup)
2 tablespoons brown sugar

Combine whipping cream and brown sugar in a small bowl, stirring to break up sugar. Beat until stiff peaks form. Refrigerate until ready to serve. Makes about 2 cups.

Chocolate & Peanut Butter Swirl

Small drops of semisweet chocolate may be called pieces, bits, chips or morsels.

1 (9-inch) Baked Pie Shell, pages 8 and 9,
   made with Chocolate Pastry, page 19
2/3 cup sugar
2 tablespoons all-purpose flour
1 tablespoon cornstarch
1/4 teaspoon salt
2-1/2 cups milk

3 egg yolks
1/2 teaspoon vanilla extract
1/2 cup creamy peanut butter
1/2 cup semisweet chocolate pieces
Sweetened Whipped Cream, page 185
1/4 cup peanuts

Prepare baked pie shell and set aside. In a medium saucepan, combine sugar, flour, cornstarch and salt. In a medium bowl, beat milk and egg yolks until smooth. Gradually stir into sugar mixture. Stir constantly over medium heat until mixture thickens and comes to a full boil. Stir and boil 1 minute. Remove from heat. Stir in vanilla and peanut butter until smooth. Stir in chocolate pieces until distributed but not melted. Let stand 3 minutes. Pour into baked pie shell. Place the point of a knife about 1 inch into filling and swirl for a marbled effect. Refrigerate 3 hours or longer. Prepare Sweetened Whipped Cream. Pipe or spoon around edge of pie. Sprinkle with peanuts. Refrigerate until ready to serve. Refrigerate leftover pie. Makes 8 servings.

Mix & Match Pie

Choose matching fruit, gelatin and yogurt flavors or make up your own combinations.

1 (9-inch) Graham-Cracker Crust, page 31
1 (3-oz.) pkg. fruit-flavor gelatin
3/4 cup boiling water
1/2 cup cold water

1 (8-oz.) pkg. cream cheese
1 (8-oz.) carton fruit-flavor yogurt
2 to 3 cups sliced fresh or
   drained canned fruit

Prepare crust and set aside. Combine gelatin and boiling water in a small bowl. Stir until gelatin is dissolved. Stir in cold water. Refrigerate until mixture has consistency of unbeaten egg whites. Beat cream cheese until smooth. Gradually add yogurt, beating well and cleaning beaters occasionally. Gradually stir in 3/4 cup gelatin mixture until blended. Pour into crust. Refrigerate until filling is set, about 1 hour. Let remaining gelatin mixture stand at room temperature. Arrange fruit on top of pie filling. If using canned fruit, drain well and pat dry before using. Spoon remaining gelatin mixture over fruit. Refrigerate 2 hours or longer. Refrigerate leftover pie. Makes 8 servings.

How to Make Chocolate & Peanut Butter Swirl

1/Stir vanilla and peanut butter into thickened milk mixture.

2/Place the point of a knife about 1 inch into filling and swirl.

Tropical Sunshine

A golden pie filled with tropical fruit and coconut.

1 (9-inch) Coconut-Graham Crust, page 31
1 (8-oz.) can crushed pineapple
1 (11-oz.) can Mandarin orange segments
Water
1 (5-5/8-oz.) pkg. vanilla instant
   pudding mix
1 (8-oz.) carton pineapple or
   orange yogurt

1/2 cup flaked or shredded coconut
1/2 pint whipping cream (1 cup)
2 tablespoons powdered sugar
2 tablespoons toasted flaked or
   shredded coconut, if desired

Prepare crust and set aside. Drain pineapple and orange segments, reserving liquids. Add water to reserved liquids to make 1 cup. Combine pudding mix, water mixture and yogurt in a medium bowl. Beat with a wire whip or rotary beater until smooth, about 1 minute. Stir in 1/2 cup coconut. Spoon evenly into crust. Spoon drained pineapple on top of pudding, spreading to crust. Arrange orange segments on top of pineapple. Whip cream with powdered sugar until stiff peaks form. Spoon onto center of pie. Spread whipped cream toward edge of pie filling, leaving a 1-1/2-inch fruit border. Sprinkle whipped cream with toasted coconut, if desired. Refrigerate 1 hour or until ready to serve. Refrigerate leftover pie. Makes 8 servings.

Desserts for Entertaining

Light chiffon pies.

Chiffon pies are ideal for entertaining because they may be prepared up to two days ahead. The lightness and subtle flavor of chiffon contrast well with sweet and crunchy crumb crusts. A crumb crust will not become as soggy over one or two days as a standard pastry crust will.

If you're preparing the pie ahead, leave off the topping and other garnish until a few hours before serving. To prevent the filling from drying out in the refrigerator, cover the pie with a foil tent. Insert wooden picks in the chiffon so the foil won't mar the filling. Press the foil lightly around edges of the pie pan. You can use a large plastic bag instead of foil. Before serving the pie, uncover it and remove the wooden picks. Use the garnish to cover any marks left by the picks.

More steps are involved in making chiffon pies than most pies. If you follow directions carefully, your chiffon pies will be the high point of the evening.

The first important step is to be sure any gelatin is thoroughly dissolved. The dissolving liquid should be clear and contain no visible gelatin particles. Check by looking at a small amount of the mixture in a metal spoon.

Before adding beaten egg whites or whipped cream, the gelatin mixture must be chilled until it resembles unbeaten egg whites. Or, if the mixture contains another thickener such as egg yolk or cornstarch, it must be chilled until it mounds when dropped from a spoon. Stir the refrigerated gelatin mixture occasionally to promote even chilling. If the mixture does not become firm enough, it will not mix with egg whites or whipped cream but will separate. If the mixture is too firm, it will break up into lumps and your filling will not be smooth. See Working with Gelatin Mixtures, page 146.

After beaten egg whites or whipped cream have been folded in, the mixture may be too thin to drop into mounds. If this happens, refrigerate it, stirring every 5 minutes, until it again holds mounds.

The volume of beaten egg whites and whipped cream will vary from time to time, changing the amount of filling. Spoon any leftover filling into dessert cups. Refrigerate it for serving the next day.

Chiffon fillings are attractive when piped into a crust with a pastry tube and a star tip. A smooth filling that mounds well but is not too firm may be piped in a spiral or rosette design. Arrange the whipped-cream topping and other garnishes so the piped filling may be seen and admired. See the photo on page 149. ◆

4th of July Backyard Picnic

Blue-Cheese Twists, page 40
Deviled Western Cutouts, page 34
Fried Chicken
Fresh Vegetable Dippers & Sour Cream Dip
Potato Pockets, page 84
4th of July Ripple Pie, page 154
Grandma's Apple Pie, page 92

Strawberry Chiffon Pie

Even better than strawberry shortcake!

1 (9-inch) Vanilla-Wafer Crust,
   or Graham-Cracker Crust, page 31
3 cups fresh whole strawberries
1/3 cup water
1 envelope unflavored gelatin
1/3 cup granulated sugar

2 egg whites
1/3 cup granulated sugar
1/2 pint whipping cream (1 cup)
1 tablespoon powdered sugar
8 Chocolate Leaves, page 187

Prepare crust and set aside. Wash and hull strawberries. Refrigerate 4 strawberries for garnish. Pour water into a saucepan. Sprinkle gelatin over water and let stand 2 to 3 minutes to soften. Mash remaining strawberries in a large bowl, leaving some large pieces. Add 1/3 cup granulated sugar to softened gelatin. Cook over medium-low heat until mixture comes to a boil and gelatin is dissolved. Stir into mashed berries. Refrigerate, stirring occasionally, until mixture is consistency of unbeaten egg whites. Beat egg whites until soft peaks form. Gradually beat in 1/3 cup granulated sugar. Continue beating until stiff peaks form. Fold into berry mixture. Refrigerate. Beat cream until stiff peaks form. Fold about half the whipped cream into berry mixture. If necessary, refrigerate and stir occasionally until mixture mounds when dropped from a spoon. Spoon into prepared crust. Fold powdered sugar into remaining whipped cream. Refrigerate pie and whipped cream 3 hours or longer. Prepare Chocolate Leaves. Garnish pie with whipped cream, reserved strawberries and Chocolate Leaves. Serve cold. Refrigerate leftover pie. Makes 8 servings.

Raspberry Snow

So smooth and light it almost melts in your mouth.

1 (9-inch) Vanilla-Wafer Crust,
   or Coconut-Graham Crust, page 31
1 (10-oz.) pkg. frozen red raspberries
   in syrup
1/3 cup water
1 envelope unflavored gelatin

1 tablespoon lemon juice
5 egg whites
1/3 cup sugar
16 small Chocolate Leaves, page 187, or
   mint sprigs

Prepare crust and set aside. Thaw raspberries. Place a strainer over a medium saucepan. Pour raspberries with syrup into strainer. With a wooden spoon, mash raspberries through strainer. Remove strainer and discard seeds. Pour water into a medium bowl. Sprinkle gelatin over water and let stand 2 to 3 minutes to soften. Bring raspberry puree to a boil. Pour into gelatin mixture. Stir until gelatin is dissolved. Stir in lemon juice. Refrigerate, stirring occasionally, until mixture is the consistency of unbeaten egg whites. Beat egg whites until soft peaks form. Gradually beat in sugar. Continue beating until stiff peaks form. Fold into raspberry mixture. If necessary, refrigerate until mixture forms high mounds when dropped from a spoon, stirring occasionally. Spoon into crust. Refrigerate 2 hours or longer. Prepare Chocolate Leaves, if desired. To serve pie, garnish with Chocolate Leaves or mint sprigs. Serve cold. Refrigerate leftover pie. Makes 8 servings.

Black-Bottom Pie

Discover a creamy chocolate surprise when you cut into the light topping.

1 (9-inch) Baked Pie Shell, pages 8 and 9,
    made with Basic Pastry, page 14
1/4 cup water
1 envelope unflavored gelatin
1/2 cup sugar
1 tablespoon cornstarch
3 eggs, separated
2 cups milk

1 (6-oz.) pkg. semisweet chocolate pieces
    (1 cup)
1/2 teaspoon rum extract or
    2 tablespoons rum
1/4 cup sugar
Chocolate Curls or Chocolate Leaves,
    page 187

Prepare pie shell and set aside. Pour water into a small bowl. Sprinkle gelatin over water and let stand 2 to 3 minutes until softened. Combine 1/2 cup sugar and cornstarch in a medium saucepan. In a medium bowl, mix egg yolks and milk until smooth. Gradually stir into sugar mixture. Stir constantly over medium heat until mixture thickens and comes to a full boil. Stir and boil 1 minute. Place chocolate pieces in a small bowl. Add 1 cup hot cooked mixture. Set aside while preparing gelatin mixture. Stir softened gelatin into remaining cooked mixture in saucepan. Stir constantly over medium heat about 1 minute until gelatin is dissolved. Pour into a medium bowl. Stir in rum extract or rum. Refrigerate, stirring occasionally, until mixture mounds when dropped from a spoon. While gelatin mixture is chilling, stir chocolate and pudding in small bowl until smooth. Spread evenly in bottom of prepared crust. When chilled gelatin mixture mounds, beat egg whites until soft peaks form. Gradually beat in 1/4 cup sugar. Continue beating until stiff peaks form. Fold into chilled mixture. Spoon over chocolate layer in crust, mounding in center. Refrigerate 2 hours or longer. Prepare Chocolate Curls or Chocolate Leaves. To serve pie, garnish with Chocolate Curls or Chocolate Leaves. Serve cold. Refrigerate leftover pie. Makes 8 servings.

Variation
Muddy Bottom Pie: Substitute 1 (6-ounce) package peanut butter pieces for chocolate pieces.

Working with Gelatin Mixtures

To speed up the setting of a gelatin mixture, place the bowl with the dissolved mixture in a slightly larger bowl of ice and water. Stir frequently to prevent lumps. If a gelatin mixture becomes too firm to fold in whipped ingredients, return it to its liquid state by heating in a saucepan over low heat and stirring constantly until mixture is smooth. It does not need to boil. Start the chilling process again. The mixture will thicken faster the second time.

Banana-Rum Pie   *Photo on page 149.*

Peel and cut bananas at the last minute to prevent them from darkening.

1 (9-inch) Baked Pie Shell, pages 8 and 9, made with Basic Pastry, page 14, or Graham-Cracker Crust, page 31	1-1/2 cups milk
1/2 cup granulated sugar	2 tablespoons rum or 1/2 teaspoon rum extract
2 tablespoons cornstarch	1 pint whipping cream (2 cups)
1 envelope unflavored gelatin	2 large bananas
1/4 teaspoon salt	2 tablespoons powdered sugar
3 egg yolks	Nutmeg

Prepare pie shell or crumb crust and set aside. Combine granulated sugar, cornstarch, gelatin and salt in a medium saucepan. In a medium bowl, mix egg yolks and milk until smooth. Gradually stir into sugar mixture. Stir constantly over medium heat until mixture thickens and comes to a full boil. Stir and boil 1 minute. Stir in rum or rum extract. Pour into a medium bowl. Refrigerate, stirring occasionally, until mixture mounds when dropped from a spoon. Beat cream until stiff peaks form. Fold 2 cups whipped cream into egg mixture. Peel and cut 1-1/2 bananas into 1/4-inch slices. Fold into filling. If necessary, refrigerate and stir occasionally until mixture mounds when dropped from a spoon. Spoon banana mixture into pie shell. Fold powdered sugar into remaining whipped cream. Spoon, spread or pipe over pie. Sprinkle with nutmeg. Refrigerate 3 hours or longer. Just before serving, peel and cut remaining banana half into 8 slices. Garnish pie with banana slices. Serve cold. Refrigerate leftover pie. Makes 8 servings.

Variation

Egg Nog Pie: Omit bananas.

After separating eggs, cover the bowl containing the egg whites. Foreign material in egg whites may prevent them from whipping to light stiff peaks.

Mai Tai Pie

Exotic flavors from the Pacific islands.

1 (9-inch) Graham-Cracker Crust,
   or Coconut Crust, page 31
1 (16-oz.) can crushed pineapple
Water
1/3 cup sugar
1 tablespoon cornstarch
1 envelope unflavored gelatin
3 eggs, separated

2 tablespoons lime juice
2 tablespoons apricot brandy
1 tablespoon dark rum
1/3 cup sugar
1/2 pint whipping cream (1 cup)
4 maraschino cherries
Mint sprigs, if desired

Prepare crust and set aside. Drain pineapple, reserving liquid. Add water to liquid to make 1 cup. Combine 1/3 cup sugar, cornstarch and gelatin in a medium saucepan. In a medium bowl, mix egg yolks and water mixture until smooth. Gradually stir into sugar mixture. Stir constantly over medium heat until mixture thickens and comes to a full boil. Stir and boil 1 minute. Set aside 1/2 cup drained pineapple. Stir remaining pineapple, lime juice, apricot brandy and rum into cooked mixture. Pour into a medium bowl. Refrigerate, stirring occasionally, until mixture mounds when dropped from a spoon. Beat egg whites until soft peaks form. Gradually beat in 1/3 cup sugar. Continue beating until stiff peaks form. Fold into pineapple mixture. Beat cream until stiff peaks form. Fold into pineapple mixture. If necessary, refrigerate and stir occasionally until mixture mounds when dropped from a spoon. Pour into crust. Coarsely chop cherries. Blot reserved pineapple with paper towels. Arrange pineapple and chopped cherries in a circle on filling. Refrigerate 4 hours or longer. Garnish with mint sprigs, if desired. Serve cold. Refrigerate leftover pie. Makes 8 servings.

Variation

Frosty Mai Tai Pie: Place finished pie in freezer instead of in refrigerator. Freeze about 4 hours until filling is set.

From top to bottom: Mai Tai Pie with Coconut Crust, page 31; Banana-Rum Pie, page 147, with Graham-Cracker Crust, page 31; and Lime Chiffon Pie, page 150, with Basic Pastry, page 14.

Lime Chiffon Pie *Photo on page 149.*

On warm summer days, freeze this pie for several hours before serving.

1 (9-inch) Baked Pie Shell, pages 8 and 9,
  made with Basic Pastry, page 14, or
  Graham-Cracker Crust, page 31
1/2 cup sugar
1 tablespoon cornstarch
1 envelope unflavored gelatin
1 cup water
4 eggs, separated

1 teaspoon finely shredded lime peel
1/4 cup lime juice
6 drops green food coloring and 2 drops
  yellow food coloring, if desired
1/2 cup sugar
1/2 pint whipping cream (1 cup)
Lime slices

Prepare pie shell or crumb crust and set aside. Combine 1/2 cup sugar, cornstarch and gelatin in a medium saucepan. In a medium bowl, mix water and egg yolks until smooth. Gradually stir into sugar mixture. Stir constantly over medium heat until mixture thickens and comes to a full boil. Stir and boil 1 minute. Pour into a medium bowl. Stir in lime peel and lime juice. Add food coloring, if desired. Refrigerate, stirring occasionally, until mixture mounds when dropped from a spoon. Beat egg whites until soft peaks form. Gradually beat in 1/2 cup sugar. Continue beating until stiff peaks form. Fold into lime mixture. Beat cream until stiff peaks form. Fold half the whipped cream into lime mixture. If necessary, refrigerate and stir occasionally until mixture mounds when dropped from a spoon. Spoon or pipe into pie shell. Spoon or pipe remaining whipped cream onto top of pie. Garnish with lime slices. Refrigerate 2 hours or longer. Serve cold. Refrigerate leftover pie. Makes 8 servings.

Variation

Daiquiri Pie: Stir in 1 teaspoon Triple Sec and 2 tablespoons light rum with lime juice and peel.

 *tip*

When using both the peel and juice of citrus fruit, shred the peel before cutting and juicing the fruit.

Peanut Butter & Jelly Pie

Fantastic after-school treat.

Nutty Graham Crust, page 31,
  made with peanuts
1 envelope unflavored gelatin
1/2 cup sugar
1/2 teaspoon salt
3 eggs, separated
1 cup water
1/2 cup creamy peanut butter

1/2 teaspoon vanilla extract
1/2 cup sugar
3 tablespoons strawberry jam or
  grape jelly
Sweetened Whipped Cream, page 185
Chocolate Curls, page 187
1/4 cup peanuts

Prepare crust using chopped peanuts for the nuts; set aside. Combine gelatin, 1/2 cup sugar and salt in a medium saucepan. Mix egg yolks and water in a small bowl until smooth. Stir into gelatin mixture. Stir constantly over medium heat until mixture comes to a full boil. Continue to boil and stir 1 minute. Remove from heat. Stir in peanut butter and vanilla until mixture is smooth. Pour into a large bowl. Refrigerate, stirring occasionally, until mixture is cooled to room temperature and mounds when dropped from a spoon. Beat egg whites until soft peaks form. Gradually beat in 1/2 cup sugar. Continue beating until stiff peaks form. Fold into peanut butter mixture. If necessary, refrigerate and stir occasionally until mixture mounds when dropped from a spoon. Pour into prepared crust. Stir jam or jelly until smooth. Spoon on top of pie, making 9 evenly spaced mounds. Place the point of a knife about 1/2 inch into peanut butter mixture and swirl for a marbled effect. Refrigerate 2 hours or longer. Prepare Chocolate Curls. Before serving, spoon or pipe Sweetened Whipped Cream around edge of pie. Garnish with peanuts and Chocolate Curls. Serve cold. Refrigerate leftover pie. Makes 8 servings.

Apricot-Cheese Pie

A wonderful chilled pie that can also be served frozen.

1 (9-inch) Graham-Cracker Crust, page 31
1 (16-oz.) can apricot halves
1 (3-oz.) pkg. apricot-flavor gelatin
1 cup boiling water

1 (8-oz.) pkg. cream cheese, softened
1/4 cup sugar
1/2 pint whipping cream (1 cup)
8 Chocolate Leaves, page 187

Prepare crust and set aside. Drain apricots, reserving 1/2 cup liquid. Chop all but 4 apricot halves. Set aside unchopped apricots for garnish. Dissolve gelatin in boiling water. Stir in 1/2 cup reserved apricot liquid. In a large bowl, beat cream cheese and sugar with electric mixer until light and fluffy. Beat in 1/4 cup gelatin mixture. Scrape bowl and beaters. Beat until mixture is smooth. Gradually add remaining gelatin mixture. Stir in chopped apricots. Refrigerate, stirring occasionally, until mixture mounds when dropped from a spoon. Beat cream until stiff peaks form. Fold into gelatin mixture. If necessary, refrigerate and stir occasionally until mixture mounds when dropped from a spoon. Pour into crust. Refrigerate 2 hours or longer. Prepare Chocolate Leaves. To serve pie, garnish with reserved apricot halves and Chocolate Leaves. Serve cold. Refrigerate leftover pie. Makes 8 servings.

Blueberry-Cheese Chiffon Pie

Freeze any leftovers and serve as you would a freezer pie.

1 (9-inch) Vanilla-Wafer Crust, page 31,
  or Baked Pie Shell, pages 8 and 9,
  made with Basic Pastry, page 14
1-3/4 cups fresh or
  thawed frozen blueberries
1 cup water
2 envelopes unflavored gelatin

1/4 cup sugar
1 (8-oz.) pkg. cream cheese, softened
1/4 cup sugar
2 egg whites
1/4 cup sugar
1/2 pint whipping cream (1 cup)

Prepare crumb crust or pie shell. Reserve 24 blueberries for garnish. Place remaining berries in a medium saucepan. Mash with a potato masher until most berries are broken. Pour in water. Sprinkle gelatin over water. Let stand 3 to 5 minutes to soften gelatin. Stir in 1/4 cup sugar. Cook over medium heat, stirring occasionally until mixture comes to a full boil and gelatin is dissolved. Cool slightly. In a large bowl, beat cream cheese and 1/4 cup sugar with electric mixer until light and fluffy. Place a strainer over another medium bowl. Pour blueberry mixture into strainer. Lightly mash pulp with a large spoon to remove all juices. Discard pulp. Add blueberry juice to cream cheese mixture 1/4 cup at a time, mixing after each addition until smooth. Refrigerate, stirring occasionally, until mixture mounds slightly when dropped from a spoon. Beat egg whites until soft peaks form. Gradually beat in 1/4 cup sugar. Beat until stiff peaks form. Fold into blueberry mixture. Spoon about 2-1/2 cups into crust. Shape with a spoon to make filling slightly higher around edges. Immediately beat cream until stiff peaks form. Set aside 1/2 cup whipped cream. Fold remaining whipped cream into remaining blueberry mixture in medium bowl. Spoon all but 1/4 cup into center of filling in crumb crust or pie shell. The lighter filling will gradually push the darker filling to the edge, leaving a 1-inch dark border around filling. Fold remaining 1/4 cup filling into reserved 1/2 cup whipped cream. Spoon onto center of pie. Using 3 reserved blueberries each, make 8 evenly spaced triangles around border. Refrigerate 3 hours or longer. Serve cold. Refrigerate leftover pie. Makes 8 servings.

Arrange garnishes on pies so they will be between the cuts for each wedge.
You won't have to cut through the garnish or remove it from the pie before serving.

How to Make Blueberry-Cheese Chiffon Pie

1/Refrigerate blueberry mixture until it mounds slightly when dropped from a spoon.

2/Add whipped cream to remaining blueberry mixture and spoon into center of pie filling.

Angelfood Pie

This light dessert is perfect after a barbecue or deep-fried dinner.

1 (9-inch) Graham-Cracker Crust, page 31
1 (8-oz.) can crushed pineapple
Water
1 envelope unflavored gelatin
1/3 cup granulated sugar
1 tablespoon finely shredded lemon peel

1 tablespoon lemon juice
3 egg whites
1/3 cup granulated sugar
1/2 pint whipping cream (1 cup)
1 tablespoon powdered sugar
Mint sprigs

Prepare crust and set aside. Drain pineapple; reserving juice. Add water to juice to make 1-1/4 cups. Pour into a medium saucepan. Sprinkle gelatin over juice mixture. Let stand 2 or 3 minutes to soften. Add 1/3 cup granulated sugar. Stir constantly over medium heat until mixture comes to a full boil and gelatin is dissolved. Pour into a medium bowl. Stir in drained pineapple, lemon peel and lemon juice. Refrigerate, stirring occasionally, until mixture is the consistency of unbeaten egg whites. Beat egg whites until soft peaks form. Gradually beat in 1/3 cup granulated sugar. Continue beating until stiff peaks form. Fold into pineapple mixture. Beat cream until stiff peaks form. Fold all but 1 cup whipped cream into pineapple mixture. If necessary, refrigerate and stir occasionally until mixture mounds when dropped from a spoon. Pour into crust. Fold powdered sugar into remaining whipped cream. Spoon or pipe around filling. Refrigerate 2 hours or longer. Garnish with mint sprigs before serving. Serve cold. Refrigerate leftover pie. Makes 8 servings.

Fourth of July Ripple Pie

A red, white and blue surprise.

1 (9-inch) Graham-Cracker Crust, page 31,
   or Baked Pie Shell, pages 8 and 9, made
   with Basic Pastry, page 14
2 cups fresh whole strawberries
1 cup fresh or thawed frozen blueberries
1/4 cup sugar
1 envelope unflavored gelatin
1/4 teaspoon salt

2/3 cup water
1 (8-oz.) pkg. cream cheese
1/4 cup sugar
1 teaspoon finely shredded lemon peel
1 teaspoon lemon juice
3 eggs, separated
1/4 cup sugar

Prepare crumb crust or pie shell and set aside. Refrigerate 4 strawberries and 1/3 cup blueberries for garnish. Chop remaining strawberries; set aside. In a small saucepan, combine 1/4 cup sugar, gelatin and salt. Stir in water. Heat until gelatin is dissolved, stirring frequently. In a large bowl, beat cream cheese, 1/4 cup sugar, lemon peel and lemon juice with electric mixer until light and fluffy. Beat in egg yolks. Add gelatin mixture 1/4 cup at a time, beating after each addition until smooth. Scrape bowl and beaters. Stir in chopped strawberries and 2/3 cup blueberries. Refrigerate, stirring occasionally, until mixture mounds when dropped from a spoon. With clean beaters, beat egg whites until soft peaks form. Gradually beat in 1/4 cup sugar. Continue beating until stiff peaks form. Fold into gelatin mixture. If necessary, refrigerate and stir occasionally until mixture mounds when dropped from a spoon. Spoon into crust, mounding in center. Refrigerate 4 hours or longer. Before serving, thinly slice reserved strawberries. Arrange slices on top of pie to resemble fans. Garnish with blueberries. Serve cold. Refrigerate leftover pie. Makes 8 servings.

Before juicing citrus fruits, roll them on the countertop with pressure from the palm of your hand. This makes them easier to juice.

Pumpkin Chiffon Pie

A summer surprise or a holiday tradition.

1 (9-inch) Graham-Cracker Crust or Gingersnap Crust, page 31	1/8 teaspoon ground ginger
1 envelope unflavored gelatin	3 eggs, separated
2/3 cup packed brown sugar	1/2 cup milk
1/2 teaspoon ground nutmeg	1 cup canned pumpkin
1/2 teaspoon ground cinnamon	6 tablespoons granulated sugar
1/2 teaspoon salt	1/2 pint whipping cream (1 cup)

Prepare crust and set aside. In a medium saucepan, combine gelatin, brown sugar, nutmeg, cinnamon, salt and ginger. Add egg yolks, milk and pumpkin. Beat with a wire whip or rotary beater until smooth. Stir constantly over medium heat until mixture comes to a full boil. Reduce heat and boil 1 minute. Pour into a medium bowl. Refrigerate, stirring occasionally, until cooled to room temperature. Beat egg whites until soft peaks form. Gradually beat in granulated sugar. Continue beating until stiff peaks form. Fold into pumpkin mixture. Reserve 1/3 cup pumpkin mixture in a small bowl. Beat cream until stiff peaks form. Add 1 cup whipped cream to reserved pumpkin mixture in small bowl. Fold in until blended; set aside. Fold remaining whipped cream into pumpkin mixture in medium bowl until blended. If necessary, refrigerate and stir occasionally until mixture mounds when dropped from a spoon. Pour into crust. Pipe or spoon reserved whipped cream mixture around edge of pie. Refrigerate 3 hours or longer. Serve cold. Refrigerate leftover pie. Makes 8 servings.

When a recipe calls for reserving fruit for garnishing, cover and refrigerate the fruit so it will retain its moisture and color.

Make-Ahead Desserts

Pies to store in your freezer.

Freezer pies fall into two categories: Mousse pies are prepared by a method similar to the method for chiffon pies. Ice-cream pies are simply crusts filled with ice cream.

A mousse is a rich and airy mixture similar to a chiffon filling. Before you prepare this type of freezer pie, review the preparation of chiffon fillings in Desserts for Entertaining, page 144. Traditionally, mousse is served either hot or chilled, but more cooks are becoming convinced that frozen mousse has a place in entertaining. Not only is a frozen mousse convenient, it is a delightful and refreshing ending to a hearty dinner. Purists may frown on serving mousse in a crust. But when you have something delicious and in demand, why worry about tradition?

With five basic recipes for ice-cream pies and the range of ice-cream flavors in supermarkets, you have a myriad of possibilities for desserts to be stored in your freezer. Just change the flavor of ice cream or sherbet and you'll have a completely different pie. If you substitute peach ice cream for pumpkin ice cream, Holiday Pie becomes Peaches & Cream Pie. The same brown-sugar-and-nut base is also delectable with caramel ice cream, butterscotch ice cream or praline ice cream.

To soften ice cream or sherbet, let it stand at room temperature for about 15 minutes. If you are using part of the ice cream, remove the amount you need from the container and place it in a chilled bowl. Return the container to the freezer and let the ice cream in the bowl soften at room temperature. To speed the softening, break up the ice cream and stir it. Do not let softening ice cream melt or it will contain ice crystals after it is refrozen.

To store freezer pies for more than one day, cover them or wrap them well to prevent drying out and flavor change. If a pie is frozen too hard to cut when it is removed from the freezer, let it stand at room temperature for 5 to 10 minutes before cutting.

If the members of your household eat in several shifts, cut a frozen pie into serving wedges. Wrap each wedge separately and return them to the freezer. When the first shift is ready for dessert, remove the required number of wedges from the freezer, unwrap and serve. ◆

Mexican Honeymoon Supper

Chablis
Tomato-Avocado Salad
Chicken Pie Suizas, page 74
Rocky Mocha Mousse, page 164

Dinner at Eight

Filo Triangles, page 38
Caesar Salad
Beef Wellingtons, page 72
Asparagus with Lemon Butter
Baked Alaska Pie, page 160

Grasshopper Pie

Garnish with red maraschino cherries for a touch of holiday spirit.

1 (9-inch) Chocolate-Cookie Crust, page 31
1 (10-1/2-oz.) pkg. miniature marshmallows
   (7 cups)
1/2 cup water
2 tablespoons crème de cacao

1/4 cup green crème de menthe
1 pint whipping cream (2 cups)
1/2 teaspoon crème de menthe
Chocolate Curls, page 187, or
   green maraschino cherries with stems

Prepare crust and set aside to cool. Place marshmallows and water in a medium saucepan. Stir frequently over low heat until marshmallows are completely melted. Remove from heat. Stir in crème de cacao and 1/4 cup crème de menthe. Pour into a medium bowl. Refrigerate until cooler than room temperature, stirring frequently. Beat cream until stiff peaks form. Fold 3 cups whipped cream into marshmallow mixture. If necessary, refrigerate until mixture holds firm mounds when dropped from a spoon. Spoon into cooled crust. Fold 1/2 teaspoon crème de menthe into remaining whipped cream. Spoon or pipe around edges of filling. Prepare Chocolate Curls, if desired. Garnish pie with Chocolate Curls or maraschino cherries. Freeze 4 hours or longer until filling is firm. Remove from freezer about 10 minutes before cutting. Makes 10 servings.

Strawberry Mousse Pie

Pretty-as-a-picture with strawberry whipped cream, whole strawberries and Chocolate Leaves.

1 (9-inch) Graham-Cracker Crust, page 31
3 cups fresh strawberries
1/4 cup water
1 envelope unflavored gelatin
2 eggs, separated

3/4 cup sugar
1/2 pint whipping cream (1 cup)
8 strawberries, if desired
8 Chocolate Leaves, if desired, page 187

Prepare crust and set aside to cool. Wash and hull 3 cups strawberries. Puree in food processor or blender. If using a masher to puree strawberries, mash well to prevent large pieces of hard-frozen fruit. Pour water into a small saucepan. Sprinkle gelatin over water. Let soften 3 to 5 minutes. Add egg yolks and 1/2 cup sugar to gelatin mixture. Stir until mixed well. Stir in strawberry puree. Stir constantly over medium heat until mixture comes to a full boil. Stir and boil 1 minute. Remove from heat and pour into a large bowl. Refrigerate until mixture mounds when dropped from a spoon. Beat egg whites until soft peaks form. Gradually beat in remaining 1/4 cup sugar. Continue beating until stiff peaks form. Fold into strawberry mixture. Remove 1/2 cup mixture and place in a small bowl. Refrigerate mixture remaining in large bowl. Beat cream until stiff peaks form. Fold 1 cup whipped cream into 1/2 cup strawberry mixture in small bowl. Fold remaining whipped cream into mixture in large bowl. If necessary, refrigerate until mixture holds high mounds when dropped from a spoon. Spoon mixture from large bowl into cooled crust, mounding in center. Pipe or spoon whipped cream mixture in small bowl over pie, mounding in center. Freeze 3 hours or longer until filling is firm. Prepare Chocolate Leaves, if desired. Remove from freezer about 10 minutes before cutting. Garnish pie with 8 strawberries and Chocolate Leaves, if desired. Makes 8 servings.

Frosty Lemon Pie

If you refrigerate this pie instead of freezing it, you'll have Lemon Chiffon Pie.

1 (9-inch) Baked Pie Shell, pages 8 and 9,
    made with Basic Pastry, page 14, or
    Nutty Graham Crust, page 31
1/2 cup sugar
1 tablespoon cornstarch
1 envelope unflavored gelatin
1 cup water

4 eggs, separated
1 tablespoon finely shredded lemon peel
1/4 cup lemon juice
2 drops yellow food coloring, if desired
1/2 cup sugar
1/2 pint whipping cream (1 cup)
1/4 cup crushed lemon drops, if desired

Prepare baked pie shell or crumb crust and set aside to cool. Combine 1/2 cup sugar, cornstarch and gelatin in a medium saucepan. In a small bowl, beat water and egg yolks until smooth. Gradually stir into sugar mixture. Stir constantly over medium heat until mixture thickens and comes to a full boil. Stir and boil 1 minute. Pour into a medium bowl. Stir in lemon peel and lemon juice. Stir in food coloring, if desired. Refrigerate until mixture mounds when dropped from a spoon. Beat egg whites until soft peaks form. Gradually beat in 1/2 cup sugar. Continue beating until stiff peaks form. Fold into lemon mixture. Beat cream until stiff peaks form. Fold half the whipped cream into lemon mixture. If necessary, refrigerate until mixture holds firm mounds when dropped from a spoon. Spoon into cooled crust. Spoon or pipe remaining whipped cream around edge of filling. Sprinkle whipped cream with lemon drops, if desired. Freeze 4 hours or longer until filling is firm. Remove from freezer about 10 minutes before cutting. Makes 8 servings.

Tropical Freeze

Marshmallows already contain the gelatin needed to help stiffen this filling.

1 (9-inch) Coconut Crust, page 31
1 (16-oz.) can fruit cocktail
Water
1/2 lb. miniature marshmallows (4 cups)
1/2 cup halved maraschino cherries

1/2 cup chopped walnuts or pecans
1/2 cup flaked or shredded coconut
1/2 pint whipping cream (1 cup)
8 pecan halves

Prepare crust and set aside to cool. Drain fruit cocktail, reserving liquid. Add water to liquid to measure 1/2 cup. Pour into a medium saucepan. Add marshmallows. Stir frequently over low heat until marshmallows are melted. Set aside 8 maraschino cherry halves. In a medium bowl, combine remaining maraschino cherries, drained fruit cocktail, nuts and coconut. Stir in melted marshmallow mixture. Mixture will lose some air as it is stirred. Refrigerate until liquid part of mixture holds firm mounds when dropped from a spoon. Beat cream until stiff peaks form. Fold into marshmallow mixture. Spoon into cooled crust. Garnish with reserved maraschino cherry halves and pecan halves. Freeze 6 hours or longer until filling is firm. Remove from freezer about 10 minutes before cutting. Makes 8 servings.

Banana-Split Pie

An ice-cream ladle is flatter than an ice-cream scoop.

1 (9-inch) Graham-Cracker Crust or
  Nutty Graham Crust, page 31
2 bananas
1/2 gal. vanilla ice cream
1/2 cup strawberry preserves

1/2 cup apricot-pineapple preserves
1/2 cup chocolate fudge ice cream topping
1/4 cup chopped walnuts or pecans
Sweetened Whipped Cream, page 185,
  if desired

Prepare crust and cool slightly. Chill in freezer about 30 minutes before making pie. Halve bananas lengthwise and then crosswise to make 8 pieces. Place banana pieces pinwheel fashion in chilled crust with curved ends against sides of crust. With a large spoon or ice-cream ladle, layer a third of the ice cream evenly over bananas. Spoon 1 tablespoon strawberry preserves on top of pie slightly off-center. Repeat with 2 additional tablespoons strawberry preserves equally distant from first spoonful. Spread lightly with back of spoon or ladle. Repeat with apricot-pineapple preserves and chocolate topping. Repeat layers using another third of the ice cream and 3 tablespoons each strawberry preserves, apricot-pineapple preserves and chocolate topping. Make a layer of remaining ice cream, mounding slightly in center. Spoon remaining 2 tablespoons of each preserve over ice cream. Drizzle remaining chocolate from center to about 1-1/2 inches from edge of filling. Sprinkle with nuts. Place in freezer immediately. Freeze 4 hours or longer until filling is firm. Prepare Sweetened Whipped Cream, if desired. Serve pie frozen. Garnish with Sweetened Whipped Cream, if desired. Pie may be returned to freezer after garnishing. Makes 8 servings.

Pink-Lemonade Pie

No squeezing lemons for this pie. Use frozen pink-lemonade concentrate.

1 (9-inch) Graham-Cracker Crust, page 31
1 (6-oz.) can pink-lemonade concentrate
2 eggs, separated

2/3 cup sugar
8 drops red food coloring
1/2 pint whipping cream (1 cup)

Prepare crust and set aside to cool. Remove 1/2 cup lemonade concentrate from can. Let stand at room temperature while whipping other ingredients. Reserve remaining concentrate for another use. In a small bowl, beat egg whites until soft peaks form. Gradually beat in 1/3 cup sugar. Continue beating until stiff peaks form, about 5 minutes. Place in a large bowl. Place egg yolks in the small bowl. Add remaining 1/3 cup sugar. Beat until thick and pale yellow, about 4 minutes. Fold beaten yolk mixture and food coloring into beaten egg whites. Beat cream until stiff peaks form. Fold partially thawed lemonade concentrate into whipped cream. Fold into egg mixture until blended. Spoon into cooled crust. Place in freezer immediately. Freeze 6 hours or longer until filling is firm. Serve frozen. Makes 8 servings.

Rainbow Pie

Make two or three. Wrap the extras and freeze them.

1 (9-inch) Coconut-Graham Crust, page 31
1/2 pint whipping cream (1 cup)
1/2 teaspoon vanilla extract

2 tablespoons powdered sugar
1 pint each lime, orange and raspberry sherbet
Small jelly beans or gum drops

Prepare crust and cool slightly. Chill in freezer about 30 minutes before making pie. Combine cream, vanilla and powdered sugar in a small bowl. Beat until stiff peaks form. Spread half the whipped cream mixture over bottom of chilled crust. Freeze 30 minutes. Place each sherbet flavor in a separate bowl. Stir each to soften to a thick spreading consistency. Spread lime sherbet over cream mixture, mounding slightly in center. Spread orange sherbet over lime, then raspberry sherbet over orange. Make each layer slightly thicker in center. Spoon or pipe remaining whipped cream over raspberry sherbet. Garnish with candy. Place in freezer immediately. Freeze 4 hours or longer until sherbet is firm. Serve frozen. Makes 8 servings.

Variation
Rainbow Loaf: Line a 9" x 5" x 3" loaf pan with foil. Prepare mixture for crust. Press evenly in bottom and up sides of pan. Bake as directed for crust. Cool. Proceed as directed above.

Baked Alaska Pie

Use three different flavors of ice cream or all one flavor.

1 (9-inch) baked pie crust, pages 8 and 9,
   made with Basic Pastry, page 14
3 pints ice cream (1-1/2 qts.)

3/4 cup chopped walnuts or pecans
1/2 cup fruit preserves or ice-cream topping
Meringue Topping, page 134

Prepare crust and cool slightly. Chill in freezer about 30 minutes before making pie. Stir ice cream to soften slightly. If using different flavors, stir each flavor in a separate bowl. Spread 1 pint ice cream in chilled crust, being careful not to break crust and smoothing out large air pockets in ice cream. Sprinkle with half the nuts and half the preserves or topping. Spread with another pint ice cream. Repeat nuts and topping. Spread with remaining ice cream. Place in freezer immediately. Freeze 4 hours or longer until filling is firm. Prepare Meringue Topping. Remove pie from freezer. Spread Meringue Topping over filling as evenly as possible to insulate ice cream. Seal carefully to edge of crust. Return pie to freezer. Preheat oven to 475F (245C). Place pie on a 12- to 14-inch pizza pan or baking sheet. This will help deflect heat evenly toward center of pie. Bake 3 to 5 minutes until topping is golden brown. Serve immediately or return to freezer. Makes 8 to 10 servings.

Rainbow Loaf

Frozen Nesselrode Pie

Cut this extra-rich dessert into small servings.

1 (9-inch) Graham-Cracker Crust, page 31
2/3 cup sugar
2 tablespoons cornstarch
1 envelope unflavored gelatin
1-1/3 cups milk
3 egg yolks
1 teaspoon vanilla extract
1/2 cup candied chopped citrus peel

1/2 cup raisins
1/2 cup halved maraschino cherries
2 tablespoons brandy, if desired
1/4 cup chestnut spread or puree, if desired
1/2 pint whipping cream (1 cup)
10 Chocolate Leaves, page 187
10 whole maraschino cherries with stems

Prepare crust and set aside to cool. Combine sugar, cornstarch and gelatin in a medium saucepan. In a medium bowl, beat milk and egg yolks until smooth. Gradually stir into sugar mixture. Stir constantly over medium heat until mixture thickens and comes to a full boil. Stir and boil 1 minute. Remove from heat. Stir in vanilla, citrus peel, raisins and halved maraschino cherries. Add brandy and chestnut spread or puree, if desired. Refrigerate until mixture is cooler than room temperature. Beat cream until stiff peaks form. Fold into fruit mixture. Spoon into cooled crust. Freeze 4 hours or longer until filling is firm. Prepare Chocolate Leaves and refrigerate or freeze. Remove pie from freezer about 10 minutes before cutting. Garnish with Chocolate Leaves and whole maraschino cherries. Makes 10 servings.

Cranberry Chiffon Freeze

For individual servings, use twelve 2-inch graham-cracker tart shells.

1 (9-inch) Graham-Cracker Crust, page 31
1 (8-oz.) can crushed pineapple (1 cup)
Water
1 (3-oz.) pkg. orange-flavor gelatin
1 (16-oz.) can whole-berry cranberry sauce

1/2 pint whipping cream (1 cup)
1/3 cup powdered sugar
2 thin orange slices, if desired
Mint leaves, if desired

Prepare crust and set aside to cool. Drain pineapple, reserving liquid. Add water to liquid to measure 1 cup. Pour into a small saucepan. Bring to a boil. Place gelatin in a medium bowl. Pour boiling water mixture over gelatin. Stir until gelatin is dissolved. Add drained pineapple and cranberry sauce, stirring to break up sauce. Refrigerate until mixture has consistency of unbeaten egg whites. Beat cream until stiff peaks form. Fold in powdered sugar. Fold into cranberry mixture until blended. If necessary, refrigerate until mixture holds firm mounds when dropped from a spoon. Spoon into cooled crust. Freeze 4 hours or longer until filling is firm. Remove from freezer about 10 minutes before cutting. If desired, cut each orange slice into 4 wedges and garnish pie with orange wedges and mint leaves. Makes 8 servings.

Holiday Ice-Cream Pie

Surprise guests at a tree-trimming party with pumpkin or eggnog ice cream in a crunchy crust.

Single-Crust Basic Pastry, page 14
1/4 cup butter
1/3 cup packed brown sugar
1/2 cup chopped pecans

1/2 gal. pumpkin or eggnog ice cream
Sweetened Whipped Cream, page 185
16 pecan halves

Prepare dough for pastry. Review Baked Pie Shells, pages 8 and 9. Preheat oven to 475F (245C). On a lightly floured surface, roll out dough to a 12-inch circle. Fit into a 9-inch pie pan. Fold dough under for a raised edge. Make a high fluting. With a fork, prick bottom and sides of un-baked pie shell at 1/2-inch intervals. In a small bowl, mix butter and brown sugar until smooth. Stir in chopped pecans. Sprinkle evenly over bottom of pie shell. Bake 8 to 10 minutes or until crust is browned and sugar mixture is bubbly. Cool slightly. Chill in freezer about 30 minutes before making pie. Stir ice cream to soften slightly. Spoon into chilled shell, mounding in center. Place in freezer immediately. Freeze 2 hours or longer until filling is firm. Serve frozen. Garnish with Sweetened Whipped Cream and pecan halves. Pie may be returned to freezer after garnishing. Makes 8 servings.

Variation

Holiday Alaska Pie: Decrease ice cream to 5 cups. Top filling with Meringue Topping or any variation, page 134, and proceed as for Baked Alaska Pie, page 160.

Chocolate-Chip Mint Pie

Folding melted chocolate into cold whipped cream creates small chips of chocolate.

1 (9-inch) Chocolate-Cookie Crust, page 31
4 (1-oz.) squares semisweet chocolate
1 pint whipping cream (2 cups)

3/4 cup powdered sugar
1/4 cup white crème de menthe or
  peppermint schnapps

Prepare crust and set aside to cool. Melt chocolate in a small saucepan over low heat. Keep melted chocolate warm. Combine cream and powdered sugar in a large bowl. Beat until stiff peaks form. Fold in crème de menthe or schnapps. Refrigerate 15 minutes. Drizzle melted chocolate over whipped cream and fold in. Spoon into cooled crust. Freeze 3 hours or longer until filling is firm. Serve frozen. Makes 8 servings.

*tip*

Chill a pie shell for a freezer pie in the freezer for about 15 minutes before adding the filling. This prevents the filling from melting or getting warm when it comes in contact with the shell.

Rocky Mocha Mousse

Chocolate and coffee combine in this rich freezer pie.

1 (9-inch) Chocolate-Cookie Crust,
   page 31
1/3 cup packed brown sugar
2 tablespoons cornstarch
1 envelope unflavored gelatin
1 tablespoon instant coffee granules
3 eggs, separated
1 cup milk

4 (1-oz.) squares semisweet chocolate
1/3 cup granulated sugar
3/4 cup chopped walnuts or pecans
3/4 pint whipping cream (1-1/2 cups)
3 tablespoons Kahlúa or other
   coffee liqueur
Chocolate Curls, page 187, or
   candied coffee beans

Prepare crust and set aside to cool. In a medium saucepan, combine brown sugar, cornstarch, gelatin and coffee granules. In a small bowl, beat egg yolks and milk until smooth. Gradually stir into coffee mixture. Stir constantly over medium heat until mixture thickens and comes to a full boil. Remove from heat. Break chocolate into pieces. Add to coffee mixture. Stir until chocolate is completely melted. Pour into a medium bowl. Place plastic wrap on surface of mixture to prevent a film from forming. Refrigerate about 1 hour until cooled to room temperature, stirring occasionally. Beat egg whites until soft peaks form. Gradually beat in granulated sugar. Continue beating until stiff peaks form. Stir about 1 cup egg whites into chocolate mixture. Fold in remaining egg whites. Spoon 2 cups chocolate mixture into cooled crust. Spread evenly. Sprinkle with nuts. Refrigerate. Beat cream until stiff peaks form. Fold in liqueur. Set aside 1 cup whipped cream mixture. Fold remaining whipped cream into remaining chocolate mixture. If necessary, refrigerate until mixture holds firm mounds when dropped from a spoon. Spoon into crust and spread over nuts, mounding in center. Spoon or pipe reserved whipped cream mixture around edge of filling. Garnish with Chocolate Curls or candied coffee beans. Freeze 4 hours or longer until filling is firm. Remove from freezer about 10 minutes before cutting. Makes 8 servings.

 *tip*

To whip well, cream must be very cold. If your kitchen is warm, place the bowl and beaters in the freezer for several minutes before whipping the cream.

How to Make Rocky Mocha Mousse

1/Spread chocolate and whipped cream mixture over nuts.

2/Garnish pie with Chocolate Curls.

Half & Half Pie

Half vanilla and half orange sherbet with a crisp chocolate coating.

1 (9-inch) Gingersnap Crust, page 31	**1/3 cup chopped walnuts or pecans**
1 qt. vanilla ice cream	**1/2 cup semisweet chocolate pieces**
1 qt. orange sherbet	**2 tablespoons vegetable oil**

Prepare crust and cool slightly. Chill in freezer about 30 minutes before making pie. Place ice cream and sherbet in separate bowls. Stir to soften to a thick spreading consistency. Spread half the vanilla ice cream in chilled crust. Top with all the sherbet, mounding in center. Spread with an even layer of vanilla ice cream. Sprinkle with nuts. Place in freezer immediately. Place chocolate pieces and oil in a small saucepan. Stir frequently over low heat until melted and smooth. Cool slightly. Remove pie from freezer. Pour chocolate mixture over mounded pie filling. Use a spoon to spread part way down the mound. Place in freezer immediately. Freeze 4 hours or longer until filling is firm. Serve frozen. Makes 8 servings.

The Bakery Shop

Display these delicacies on your prettiest platter.

Turn the pages of this section and you might—just for a minute—forget where you are and imagine yourself in a bakery shop in the heart of Paris, Vienna or Rome. And you'll be surprised at how easy it is to duplicate some of their specialties.

Start with Glazed Fruit Tartlets made with Sweet Butter Pastry. They're so appealing and colorful that they'll disappear quickly. Your next accomplishment could be Pecan Tarts or Custard Tarts. The shells for these are larger than the tartlet shells because they are made by molding circles of dough into muffin cups. For a still larger shell, use the recipe for Tart Shells. They are made by molding circles of dough around the outside of muffin cups. Fill these larger tart shells with a cream filling, chiffon filling or freezer pie filling. At this point, your bakery shop repertoire could include Peach Dumplings in Almond Pastry.

Once you've built your confidence with several tart and dumpling successes, move on to choux pastries. Cream Puffs and Profiteroles are not at all difficult if you follow the directions. And they are truly the epitome of elegant desserts.

Your first venture with puff pastry should be one of the fruit turnovers. The fillings are uncomplicated so you can concentrate on the pastry itself. The recipe for Assorted Sweet Turnovers calls for ordinary staples such as peanut butter, jelly, marmalade and canned pie filling. Spicy Banana Turnovers are filled with sliced bananas and spiced with cinnamon.

For something completely different, try Pistachio Coils. They are made with filo sheets. If pistachio nuts aren't available, use pecans or walnuts.

You'll soon be an expert at making rich Napoleons and exotic Baklava. During the holidays, surprise everyone with a Christmas Wreath made with choux pastry and Cream Horns made with puff pastry.

For a Bakery Shop party, take advantage of your freezer. Up to 1 month ahead, prepare cream-puff shells, tart shells and shells for cream horns. Wrap them well and store them in the freezer where they won't become crushed. Freeze unbaked fruit turnovers. The day before your party, prepare Pistachio Coils and Baklava. On the day of the party, thaw and fill the shells you've stored. Thaw and bake the turnovers. Arrange the finished pastries on doilies on your most ornate china or glass plates. Serve them from a buffet or a tea cart with tea and coffee. Then sit back and enjoy the applause. ◆

Celebration Dinner for Four

Champagne
Hors d'Oeuvre Puffs, page 37
Shrimp Cocktail
Chicken Sesame, page 73
Snow Peas & Mushrooms
Julienne Carrots
Profiteroles, page 178

Assorted Sweet Turnovers

When you have puff pastry scraps, make these coffee-break or after-school snacks.

1 cup Classic Puff Pastry, page 22, or
   Quick Puff Pastry, page 24
1 egg white
1/4 teaspoon salt

Assorted fillings for each turnover,
   see below
1 teaspoon sugar

Assorted Fillings for each turnover:
1 tablespoon peanut butter and
   1 teaspoon jelly
1 rounded tablespoon marmalade or other jam

1 rounded tablespoon canned pie filling
1 rounded tablespoon applesauce

Review Puff Pastry Techniques, page 21. Prepare dough for pastry. On a lightly floured surface, roll out dough to a 15'' x 10'' rectangle. With a large knife or pastry cutter, cut rectangle into six 4-1/2-inch squares. To make glaze, mix egg and salt in a small bowl until foamy. Lightly brush glaze around edge of each square, making a 1/4-inch border and being careful not to let glaze drip over edge. Place desired filling on square and spread to a triangle on half the square. Fold half the square over filling, matching opposite points and making a triangle. Firmly press edges together with your fingers. Crimp with a fork, if desired. Cut two 1-inch slits in top of each turnover. Place turnovers on ungreased baking sheets. Refrigerate 15 minutes. Preheat oven to 425F (220C). Bake turnovers 12 to 15 minutes until lightly browned. Brush with glaze and sprinkle generously with sugar. Bake 2 to 3 minutes longer. Cool slightly. Makes 6 servings.

Spicy Banana Turnovers

Especially delicious when they are piping hot.

1 cup Classic Puff Pastry, page 22, or
   Quick Puff Pastry, page 24
1 tablespoon sugar
1/8 teaspoon ground cinnamon

1 egg white
1/4 teaspoon salt
1 medium banana
1 tablespoon butter

Review Puff Pastry Techniques, page 21. Prepare dough for pastry. On a lightly floured surface, roll out dough to a 15'' x 10'' rectangle. With a large knife or pastry cutter, cut rectangle into six 4-1/2-inch squares. Mix sugar and cinnamon in a small bowl. To make glaze, mix egg white and salt until foamy. Lightly brush glaze around edge of each square, making a 1/4-inch border and being careful not to let glaze drip over edge. Peel banana, cut in half lengthwise and slice thinly. Divide slices equally among the 6 squares, shaping into a triangle on half of each square. Using 2 teaspoons sugar mixture, sprinkle evenly on each banana triangle. Cut butter into 6 equal pieces. Place 1 butter piece on each banana triangle. Fold half of square over filling, matching opposite points and making a triangle. Firmly press edges together with your fingers. Crimp with a fork, if desired. Cut two 1-inch slits in top of each turnover. Place on an ungreased baking sheet. Refrigerate 15 minutes. Preheat oven to 425F (220C). Bake turnovers 12 to 15 minutes until lightly browned. Lightly brush with glaze and sprinkle with remaining sugar mixture. Bake 2 to 3 minutes longer until glossy. Cool slightly. Makes 6 servings.

Apple Turnovers

If you have overripe apples in your fruit bowl, make a batch of old-fashioned turnovers.

2 cups Classic Puff Pastry, page 22, or
   Quick Puff Pastry, page 24
3 medium apples
About 1/2 cup water
1/4 cup packed brown sugar

2 tablespoons butter
1/4 teaspoon ground cinnamon
1 egg white
1/4 teaspoon salt
Drizzle Icing, page 93

Review Puff Pastry Techniques, page 21. Prepare dough for pastry. Peel, core and chop apples. Place in a medium saucepan. Add 1/2 cup water. Cover and place over medium-low heat. Cook, stirring occasionally, until apples are very soft, about 25 minutes. If necessary, add more water 1 tablespoon at a time to prevent scorching or remove cover so liquid can evaporate. When apples are soft and their consistency resembles applesauce, stir in brown sugar, butter and cinnamon. Cook 3 to 5 minutes. Cool to room temperature. Cut dough into 2 equal portions. On a lightly floured surface, roll out 1 portion to a 15" x 9" rectangle. With a large knife or pastry cutter, cut rectangle into six 4-1/2-inch squares. To make glaze, mix egg white and salt until foamy. Lightly brush glaze around edge of each square, making a 1/4-inch border and being careful not to let glaze drip over edge. Place 1 rounded tablespoon cooked apples slightly off-center on each square. Spread slightly to make a triangle on half of each square. Fold half of square over filling, matching opposite points and making a triangle. Firmly press edges together with your fingers. Crimp with a fork, if desired. Cut two 1-inch slits in top of each turnover. Place on an ungreased 17" x 11" baking sheet. Refrigerate 15 minutes. Preheat oven to 425F (220C). Bake turnovers 12 to 15 minutes until lightly browned. Lightly brush with glaze. Bake 2 to 3 minutes longer until glossy. Cool slightly. Prepare Drizzle Icing. Immediately drizzle over turnovers. Makes 12 servings.

Tart Shells   *Photo on pages 2 and 3.*

Mound with any cream, chiffon or freezer pie filling, pages 132 to 165.

Double-Crust Basic Pastry, page 14, or
   Almond or Pecan Pastry, page 20

Prepare dough for pastry. Review Rolling Out, page 8. Cut dough into 4 equal portions. On a lightly floured surface, roll out 1 portion to a 10-inch circle. Using a small plastic lid or inverted bowl as a guide, cut three 4-1/2-inch circles. Set aside. Lightly knead scraps. Let rest 1 minute. Roll out and cut another 4-1/2-inch circle. Repeat with each portion of dough, making a total of 16 circles. Use muffin pans with 2-3/4-inch cups as tart molds. Turn the pans upside down on a large baking sheet. If you don't have 16 muffin cups, wrap and refrigerate extra circles while preparing first batch. Center 1 circle over 1 inverted muffin cup. Gently press circle down around sides, pinching 4 equally spaced pleats. Repeat with remaining circles, placing each one over a separate muffin cup. Prick bottoms with a fork. Refrigerate 15 minutes. Preheat oven to 450F (230C). Bake tarts on inverted pans 10 to 12 minutes until lightly browned. Remove from oven and cool before filling. Makes 16 tart shells.

Glazed Fruit Tartlets   *Photo on page 181.*

Creamy filling is layered with fruit and topped with an apple glaze.

Sweet Butter Pastry, page 19
Creamy Filling, see below
Apple Glaze, below
2 to 3 cups any combination of the following
     fruit: drained canned orange segments or
     fresh orange slices; fresh or drained
     canned grapes, peach or apricot slices;
     fresh or frozen blueberries or raspberries;
     fresh bananas or strawberries; drained
     canned mixed fruit or maraschino cherries

Creamy Filling:
1 (3-oz.) pkg. cream cheese   **1/4 cup fruit-flavor yogurt**
1 tablespoon sugar

Prepare dough for pastry. Preheat oven to 375F (190C). Shape dough into a 5-inch square. Cut square into thirds in one direction. Divide each third into 6 portions, making 18 portions. Use your fingers to press each portion into a 3" x 2" tartlet pan or a 2-3/4-inch muffin cup. If using tartlet pans, press dough evenly into fluting and use your fingers to trim off at edge of pan: If using muffin cups, press evenly on bottom and up sides almost to top of each cup. With a fork, prick bottom of each shell 2 or 3 times. Bake 15 to 20 minutes until golden brown. Remove shells from pans. Cool completely. Prepare Creamy Filling and Apple Glaze. Spread 1 tablespoon Creamy Filling in bottom of each shell. Arrange fruit in an even layer or mound in center on filling. Immediately spoon 1 to 2 teaspoons cooled Apple Glaze over fruit. Serve immediately or refrigerate and serve within 8 hours. Makes 18 servings.

Creamy Filling:
In a small bowl, combine cream cheese and sugar. Mix until smooth. Gradually stir in yogurt until mixture is smooth.

Apple Glaze

Especially for Glazed Fruit Tartlets, above, and French Puff Tart, page 105.

1/2 cup sugar   **1 cup apple juice**
4 teaspoons cornstarch

Combine sugar and cornstarch in a medium saucepan. Gradually stir in apple juice. Stir constantly over medium heat until mixture thickens and comes to a full boil. Stir and boil 1 minute. Cool to room temperature.

Custard Tarts

Miniature custard pies can be made with any of the variations listed below.

Double-Crust Basic Pastry, page 14
2-2/3 cups milk
4 eggs
1/2 cup sugar

1/4 teaspoon salt
1 teaspoon vanilla extract
1/4 teaspoon ground nutmeg

Prepare dough for pastry. Review Rolling Out, page 8. Cut dough into 2 equal portions. On a lightly floured surface, roll out 1 portion a little larger than a 12" x 8" rectangle. Using a small plastic lid or inverted bowl as a guide, cut six 4-inch circles. Set scraps aside. Roll out remaining portion of dough and cut 6 more circles. Gently knead scraps together. Roll out and cut 6 more circles to make a total of 18 circles. Gently ease each circle into a 2-3/4-inch muffin cup, making evenly spaced tucks around edge of each circle. If necessary, stretch dough to make a 1/4-inch or higher rim above cup. Preheat oven to 400F (205C). In a medium saucepan, heat milk to scalding or just below boiling, about 180F (80C). In a medium bowl, combine eggs, sugar, salt and vanilla. Beat with a wire whip or rotary beater until smooth. Gradually stir in hot milk. Mix until blended. Pour a scant 1/4 cup egg mixture into each tart shell. Bake 25 to 30 minutes until custard is set and crust is light golden brown. Serve warm or chilled. Refrigerate cooled tarts. Makes 18 servings.

Variations

Substitute the filling from one of the following recipes: Valencia Custard Pie, page 127; Coconut Custard Pie, page 128; Pumpkin Pie, page 129; Maple Pumpkin Pie; page 131; Pumpkin & Sour Cream Pie, page 130. To make miniature Almond-Peach Custard Pies, page 126, coarsely chop the peach slices and proceed as directed.

Recipes in this book were developed with large eggs. Different size eggs may cause a difference in the consistency of the finished pie or pastry.

Pecan Tarts

Little nut pies to bake, freeze and have on hand during the holiday season.

Double-Crust Basic Pastry, page 14
1/3 cup butter, melted
3 eggs
1 cup sugar

1/2 teaspoon salt
1 teaspoon vanilla extract
1 cup light corn syrup
1 cup chopped pecans

Prepare dough for pastry. Review Rolling Out, page 8. Cut dough into 2 equal portions. On a lightly floured surface, roll out 1 portion a little larger than a 12" x 8" rectangle. Using a small plastic lid or inverted bowl as a guide, cut six 4-inch circles. Set scraps aside. Roll out remaining portion of dough and cut 6 more circles. Gently knead scraps together. Roll out and cut 6 more 4-inch circles for a total of 18 circles. Gently ease each circle into a 2-3/4-inch muffin cup, making evenly spaced tucks around edge of circle. If necessary, stretch dough to make a 1/4-inch or higher rim above cup. Preheat oven to 375F (190C). Combine butter, eggs, sugar, salt and vanilla in a medium bowl. Beat with a wire whip or rotary beater until smooth. Stir in corn syrup until blended. Place 1 scant tablespoon pecans in each tart shell. Add about 3 tablespoons egg mixture. To making filling cups easier, use a 1/4-cup measure minus 1 tablespoon filling to fill each cup. Bake about 25 minutes until filling is set and crust is light golden brown. Makes 18 servings.

Variations

Substitute the filling from Spicy Walnut Pie, page 121, for the custard-nut filling.

Peach Dumplings

Nutty pastry filled with peaches and a golden sauce.

Double-Crust Almond Pastry, page 20, or
   Basic Pastry, page 14
1/3 cup apricot-pineapple preserves
2 teaspoons quick-cooking tapioca

1/3 cup sugar
1/4 teaspoon ground nutmeg
2-1/2 cups sliced peeled fresh peaches
Spicy Thickened Cream, page 180

Prepare dough for pastry. Review Rolling Out, page 8. In a medium bowl, combine preserves, tapioca, sugar and nutmeg. Add peach slices and toss to coat with preserve mixture. Lightly grease a 17" x 11" baking sheet. Set aside. Preheat oven to 375F (190C). On a lightly floured surface, roll out dough to an 18" x 12" rectangle. With a knife or pastry cutter, cut into six 6-inch squares. Place 1/2 cup peach mixture in center of each square. Lightly moisten edge of each square with water. Fold corners to center, gently pressing edges together near top. Carefully place dumplings on prepared baking sheet. Bake about 40 minutes until pastry is golden. Prepare Spicy Thickened Cream. Serve dumplings warm. Pour cream over each dumpling. Makes 6 servings.

Whole-Apple Dumplings

Basting these dumplings with Cinnamon Sauce gives them a glossy, crisp crust.

Double-Crust Basic Pastry, page 14
1/4 cup packed brown sugar
2 tablespoons granulated sugar
1/4 teaspoon ground cinnamon
1/4 teaspoon ground nutmeg
1/4 teaspoon ground allspice

6 medium apples
   (about 2-1/2 inches in diameter)
1/4 cup raisins, if desired
2 tablespoons butter
Cinnamon Sauce, see below

Cinnamon Sauce:
1/3 cup granulated sugar
1/3 cup packed brown sugar
1/2 teaspoon ground cinnamon

2 tablespoons butter
1-1/2 cups water

Prepare dough for pastry. Review Rolling Out, page 8. Combine brown sugar, granulated sugar, cinnamon, nutmeg and allspice in a small bowl. Peel and core apples, leaving them whole. After preparing each apple, roll in sugar mixture to prevent browning. Set aside. Grease a 13" x 9" baking pan. Set aside. Divide pastry into 6 equal portions. Roll out each portion a little larger than a 7-inch square. With a knife or pastry cutter, trim to a 7-inch square. Reserve scraps. Place a sugared apple in center of each square. If desired, spoon 1/6th of the raisins into center of each apple. Spoon 1 teaspoon butter and about 1 teaspoon remaining sugar mixture into each center. Lightly moisten edges of squares with water. Fold corners up over apple. Gently press together, joining edges of square. Place dumplings in prepared pan. Preheat oven to 375F (190C). Fold down the 4 points at sides of each dumpling in the same direction to make a pinwheel pattern. Roll out remaining scraps. Cut leaves with a pastry cutter or hors d'oeuvre cutter. Brush tops of dumplings with water. Press leaves on tops and part way down sides. Pinch a piece of dough to the top for a stem. Bake 30 minutes. While dumplings are baking, prepare Cinnamon Sauce. Pour over dumplings, basting each 2 or 3 times. Bake about 15 minutes longer until pastry is golden brown, basting dumplings once with sauce. Remove from oven. Baste again. Use a metal spatula to place dumplings on a platter or in dessert bowls. Serve hot. Spoon Cinnamon Sauce over each serving. Makes 6 servings.

Cinnamon Sauce:
Combine all ingredients in a small saucepan. Bring to a full boil. Boil 5 minutes.

*tip*

After chopping nuts for garnish, place them in a strainer and toss gently.
This removes small pieces of nuts and skins so your garnish will look more professional.

Cream Horns   *Photo on page 181.*

For delightful crispness, fill these pastry horns as close to serving time as possible.

1 cup Classic Puff Pastry, page 22, or	**2 tablespoons strawberry jam or**
Quick Puff Pastry, page 24	**raspberry jelly**
1 egg white	**Sweetened Whipped Cream, page 185**
1/4 teaspoon salt	**1 tablespoon chopped walnuts or pecans,**
Granulated sugar	**chocolate sprinkles or crushed nut brittle**

Review Puff Pastry Techniques, page 21. Have ready nine 4" x 1-1/2" metal horn molds or make as directed below. Prepare dough for pastry. On a lightly floured surface, roll out dough to a 15" x 10" rectangle. Cut nine 15" x 1" strips. Starting with 1 corner of 1 strip, wrap end tightly around tip of mold. Wind strip spiral-fashion up mold, overlapping 1/2 inch. Place with end of strip down on an ungreased baking sheet. Repeat with remaining strips and molds. Refrigerate 15 minutes. Preheat oven to 425F (220C). Bake horns 10 to 12 minutes until golden brown. Mix egg white and salt until slightly foamy. Brush on baked horns and sprinkle generously with sugar. Bake 2 to 3 minutes longer. Remove from oven. Remove molds from horns. Turn off oven. Return horns to oven 10 minutes to dry out. Leave oven door slightly ajar. Remove from oven and cool completely. Stir jam or jelly until spreadable. Using a small brush, coat inside of horns with jam or jelly. Prepare Sweetened Whipped Cream. Spoon or pipe into horns. Sprinkle whipped cream with nuts, chocolate sprinkles or brittle. Refrigerate until ready to serve. Makes 9 servings.

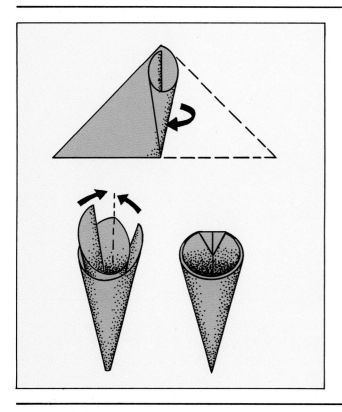

How to Make Pastry Horn Molds

Cut a piece of foil 12 inches square. Fold edges to make an 8-inch square. Fold in half on the diagonal to make a triangle. Holding your finger in the center of the long side, curve one of the side points around to meet top point of triangle, making a cone. Remove your finger and wrap other point around cone. Fold down open end of cone, where 3 points meet, about 1 inch.

Napoleons

The French name for this pastry is mille feuille and it means a thousand leaves.

Napoleon Cream, see below
Pastry Rectangles, below
1 (1-oz.) square semisweet chocolate

1 teaspoon shortening or butter
1 cup powdered sugar
4 to 5 teaspoons milk

Napoleon Cream:
1/3 cup sugar
2 tablespoons cornstarch
1/4 teaspoon salt

2 egg yolks
1-1/2 cups milk
1/2 teaspoon vanilla extract

Prepare Napoleon Cream. Prepare Pastry Rectangles. Select flattest rectangle for top and set aside. Spread half the Napoleon Cream on each of remaining 2 rectangles. Place one filled rectangle on a baking sheet. Place second filled rectangle on first one. Top with reserved rectangle. Melt chocolate and shortening or butter over very low heat, stirring until smooth. Cool slightly. Combine powdered sugar and 4 teaspoons milk to make icing. Stir until smooth. Add more milk 1/2 teaspoon at a time until mixture makes a thick ribbon when dropped from a spoon. Spoon chocolate into a pastry tube with a 1/8-inch, round tip. Spread white icing on pastry. Immediately pipe chocolate in parallel lines across icing about 3/4 inch apart. Immediately draw a small knife lengthwise down center of icing. This will pull chocolate into points. Draw the knife in the opposite direction on each side of the center line. Refrigerate 30 minutes or longer. Cut with a serrated knife. Makes 8 servings.

Napoleon Cream:
In a medium saucepan, combine sugar, cornstarch and salt. In a small bowl, mix egg yolks and milk until smooth. Gradually stir into sugar mixture. Stir constantly over medium heat until mixture comes to a full boil. Stir and boil 1 minute. Stir in vanilla. Pour into a small bowl. Place plastic wrap on surface of mixture to prevent a film from forming. Refrigerate about 1 hour.

Pastry Rectangles

Flaky pastry layers to use with Napoleons, above, and Neapolitan Napoleons, opposite.

1 cup Classic Puff Pastry, page 22, or
   Quick Puff Pastry, page 24

Review Puff Pastry Techniques, page 21. Prepare dough for pastry. Select a 14" x 10" rimmed baking sheet. On a lightly floured surface, roll out dough to a 16" x 12" rectangle or 2 inches larger than baking sheet. If dough is difficult to roll, let rest 3 to 5 minutes. Keep work surface lightly floured to prevent dough from stretching unevenly. Invert baking sheet. Fold dough rectangle in half. Drape over one half of inverted baking sheet. Unfold to cover baking sheet. With a fork, prick dough at 1/2-inch intervals. Refrigerate 15 minutes. Preheat oven to 450F (220C). Bake rectangle 3 minutes. Deflate any large bubbles with a fork. Bake about 9 minutes longer until light golden brown. Remove baked rectangle from baking sheet and cool on a wire rack. Trim edges to make a flat 12" x 9" rectangle. Cut lengthwise into 12" x 3" rectangles. Makes 3 rectangles.

How to Make Napoleons

1/Prepare Pastry Rectangles by draping dough over the bottom of a baking sheet. Prick at 1/2-inch intervals with a fork.

2/Draw a small knife lengthwise down center and each side of icing, crossing chocolate lines and pulling them into points.

Neapolitan Napoleons   *Photo on page 181.*

Chocolate and vanilla pudding layered with fresh strawberries.

Pastry Rectangles, opposite
1/4 cup sugar
1 tablespoon cornstarch
Dash salt
2 egg yolks
1 cup milk

1/4 teaspoon vanilla extract
1 (1-oz.) square semisweet chocolate
1/2 pint whipping cream (1 cup)
3 cups fresh small strawberries
Chocolate Curls, page 187, or
    chocolate sprinkles

Prepare Pastry Rectangles. Select flattest rectangle for top and set aside. Place sugar, cornstarch and salt in a medium saucepan. Combine egg yolks and milk. Stir into sugar mixture. Stir constantly over medium heat until mixture comes to a full boil. Stir and boil 1 minute. Stir in vanilla. Remove 1/2 cup mixture and set aside. Add chocolate to remaining hot mixture in saucepan. Stir until chocolate is melted. Place plastic wrap on surface of both mixtures to prevent films from forming. Cool. Whip cream until firm peaks form. Fold into reserved vanilla mixture. Refrigerate about 1 hour. Wash and hull berries. Cut points off any long berries. Spread chocolate mixture on 1 pastry rectangle. Spread 1/2 cup vanilla mixture on another rectangle. Arrange berries in 3 rows on vanilla mixture. Spread enough vanilla mixture over berries to just cover and fill in spaces. Place berry-covered rectangle on chocolate rectangle. Top with reserved rectangle. Spoon or pipe remaining vanilla mixture on top rectangle. Garnish with any leftover berries and Chocolate Curls or sprinkles. Cut with a serrated knife. Makes 8 servings.

Jalousie

Jalousie is French for louvered shutters, which is what this pastry resembles.

1 cup Classic Puff Pastry, page 22, or
  Quick Puff Pastry, page 24
1/4 cup apple butter, strawberry jam or
  apricot jam

1 egg white
Granulated sugar

Review Puff Pastry Techniques, page 21. Prepare dough for pastry. On a lightly floured surface, roll out dough to a rectangle 1/8 inch thick. Cut a 10'' x 4'' rectangle from the center. Fold rectangle in half lengthwise. With a sharp knife, cut across rectangle from fold to within 1/2 inch of cut edges at 1/4-inch intervals. Lightly knead trimmings together. Let rest 3 to 5 minutes. Roll out a little larger than a 10'' x 4'' rectangle. This rectangle will be thinner than the first. Place on a baking sheet. Spoon apple butter or jam lengthwise down center of rectangle and spread to within 1 inch of edge. Lightly brush edge with water. Unfold cut rectangle and straighten. Carefully lift it onto rectangle on baking sheet, matching edges. Press edges together with your fingers. Cut off about 1/8 inch all around to make edges even. Refrigerate 15 minutes. Preheat oven to 425F (220C). Bake pastry 25 minutes. Beat egg white until slightly foamy. Brush over pastry. Sprinkle generously with sugar. Bake about 5 minutes longer until golden brown. Cool slightly before serving. Makes 8 servings.

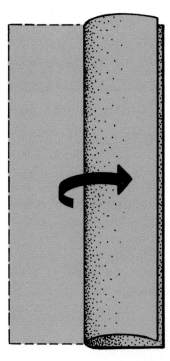

Folded dough rectangle for Jalousie.   Rectangle cut at 1/4-inch intervals.

Almond Pithiviers

The photo for Ham Pithiviers, page 45, shows how the finished pastry should look.

**2 cups Classic Puff Pastry, page 22, or
   Quick Puff Pastry, page 24
1 cup finely ground blanched almonds
2 tablespoons butter, softened
1/3 cup granulated sugar
2 tablespoons apricot preserves**

**2 egg yolks
1 tablespoon rum
1 tablespoon milk or cream
Egg Glaze, page 20
1 teaspoon powdered sugar**

Review Puff Pastry Techniques, page 21. Prepare dough for pastry. In a medium bowl, combine almonds, butter, granulated sugar, preserves, egg yolks, rum and milk or cream. Stir until blended. Cut dough into 2 equal portions. On a lightly floured surface, roll out 1 portion to a 9-inch square. Using an 8-inch cake pan as a guide, cut an 8-inch circle from center of square. Place circle on an ungreased baking sheet. Prepare Egg Glaze. Lightly brush glaze around edge of circle, making a 1-inch border and being careful not to let glaze drip over edge. Place almond mixture in center of circle and spread to inside edge of glazed border. Roll out remaining dough to a 9-inch square and cut an 8-inch circle. Place over almond mixture, stretching as necessary to match edges and deflating any air pockets. Press edges together firmly with your fingers to seal. Use the point of a knife to make a small hole in center of top pastry. Scallop edge with the back of a knife at 1/4-inch intervals. Brush top with Egg Glaze, being careful not to let glaze drip over edge. With a small sharp knife, make a design on pastry using 1/16-inch-deep cuts. Do not cut all the way through dough. Long curved lines radiating from the center are traditional but any pattern may be used. Refrigerate 30 minutes or longer. Preheat oven to 450F (230C). Bake pastry 15 minutes. Reduce heat to 400F (205C). Bake about 20 minutes longer until pastry is puffed and golden brown. Place powdered sugar in a small strainer or sifter. Sprinkle over top of pastry. Return to oven. Bake about 10 minutes longer until sugar is melted. Cool slightly. Serve warm. Makes 8 servings.

 *tip*

*   Keep Main-Dish Pastry Puffs, page 174, in your freezer. When you need a quick and elegant dessert, reheat them in a 350F (175C) oven for about 5 minutes, and serve them topped with sliced fruit and whipped cream.*

Profiteroles

Tiny cream puffs filled with cream or ice cream and topped with chocolate sauce.

1 pint vanilla ice cream or
    Vanilla Pastry Cream, below
	1 tablespoon Kahlúa or other coffee liqueur,
	    if desired

Choux Pastry made with 3 eggs, page 28	Sweetened Whipped Cream, if desired,
2 tablespoons sugar	page 185
1 (12-oz.) jar chocolate ice-cream topping or	Chocolate Dipped Maraschino Cherries,
1/2 cup chocolate syrup	if desired, page 187

If using Vanilla Pastry Cream, prepare at least 2 hours before serving. Lightly grease a 17" x 11" baking sheet. Preheat oven to 400F (205C). Prepare dough for pastry, adding sugar with first egg. Drop by slightly rounded teaspoons about 1 inch apart on prepared baking sheet. Bake about 30 minutes until puffed and dry. Remove from baking sheet. Cool. With a sharp knife, cut off tops. Generously fill bottoms of puffs with ice cream or Vanilla Pastry Cream. Replace tops. Refrigerate cream-filled puffs up to 2 hours. Puffs filled with ice cream are best served immediately but may be prepared up to 5 days ahead and frozen in a food-storage container. Combine chocolate sauce or syrup and liqueur, if desired. Place 4 or 5 filled puffs in a parfait dish or dessert glass. Spoon chocolate mixture over puffs. If desired, garnish with Sweetened Whipped Cream and Chocolate-Dipped Cherries. Serve immediately. Makes 8 or 9 servings.

Vanilla Pastry Cream

Basic vanilla pudding for filling éclairs, tarts and other sweet pastries.

1/2 cup sugar	4 egg yolks
2 tablespoons cornstarch	2 cups milk
1/4 teaspoon salt	1/2 teaspoon vanilla extract

Combine sugar, cornstarch and salt in a medium saucepan. In a medium bowl, beat egg yolks and milk until smooth. Gradually stir into sugar mixture. Stir constantly over medium heat until mixture thickens and comes to a full boil. Stir and boil 1 minute. Stir in vanilla. Pour into a small bowl. Place plastic wrap on surface of pudding to prevent a film from forming. Refrigerate 2 hours or longer. Makes about 2 cups.

Variations

Chocolate Pastry Cream: Add 3 (1-ounce) broken squares semisweet chocolate with the vanilla. Stir until chocolate is melted.

Coffee Pastry Cream: Add 2 teaspoons instant coffee granules with the sugar.

Light Pastry Cream: Increase cornstarch to 3 tablespoons. Cook as directed. Cool to room temperature. Beat 1/2 pint (1 cup) whipping cream until stiff. Fold into cooled milk mixture.

Light Chocolate Pastry Cream: Prepare Chocolate Pastry Cream as directed above. Cool to room temperature. Beat 1/2 pint (1 cup) whipping cream until stiff. Fold into cooled milk mixture.

How to Make Profiteroles

1/Drop slightly rounded teaspoonfuls of dough onto lightly greased baking sheet.

2/Top puffs with chocolate topping or syrup. Garnish with whipped cream and Chocolate-Dipped Cherries.

Cream Puffs   *Photo on page 181.*

The easiest, most elegant dessert you could ever imagine!

Double recipe Sweetened Whipped Cream, page 185, single recipe Chocolate Whipped Cream, page 182, or Light Chocolate Pastry Cream, opposite

Choux Pastry made with 3 eggs, page 28 Powdered sugar

If using pastry cream, prepare at least 2 hours before serving. Lightly grease a baking sheet. Preheat oven to 400F (205C). Prepare dough for pastry. Using a 1/4-cup measure, drop mounds of dough about 3 inches apart on prepared baking sheet. Or, spoon dough into a pastry tube fitted with a 1/2-inch plain tip and pipe into 8 to 10 mounds about 2 inches in diameter and 1-1/2 inches high. Bake 35 to 40 minutes until golden brown, including any cracks formed during baking. Remove from oven. Cool. Prepare whipped cream if using for filling. Slit cooled puffs horizontally about 1/3 down from the top. Remove any soft dough inside puffs. Spoon or pipe filling into puffs. Replace tops. Sprinkle with powdered sugar. Serve immediately or refrigerate and serve within 2 hours. Makes 8 to 10 servings.

Éclairs   *Photo opposite.*

Oblong cream puffs are filled with pastry cream and iced with chocolate.

**2 cups Vanilla Pastry Cream, Chocolate
Pastry Cream or Coffee Pastry Cream,
page 178**

**Choux Pastry made with 3 eggs, page 28
Chocolate Icing, see below**

Chocolate Icing:
**2 (1-oz.) squares semisweet chocolate or
1/3 cup semisweet chocolate pieces
1 tablespoon butter**

**1/2 cup powdered sugar
1 to 2 tablespoons hot water**

At least 2 hours before serving, prepare pastry cream. Lightly grease a baking sheet. Preheat oven to 400F (205C). Prepare dough for pastry. Spoon into a pastry bag fitted with a 1/2-inch plain tip. Pipe dough onto prepared baking sheet in 4'' x 1'' fingers. Leave about 2 inches between fingers. Or, spoon 3 tablespoons dough onto baking sheet and use a small spatula to shape into fingers. Bake about 40 minutes until golden brown, including any cracks formed during baking. Remove from oven. Cool. Prepare Chocolate Icing. Spoon pastry cream into a pastry bag fitted with a 1/4- or 3/16-inch plain tip. Use a knife point to make a small hole in both ends of each baked pastry. Pipe cream into pastry through holes. Or, slice top off each baked pastry and spoon in filling; replace tops. Ice each filled pastry with about 2 teaspoons Chocolate Icing. Serve immediately or refrigerate and serve within 2 hours. Makes 10 to 12 servings.

Chocolate Icing:
In a small saucepan, melt chocolate and butter over low heat. Stir in powdered sugar and 1 tablespoon hot water. Stir until smooth. Add more hot water 1/2 teaspoon at a time until mixture drops off spoon in a thin ribbon.

Spicy Thickened Cream

Old-fashioned flavor for topping fruit pastries or pumpkin pies.

**1/2 pint whipping cream (1 cup)
1 tablespoon powdered sugar**

**1/8 teaspoon ground cinnamon
1/8 teaspoon ground nutmeg**

Beat cream until slightly thickened. Cream should not form soft peaks but mound very slightly when beaters are lifted. Fold in powdered sugar, cinnamon and nutmeg. Refrigerate until ready to serve. Makes about 1-1/2 cups.

On the top shelf, left to right: Pecan Coils, page 186; Cream Horns, page 173; and Cream Puffs, page 179, with Chocolate Whipped Cream, page 182. On the middle shelf, left to right: Cream Puffs, page 179, with Sweetened Whipped Cream, page 185; Éclairs, above; and Neapolitan Napoleons, page 175. On the bottom shelf, left to right: Glazed Fruit Tartlets, page 169, and Baklava, page 184.

Paris-Brest

A large ringed cream puff to fill with your favorite cream filling.

**Light Pastry Cream or Light Chocolate
 Pastry Cream, page 178, or
 double recipe Sweetened Whipped Cream,
 page 185**

**Choux Pastry made with 4 eggs, page 28
3 tablespoons sliced almonds
Powdered sugar**

If using pastry cream, prepare at least 2 hours before serving. Preheat oven to 400F (205C). Prepare dough for pastry. Spoon into a pastry bag fitted with a 1/2-inch plain tip or a star tip with a large opening. Lightly grease and flour a 17" x 11" or 14-inch, round baking sheet. Invert an 8-inch bowl or plate in center of prepared baking sheet and twist to mark a circle in the flour. Remove bowl. Being generous with dough, pipe 3 rings: the first, just inside the circle; the second, just outside the circle but slightly overlapping the first; the third, on top of the seam created by the first two. Sprinkle ring with almonds. Be sure none are sticking straight up as they will become too brown. With your fingers, lightly press almonds onto ring. Bake 40 to 45 minutes or until ring is golden brown, including any cracks formed during baking. Turn oven off. With a fork, prick ring in several places and leave in oven 5 minutes with oven door ajar. Remove from oven and cool completely. Prepare Sweetened Whipped Cream if using for filling. With a serrated knife, cut off top third of ring. Remove any soft dough inside ring. Pipe or spoon pastry cream or whipped cream into ring. Replace top of ring. Sprinkle generously with powdered sugar. Serve immediately or refrigerate and serve within 3 hours. Makes 8 to 10 servings.

Chocolate Whipped Cream

Melting chocolate in the cream assures a smooth mixture.

**1 (1-oz.) square semisweet chocolate or
 3 tablespoons semisweet chocolate pieces**

**1/2 pint whipping cream (1 cup)
2 tablespoons powdered sugar**

Place chocolate and 1/2 cup cream in a small saucepan. Stir frequently over low heat until chocolate is melted. Remove from heat and stir until mixture is blended and no chocolate specks remain. Pour into a small deep bowl. Add remaining cream. Refrigerate until cold. Beat until soft peaks form. If whipped cream is to be piped through a pastry tube, beat until stiff peaks form. Fold in powdered sugar. Refrigerate until ready to serve. If necessary, stir before serving. Makes about 2 cups.

Variation

Mocha Whipped Cream: Add 1 teaspoon instant coffee granules to chocolate and cream before heating.

Christmas Wreath *Photo on pages 2 and 3.*

Deck the halls with holly. Then garnish a Paris-Brest with colored fruit to look like holly.

Light Pastry Cream, page 178
Choux Pastry made with 4 eggs, page 28
1/4 cup chopped red maraschino cherries

1/4 cup chopped green candied pineapple
Whole maraschino cherries and
green candied pineapple

At least 2 hours before serving, prepare Light Pastry Cream. Preheat oven to 400F (205C). Prepare dough for pastry. Spoon into a pastry bag fitted with a 1/2-inch plain or star tip with a large opening. Lightly grease and flour a 17" x 11" or 14-inch, round baking sheet. Invert an 8-inch bowl or plate in center of prepared baking sheet and twist to mark a circle in the flour. Remove bowl. Being generous with dough, pipe 3 rings: the first, just inside the circle; the second, just outside the circle but slightly overlapping the first; the third, in a rick-rack pattern on top of the seam created by the first two. Bake 40 to 45 minutes until golden brown, including any cracks formed during baking. Turn oven off. With a fork, prick ring in several places. Leave in oven 5 minutes with oven door ajar. Remove from oven and cool completely. With a serrated knife, cut off top third of ring. Remove any soft dough inside ring. Fold chopped cherries and chopped pineapple into Light Pastry Cream. Spoon into ring, reserving about 3 teaspoons for garnish. Replace top of ring. Dab reserved pastry cream in 3 equally spaced spots around top of ring, making dabs about 2 inches long. Cut maraschino cherries in half. Place a cherry half in center of each dab. Thinly slice green pineapple and cut leaves from slices. Place leaves at sides of cherries to resemble holly and berries. Serve immediately or refrigerate and serve within 3 hours. Makes 8 to 10 servings.

Individual Paris-Brests

Cream puffs in the shape of rings.

Vanilla Pastry Cream, page 178, or
   Sweetened Whipped Cream, page 185
Choux Pastry made with 3 eggs, page 28

2 tablespoons sliced almonds
Powdered sugar

If using Vanilla Pastry Cream, prepare at least 2 hours before serving. Lightly grease a 17" x 11" baking sheet. Preheat oven to 400F (205C). Prepare dough for pastry. Spoon into a pastry bag fitted with a 1/2-inch plain tip or a star tip with a large opening. Pipe rings with an outside diameter of 3 inches. Make 8 or 9 rings. Coarsely chop almonds. Sprinkle almonds on rings. With your fingers, lightly press almonds onto rings. Bake about 35 minutes until golden brown, including any cracks formed during baking. Remove from oven. Cool. Prepare Sweetened Whipped Cream, if using for filling. With a serrated knife, slice cooled rings in half horizontally. Remove any soft dough inside rings. Spoon or pipe Vanilla Pastry Cream or Sweetened Whipped Cream into tops and bottoms of rings. Replace tops. Sprinkle rings generously with powdered sugar. Serve immediately or refrigerate and serve within 3 hours. Makes 8 or 9 servings.

Baklava   *Photo on page 181.*

Finely chop your favorite nuts to layer in this Middle Eastern sweet.

3 cups finely chopped walnuts
1 teaspoon ground cinnamon, if desired
About 3/4 cup butter
1/4 cup vegetable oil

1 lb. fresh or thawed frozen filo sheets
40 whole cloves, if desired
Honey syrup, see below

Honey Syrup:
3/4 cup sugar
3/4 cup water

1 teaspoon lemon juice
1/3 cup honey

Review Filo Pastry Techniques, page 27. Combine walnuts and cinnamon, if desired. Set aside. Melt 3/4 cup butter and stir in oil. Lightly brush a 13" x 9" baking pan with butter mixture. Place 1 filo sheet in prepared pan, folding to fit in pan. Lightly brush with butter mixture. Repeat with 5 more filo sheets. Sprinkle the last sheet with a third of the nut mixture. Place 1 filo sheet on top of the nut layer, folding to fit in pan. Lightly brush with butter mixture. Repeat with 3 more filo sheets. Sprinkle the last sheet with half the remaining nut mixture. Place 1 filo sheet on top of nut layer, folding to fit pan. Lightly brush with butter mixture. Repeat with 3 more filo sheets. Sprinkle last sheet with remaining nut mixture. Top with remaining filo sheets, folding to fit pan and brushing each sheet with butter mixture. Press top layer firmly all over to lightly compact layers. Trim any pastry that sticks above top layer. Brush top with melted butter mixture. If necessary, melt more butter. Preheat oven to 350F (175C). With the tip of a very sharp knife, score a diagonal line from corner to corner. Do not cut through layers. On the same diagonal, score a line from the center points of adjoining sides. Score a line between first line and second line. Score another line between the second line and the corner. Repeat on the other side of the first diagonal line. Repeat all diagonals in the opposite directions to make 24 full diamonds and 16 half diamonds. If desired, insert a clove in center of each piece. Bake 30 minutes. Immediately after placing Baklava in oven, prepare Honey Syrup. After Baklava bakes 30 minutes, reduce heat to 300F (150C). Bake 30 to 40 minutes longer until light golden brown. Remove from oven. Cut pastry on scored lines. Pour Honey Syrup evenly over cut pastry. Cool. Makes 40 servings.

Honey Syrup:
Combine sugar and water in a medium saucepan. Stir frequently over medium heat until mixture comes to a full boil. Reduce heat and simmer 5 minutes. Stir in lemon juice and honey. Cool slightly.

How to Make Baklava

1/Layer a third of the filo and melted butter in baking pan. Sprinkle with a third of the nut mixture.

2/Before baking, score diagonal lines on the surface to make a diamond pattern.

Sweetened Whipped Cream

A smooth topping for dessert pies. Double the recipe for filling Cream Puffs, page 179.

1/2 pint whipping cream (1 cup)
2 tablespoons powdered sugar

1/2 teaspoon vanilla extract, if desired

Chill mixing bowl if temperature of kitchen is warm. In a small bowl, beat cream until soft peaks form. If whipped cream is to be piped through a pastry tube, beat until stiff peaks form. Fold in powdered sugar. Add vanilla, if desired. Refrigerate until ready to serve. If necessary, stir before serving. Makes about 2 cups.

Variations

Substitute 1/2 teaspoon peppermint, almond or rum extract for the vanilla.

Substitute 2 tablespoons Kahlúa, crème de menthe, crème de cacao, Amaretto or kirsch for the sugar and vanilla.

Pistachio Coils   *Photo on pages 2 and 3.*

In some Middle Eastern countries, these are called birds' nests.

About 1 cup butter, melted
12 fresh or thawed frozen filo sheets
1-1/4 cups chopped unsalted shelled
   pistachio nuts

Lemon-Honey Syrup, see below

Lemon-Honey Syrup:
1/2 cup sugar
1/2 cup water

2 teaspoons lemon juice
1/4 cup honey

Review Filo Pastry Techniques, page 27. Preheat oven to 400F (205C). Select a 14'' x 10'' rimmed baking sheet. Lightly brush with melted butter. Place filo sheets near work surface and cover with plastic wrap. Set aside 1/4 cup nuts. Place 1 filo sheet on work surface. Brush lightly with melted butter. Fold in half lengthwise. Brush again with butter. Spread 1 rounded tablespoon nuts in a strip about 1 inch from long edge and to within 2-1/2 inches of each short edge. Fold long edge over nuts. Fold in each short edge 1 inch. Starting with the long folded edge, roll up jelly-roll fashion. Then, starting at one end, roll up loosely to make a coil. Make a slight depression in center with your finger. Depression will help hold syrup to be added later. Tuck outside end under coil. Place on prepared baking sheet. Repeat with remaining filo sheets and nuts. Brush tops of coils with melted butter. If necessary, melt more butter. Bake 15 to 20 minutes until coils are golden brown. While coils are baking, prepare Lemon-Honey Syrup. Drain off excess butter from baked coils. Spoon half the Lemon-Honey Syrup over coils. Sprinkle center of coils with remaining nuts. Spoon remaining syrup over nuts and coils. Cool to room temperature. Makes 12 servings.

Lemon-Honey Syrup:
Combine sugar and water in a medium saucepan. Stir frequently over medium heat until mixture comes to a full boil. Reduce heat and simmer 5 minutes. Stir in lemon juice and honey. Cool slightly.

Variations

Pecan or Walnut Coils: Photo on page 181. Substitute pecans or walnuts for the pistachio nuts.
Cream Coils: Substitute Vanilla Pastry Cream, page 178, for 1 cup nuts used for filling. Use about 2 tablespoons Vanilla Pastry Cream in each coil.
Fruit-Nut Coils: Substitute 1/2 cup chopped dates or dried figs for 1/2 cup chopped nuts. Combine with remaining 1/2 cup chopped nuts.

*tip*

Sweet pastries made with choux pastry and pastry cream may be filled about 2 hours before serving. If they stand longer, the pastry may become soggy.

Chocolate Garnishes

Melting Chocolate—Melt semisweet chocolate in a heavy saucepan over very low heat or in a double boiler over simmering water. Stir occasionally until the chocolate is smooth.

Chocolate-Dipped Strawberries—Use large strawberries with long stems. One (1-ounce) piece of semisweet chocolate, melted, will cover 5 to 8 strawberries. Wash and dry the strawberries. Line a plate with waxed paper. Pour or spoon melted chocolate into a small deep dish. Dip or roll each strawberry from its tip to 1/4 to 1/2 inch from its stem. If necessary, spread the chocolate with a small spatula. Place the coated strawberries on the waxed paper and refrigerate until you are ready to garnish.

Chocolate-Dipped Maraschino Cherries—Use maraschino cherries with stems. One (1-ounce) piece semisweet chocolate, melted, will cover 8 to 10 cherries. Remove cherries from their juice and blot dry on a paper towel. Line a plate with waxed paper. Pour or spoon melted chocolate into a small deep dish. Dip or roll each cherry in chocolate, leaving about 1/4 inch of cherry showing above the stem. If necessary, spread the chocolate with a small spatula. Place coated cherries on the waxed paper and refrigerate until you are ready to garnish.

Grated Chocolate—Use 1 (1-ounce) piece of semisweet or unsweetened chocolate. Shred the chocolate over waxed paper or aluminum foil using the large holes of a shredder. Grated chocolate may be wrapped well and refrigerated or frozen. Sprinkle grated chocolate over finished pastry from a spatula or spoon.

Chocolate Leaves—For large leaves use fresh camellia, citrus or rose leaves. For small leaves use fresh ivy or mint leaves. One (1-ounce) piece of semisweet chocolate, melted, will cover 6 to 8 leaves. Wash and dry the leaves. With a small spatula, spread melted chocolate at least 1/16 inch thick on the back of each leaf. Do not spread chocolate over leaf edges. Run your finger around the edge of each leaf to wipe off any excess chocolate. Place leaves chocolate side up on a plate. Refrigerate until the chocolate is firm. Chocolate-covered leaves may be covered and frozen. To use, carefully peel each leaf from the hardened chocolate starting at the stem end. The side closest to the leaf is the right side. Place leaves right side up on a plate. Refrigerate until you are ready to garnish. Or, garnish the dessert and refrigerate it until serving time.

Chocolate Curls—Use 1-ounce pieces of chocolate. For larger curls, use large semisweet or milk chocolate candy bars. Curls are easy to make if chocolate is slightly warmer than room temperature. Bring it to the correct temperature in a gas oven with a pilot light, in a warmed electric oven that has been turned off, or in a sunny window. Leave the chocolate there for 10 to 15 minutes. Use a vegetable peeler to shave off curls. For longer curls, pull the peeler across chocolate on a diagonal. Use a wooden pick to lift the curls. See the photo on page 165. Curls may be refrigerated. Or, place them in a pie plate, cover and freeze.

Index

Index

Index